Lois & Pat

Merry Xmas & Happy New Year
Thank You for all your
help.

Love Brad.

A
PICTORIAL HISTORY
OF THE
AMERICAN INDIAN

by OLIVER LA FARGE

Laughing Boy

Sparks Fly Upward

Long Pennant

All the Young Men

The Enemy Gods

As Long as the Grass Shall Grow

The Copper Pot

Raw Material

The Eagle in the Egg

The Mother Ditch

Cochise of Arizona

Behind the Mountains

A Pictorial History of the American Indian

Technical Subjects

The Year-Bearer's People

The Changing Indian

Santa Eulalia

by ALVIN M. JOSEPHY, JR.

The Patriot Chiefs

The Nez Perce and the Opening of the Northwest

The Indian Heritage of America

The American Heritage Book of Indians (editor)

with others

The American Heritage Book of the Pioneer Spirit

The American Heritage Pictorial History of U.S. History

A PICTORIAL HISTORY OF THE
AMERICAN INDIAN

by OLIVER LA FARGE
Revised by ALVIN M. JOSEPHY, JR.

BONANZA BOOKS · NEW YORK

Copyright © MCMLXVI by Oliver La Farge and Crown Publishers, Inc.
Copyright © MCMLXXIV by the estate of Oliver La Farge,
Alvin M. Josephy, Jr., and Crown Publishers, Inc.
All rights reserved.

This edition is published by Bonanza Books,
a division of Crown Publishers, Inc.
a b c d e f g h

Manufactured in the United States of America

Library of Congress Cataloging in Publication Data

La Farge, Oliver, 1901–1963.
    A pictorial history of the American Indian.

    Includes index.
    1. Indians of North America—Pictorial works.
2. Indians of North America.   I. Josephy, Alvin M.,
1915–   II. Title.
E77.5.L3 1980   970.004'97   80-14930
ISBN 0-517-01695-8

Contents

Publisher's Acknowledgment

Picture sources and credits appear at the end of the picture captions. The author and publishers are most grateful to all of the individuals and organizations who supplied the photographs, drawings, cuts and other pictorial matter for the book. For extraordinary services, thanks are due especially to:

American Heritage and Mrs. Joan Mills

American Museum of Natural History
and the late Harry Tschopick

Associated Press Wide World Photo Division

Bureau of Indian Affairs and Lem Banks
and Mrs. Eugenia A. Langford

Bureau of Reclamation

Harold S. Colton, author of *Hopi Kachina Dolls*

Richard Erdoes

Bruce Inverarity,
author of *The Art of the Northwest Coast Indians*

Terrence Moore

The New Mexico State Museums
and Stanley Stubbs and Dr. Marjorie Lambert

Ken Norgard

The Pennsylvania Historical Society

The Smithsonian Institution

The University of California Press

The University of New Mexico Press

A
PICTORIAL HISTORY
OF THE
AMERICAN INDIAN

I. They Discovered America

The first people to inhabit both North and South America were ancient ancestors of many of today's Indians. They came slowly in small hunting groups, crossing from northeastern Siberia to Alaska over many thousands of years during the Ice Age.

Although no one yet knows when the first of them arrived, scientists are beginning to fit together many pieces that may eventually provide the answer. It now seems certain, for instance, that man did not evolve from earlier species in the New World as he did in the Old, for no remains earlier than those of modern man have ever been found in the Americas. What appears to have happened is that about 35,000 to 50,000 years ago, when modern men, sometimes called *homo sapiens sapiens,* or humans just like ourselves, were beginning to supplant the earlier Neanderthal types of man in the Old World, groups of people migrated into parts of the earth that had never been occupied before. Developing more efficient social organizations and improving their technology to make more effective tools, implements, and other useful objects, they

One of the earliest groups of men of whom many traces have been found in different parts of North America is "Folsom Men." They were named for the site in the Southwest where their particular type of spear point, in use about 12,000 to 15,000 years ago, was first discovered. Although their weapons were primitive, they were mighty hunters, and killed many of the now extinct giant bison as well as other great animals.

Mesa Verde National Park.

followed the big game herds of Ice Age animals, like mammoths and mastodons, daring to venture into unknown areas of harsher climate and terrain.

In time, they reached eastern Siberia, which was then connected by land to Alaska. Even that "land bridge" between the two continents is only now beginning to be understood. Actually, what we think of as a single long "Ice Age" was a series of changes in climate. There were certain cold periods when glaciers covered many parts of the northern portion of the earth. Since much of the oceans' waters were congealed in the glaciers, the sea level at those times fell as much as three hundred feet or more, exposing large new land areas. Submarines going to the North Pole have revealed that the present sea bottom between Alaska and Siberia, from the Aleutians to Bering Strait, is less than three hundred feet deep. So all, or most, of that area must have been above water like a huge plain, forming a land connection between Asia and North America, at times almost a thousand miles wide from north to south. At other times, however, the climate warmed, the glaciers melted, the seas rose again, the land connection was broken, and the two continents were separated by water as they are today.

Some 35,000 years ago and more, when man is known to have been migrating through eastern Siberia, the continents were joined. Despite the presence of great glaciers, there were many areas in the north, including the "land bridge" and much of Alaska, that were free of ice barriers, and it is probable that at this time men first entered North America. Exactly who they were and what parts of Asia they had originally come from may never be known. It is not even certain that the so-called "races" of man, as we think of them, had yet evolved. Some students think that the earliest Americans may have been proto-Mongoloids —that is, that they had left Asiatic groups which, staying behind, later took on the physical characteristics of the present-day Mongoloid peoples. If that is true, then the first arrivals in the New World would have left Asia before they had taken on pronounced Mongoloid features and may be thought to have evolved in the Americas as a "race" unto themselves. Many thousands of years later, as will be seen, other peoples came from Asia, and since their Indian descendants possess more pronounced Mongoloid features, it suggests that the Asians whom they had left had become more Mongoloid in appearance than were the relatives of the earlier arrivals.

The notion that people were in the Western Hemisphere as long ago as 35,000 to 50,000 years is somewhat new and, of course, is still not accepted by everyone. No human remains that old have yet been found in the Americas. But, more and more, archeologists are turning up evidence to support the belief. In both North and South America they have found traces of peoples' presence— their stone, bone, and flint tools and spear points, the fires they built, and the bones of animals they killed—dating so far back that, for men to have been at those sites when they are believed to have been there, they would have had to enter Alaska at about the time of which we are speaking. In Mexico and the southwestern and western parts of the United States, for instance, a number of discoveries— all of them still controversial, but firmly endorsed by many reputable archeologists—suggest man's occupation of various locations between roughly 30,000 and 40,000 years ago. In Peru, stone tools have been found indicating that man lived there 22,000 years ago, if not earlier. And in Canada's northern Yukon, bone artifacts have been discovered that are definitely the work of man some 27,000 years ago.

Sometime after the first peoples reached the Americas, it is thought, they became cut off from Asia. As a result of changes in climate, the glaciers moved, blocking further entrance from Siberia and, in a manner of speaking, sealing the first Americans in their new world. Then, about 25,000 years ago came a warming period when the glaciers melted, and the two continents were again separated by water. For a long time—perhaps until about 15,000 years ago—no additional newcomers were able to come from Asia. The peoples already in America, still pursuing the big game animals on which they lived, followed ice-free passages up the Yukon River to the Mackenzie Basin of the Yukon, then south through that valley and into the warmer countries of the present-day United States and Mexico. From there, some of them may have made their way through Central America to South America. All the time, they were developing new tools of their own, including a distinctive bifacially worked, leaf-shaped spear point.

From about 15,000 to 10,000 years ago, when the weather again became cold and the two continents were once more joined together, new groups were again able to cross into America from Siberia, and now we begin to find human remains and other evidence of man's presence almost everywhere in the Western Hemisphere. Archeological discoveries, tested by what is called the radio-carbon method (which tells the age of certain materials by measuring their remaining radioactivity) or by more recent means, including the determination of the hydration of obsidian finds, have established that people were in widespread sections of the present-day United States, Mexico, and Central and South America about 12,000 years ago. In our own country, for example, burial sites with human remains 21,500 years old have been found in California,

A burial from Grand Gulch, Utah, of the high, prehistoric Pueblo period, 800 or 900 years ago. The very dry climate of the Southwest dried the body into a natural mummy. The body is wrapped in a fine piece of woven cotton with a very elaborate design. The design continues the tradition started by the Basketmakers, and any modern Southwestern weaver would be proud to produce an equally handsome textile.

Courtesy of the American Museum of Natural History.

10,000 to 11,000 years old in Washington State, and 10,000 years old in Florida.

They were all Stone Age people, who lived principally by hunting big Ice Age animals with spears and spear-throwers. Their prey included huge bison and sloths, as well as mammoths and large caribou. Some of the people probably also fished, caught birds with bolas (nets weighted with stones), and gathered shellfish and wild grasses and vegetables.

Since the different peoples on the two continents were descended from ancestors who had come from different parts of Asia at different times, and since many of the groups had gone through evolutionary processes of their own while they had been in the Americas, they were not all alike. Some were tall, some short; some had long heads, some had round heads. Some were darker complexioned than others. On the whole, however, most of them had very slight beards, their hair was black and straight, their eyes were longish, their cheekbones were high, and their faces were often broad.

The fact that over the course of thousands of years many different peoples had come into the Americas is shown also by the Indian languages. Modern Indians speak languages of many different families. These families are no more like one another than are English, Tibetans, and Zulus. People often ask Indians if they speak Indian. It is a foolish question, like asking, "Do you speak European?" Actually, when Columbus arrived in the New World, it is estimated that Indians on the two continents (numbering, perhaps, more than 20,000,000) were speaking almost 2,500 different mutually unintelligible languages. Of course, over thousands of years, these many tongues had probably developed from a relatively small number of original languages that the people had brought with them from Asia. Modern linguistic scholars, in fact, believe that all the native languages in North America can be traced back to six superstock tongues and all in South America to three; and one eminent student, Morris Swadesh, has maintained that, on the two continents, every known native tongue save four derived originally from five basic parental languages introduced from Asia.

At any rate, by 10,000 to 12,000 years ago, North and South America were populated. Then the Ice Age, as we know it, ended, and Siberia and Alaska became separated by the body of water we now call Bering Strait. Great changes came to North America. As the climate warmed, many areas became dryer. The vegetation changed, and northern-type evergreen trees retreated north, being replaced by grasslands and forests of hardwoods like oak, hickory, and elms. At the same time, the great Ice Age animals became extinct in one area after another, though no one yet knows for certain whether the hunting peoples on the continent with improved weapons simply wiped them out—as we almost did to the buffalo and have actually done to other species—or whether the big animals could not cope with the changing climate.

But gradually the different peoples had to look for new food supplies. They trapped and hunted smaller game, like deer and rabbits, developing many different kinds of new and smaller spear points with which to kill their prey. They also relied more on fish, birds, shellfish (where it

was available), and wild-growing herbs, grasses, and vegetables. In the many different environments, including jungles, coastal areas, arid regions, prairies, and woodlands, food-gathering and other needs and problems of daily life began to bring about differences in the cultures of the various peoples. They began to invent and design different kinds of implements, tools, and utensils to fit their own particular requirements. Their organizations, beliefs, and ceremonies began to take on features that differed from those of peoples in other environments. Thus, slowly, many distinctive ways of life emerged, so that thousands of years later, when the Europeans reached the New World, they found not one Indian culture, but many of them. The customs and ways of life of Indians in the barrens of northern Canada, for instance, had become totally different from those of Indians who lived along the Atlantic coast, and both had become different in almost all ways from those who lived in the deserts of the Southwest, or on the islands of the Caribbean, or in other vastly different regions.

Back in the Old World, in the Middle East, the Nile Valley, and elsewhere, many discoveries were made beginning roughly about 10,000 years ago, but these never reached across to the Western Hemisphere. The early Americans had to make their own discoveries. They were up against some real handicaps. There were few animals that could be tamed (Ask any cowboy who has tried to herd buffaloes!). The only large ones were the llamas in Peru, big enough to carry light packs, but too small to pull wagons in the Andean mountain country. The Old World had horses, cattle, tameable elephants in Asia, camels, sheep, goats, and pigs, as well as chickens, ducks, and geese. The Indians had domesticated dogs that had come with them from Asia, and they learned to tame and raise turkeys, but birds cannot be used to do work.

In the Old World, also, there were many kinds of grain, such as wheat, rye, oats, barley, and millet, that could be planted by scattering the seeds in fertile ground. The Old World people discovered how to grow these crops. And here, in agricultural development, many of the New World peoples more than kept pace with them, though with different crops. At almost the same time that men in the Middle East were learning how to grow grains, peoples in several parts of the New World were similarly—though independently—beginning to learn the secrets of agriculture. The groups in the Americas who first became horticulturists may have been some of those who relied heavily on the use of wild-growing grasses and vegetables. Somehow, about 10,000 years ago, certain of them in Peru learned how to grow various kinds of beans. A little bit later, people in northeastern Mexico began to cultivate pumpkins and peppers. And about 7,000 years ago groups in central Mexico were growing squash and maize, which most of us call corn.

Gradually, agriculture caught on in two major areas of the Americas—the Andean region of Peru and what we sometimes term Middle America, or central and southern Mexico, Guatemala, and parts of neighboring Central American countries. Increasingly, domesticated crops—particularly maize—became the principal part of the diet of the peoples in those two general areas. The story of the

Indians' discovery of maize—a crop never known in the Old World before Columbus—is especially intriguing. Anyone who has ever planted corn knows that you can't sow it broadcast; you have to set each grain in a hole. It took a lot of experimenting and centuries of time to develop the original wild grass into a plant that would yield a decent crop. In fact, there is reason to believe that maize is the result of a cross between two wild plants, neither of which yielded very much. All in all, we can see that the people who developed our American corn were intelligent, and overcame many obstacles.

In addition to the plants named above, the peoples of the New World developed numerous other crops of their own. They included many types of beans, gourds, potatoes, tomatoes, peanuts, chocolate, various fruits, tobacco, and cotton, as well as many kinds of medicinal plants. In South America, also, some Indians learned to cultivate manioc, which later, like the Indians' corn and potatoes, became a staple for peoples all over the world. The discovery of agriculture brought great changes to the groups that practiced it. For one thing, they had to tend their crops, and that meant settling down near them, at least for part of the year. That gave rise to semipermanent, and then permanent, settlements, composed of buildings rather than caves and rock-shelters. Populations became concentrated and gradually grew in size. Now, for the first time, the harvests gave surplus food that could be stored for winter and lean periods. People no longer had to give all their time to finding food. There was now time for leisure activities, for the making of aesthetically pleasing implements and utensils, and for developing intellectual pursuits. The larger and more concentrated populations demanded more complex social, political, religious, and economic organizations. Where once a father or grandfather headed a small nomadic hunting band no larger than a family or an extended family, there was now a need for organizations that would hold together a whole village of many families for the best interests of all of them.

Gradually, in Middle America and in the Andes Mountains region of South America, where agriculture became intensively practiced, there arose richly complex Indian cultures, and then civilizations, headed by religious and civil leaders. These flowered with such brilliance that they almost rivaled Greece and Rome at their height. The creators or elaborators of these civilizations whose names are best known to us are the Toltecs (the pyramid builders of Teotihuacan), the Olmecs, Mayas, and Aztecs of Mexico, the Chibchas of Colombia, and the Incas of Peru. There were great cities and religious centers, monumental buildings and engineering projects, handsome architecture and murals, fine arts in ceramics and other materials, forms of writing, mathematics, and astronomy. These were not "Stone Age" peoples, as we usually employ that term. They were on the edge of the change to metals. They worked gold, silver, and copper, but as yet mostly for ornaments.

Think back to Europe four thousand years ago, when the civilization of Egypt was already strong and was beginning to spread into the lands around the eastern Mediterranean. Almost all of Europe was occupied by primitives, even though they did know how to work some metal. An Egyptian, traveling north, would have said that the Europeans, and especially the fair-skinned, northern ones, were savages. It was like that in North America.

Model showing a settlement of the fully developed Basketmaker culture, about A.D. 450–750. Starting from the storage pits shown in the earlier picture, the people have developed houses partly made by digging in the ground, partly by building above with poles and sticks and plastering them heavily with adobe. Houses are entered through the roof. The man in the left foreground has a bow and arrow. There are pottery jars as well as baskets. Note the tame turkeys, one standing by the boy behind the man holding the bow.

Mesa Verde National Park.

In the Old World, time and again barbarians attacked the centers of civilization, conquered them, became civilized themselves, and carried on the line of progress. The same thing happened in the Americas. Notably, barbarous people speaking a language of the Uto-Aztecan family came down from the north to invade the cities of central Mexico. There they conquered the ancient Toltecs, acquired their civilization, and became the Aztecs.

The influence of the civilized centers constantly spread outward, as it did in the Old World. The influence came into what is now the United States through two principal entrance areas, the Southeast and the Southwest.

By "the Southwest," students of Indian history mean Arizona and New Mexico and narrowish strips of the neighboring territory on all sides, especially a strip of northern Mexico and of southern Colorado and Utah. A thousand miles of harsh desert and mountain country lay between this area and the cities to the south, but trade went on across it, not directly between the Southwesterners and the central Mexicans, but indirectly. Goods passed each way from tribe to tribe in a long series of exchanges. The civilized people got turquoise and, about two thousand years ago, bows and arrows from the north; the northerners received, among other things, parrot feathers and seeds. Equally important, ideas were passed on along with the goods—the *idea* of farming, of weaving, of making pottery, of putting on masks so as to represent sacred beings.

We know a good deal more about the very early history of the Southwest than we do about other parts of the country, for two reasons. Even two thousand years ago the Southwest was fairly dry, although not as arid as it is now. In dry country, the remains that people leave behind them last much longer in the ground, and in dry country, where vegetation is sparse, it is easy for archaeologists to spot the right places to dig in. Also, many of the tribes living in the Southwest today are the direct descendants of those that were there more than a thousand years ago. Oraibi, a Hopi village, has been continuously inhabited since A.D. 1100. The modern Indians retain the languages and a great deal of the ways of their ancestors, as well as many traditions about them.

Wherever conditions allowed in the Southwest, the people went in heavily for farming, beginning with native beans and corn from the south. Many of them learned to irrigate; others became expert dry farmers. They made fine basketry, raised and wove cotton, and made truly beautiful pottery. They made fine jewelry of turquoise and shell and carved small objects of various local stones.

The earliest known farmers in the Southwest, part of one of the longest continuous cultural lines that archeologists have traced, were the people of what is called the "Cochise tradition" of southern Arizona and New Mexico. For many thousands of years after the Ice Age these people had been especially gatherers of wild foods. Part of a culture that existed in the somewhat arid lands of the Far West all the way from Oregon through the Great Basin and California to central Mexico, and that is now termed the Desert Culture, they had roamed within limited areas, hunting and trapping small animals, but utilizing every

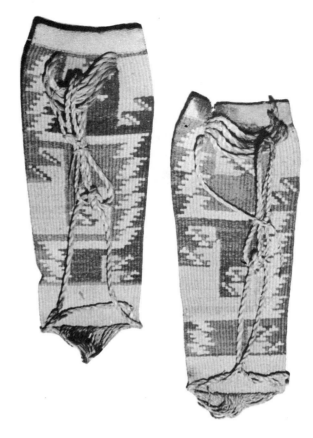

Before the Indians of the Southwest learned to cultivate cotton, they wove sandals like these out of thread made from yucca fiber. Fifteen hundred years ago or more the Basketmakers decorated their sandals, bags, and baskets with designs similar to those that the modern Indians use today. *University of Colorado Museum.*

Mimbres pottery from southern New Mexico. The Mimbres culture, distinct from the Pueblo but related to it, is noted for its fine designs and lively treatment of formalized animal figures. This culture had vanished before the white men came.

Museum of New Mexico.

15

Mimbres bowls with holes broken in the bottom. This was done when a bowl was placed in a burial; thus the bowl was "killed," so that its spirit could accompany the human's in the afterlife.
Courtesy of American Museum of Natural History.

Black-on-white jar of the Hohokam culture of southern Arizona. Although differing from the prehistoric Pueblo in many ways, this culture was equally advanced. Some of the Indians who still farm parts of Arizona may be descended from the ancient Hohokam people. *Arizona State Museum.*

food available, including rodents, certain insects, piñon nuts, berries, and grass seeds.

Finally, more than 3,500 years ago, the idea of agriculture, spreading north from Mexico, reached some of the Cochise peoples in southern Arizona and New Mexico. By 3,000 years ago they were raising a very primitive form of corn. After almost another 1,000 years, they were producing a much improved strain of corn, as well as beans, and their cultivated crops had supplanted wild foods as the mainstay of their diet. From these people derived the Mogollon and Hohokam cultures; and from the Hohokam people, it is believed, the modern Pimas and Papagos are descended. Slightly later, other peoples just to the north, in the "Four Corners" country, where Arizona, New Mexico, Colorado, and Utah meet, also began to farm. Termed

Anasazis, a Navaho word meaning "ancient ones," they were among the ancestors of the Hopi and Pueblo Indians.

There was a good deal of difference among the cultures of these various southwestern farmers, who also included related groups such as the Mimbres and the Sinagua peoples. The best known are those who became the Pueblos, not only because of their spectacular ruins but because

The transition period between the Basketmaker and true Pueblo cultures. Houses are built up against each other. Some are of poles plastered over with adobe, some of stone and adobe. They are entered through the roofs or through doors, but the small kivas in the foreground are entered only through the roofs. Extensive cornfields stretch back of the settlement.
Mesa Verde National Park.

Interior of a great kiva or combined ceremonial building and men's club at Chetro Ketl, New Mexico, of the great period of prehistoric Pueblo culture, partially excavated. Although this basic form of kiva derives from the simple pit houses of the later Basketmakers, by this time they had been greatly elaborated. The kivas were used for councils, for lounging places for men, for preparing ceremonies, and for the holding of many complete ceremonies. *Courtesy Museum of New Mexico.*

Restoration of a small, prehistoric kiva in a cliff dwelling at Rito de los Frijoles, New Mexico, showing the part that is above ground. The kiva is entered by the ladder sticking up from it, the same mode of entry as in the later Basketmaker houses shown above. *U. S. Indian Service.*

their culture is so well continued by the modern Hopis and Pueblos. The main line of the Pueblos started along the Colorado and Utah border, then later moved southward. They built villages of stone houses cemented with *adobe,* a local clay. In each village were one or more *kivas,* which were men's clubs and also centers of religious ceremonial. Kivas were built entirely or partly underground and were entered through a hole in the roof. Their basic form derived from an early type of "pit house," built before the Southwesterners had learned to be masons, but later they were elaborated beyond any obvious resemblance to those early structures. In late times, some of them were decorated with stylized but handsome murals of ritual subjects.

In the Southwest there are few hills; instead there are *mesas.* These are hills with perpendicular sides of rock and flat tops. Big sections of these sides scale off, leaving deep ledges overhung by the upper parts of the cliffs. In early times, 2,000 years ago, the Southwestern Indians often built their houses on these ledges for shelter from the weather. Later, they built their towns in them, although often that meant that the women had to climb up and down steep cliffs every day to carry water, and all the crops and other food had to be dragged or carried up. Towns placed on such ledges are known as "cliff dwellings." They are picturesque, but they must have been mighty inconvenient.

The reason for moving into such places was probably that, between A.D. 1000 and 1200, new, aggressive tribes began drifting into the Southwest. Among these were the ancestors of the Navahos and Apaches, who later became

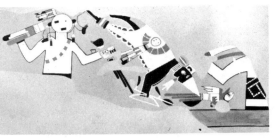
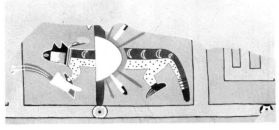

Mural decoration from the wall of a pre-historic Hopi kiva. These paintings, renewed from time to time, show stylized sacred figures and symbols. They are painted in warm, soft earth colors.
Peabody Museum, Harvard University.

Ruins of the Cliff Palace, a cliff dwelling in Mesa Verde National Park, Colorado. This area was a center of early high development of Pueblo culture. The round buildings near the front of the ledge are the kivas, the roofs of which have fallen in.
Courtesy of American Museum of Natural History.

so famous. These people, who had broken off from tribes settled in northwestern Canada and Alaska, were primitive and poor, but they had an Arctic-type bow, originally of Asiatic origin, that was stronger than any bow known in the Southwest. This gave them a military advantage. The newcomers did not make regular war upon the Pueblo people. They traded with them, they learned from them, they stole from them, and from time to time they raided them. They were enough of a nuisance to make the Pueblos want to have their settlements strong and defensible.

Later, when they moved out of the section in which their culture first developed, they built their towns on high places, or arranged them so that the houses themselves made a defensive wall.

The Southwestern culture was essentially peaceful and democratic. Few indications of fighting have been found, for all the troubles the semi-civilized people may have had with the nomadic, primitive bands that had seeped into the country. We do not find the elaborate, special burials of a few individuals that occur where there is much distinction of rank, nor are there special houses finer than others. The modern Pueblo Indians, too, are peaceful and

A fine black and white jar found in a kiva in a cliff dwelling at Mesa Verde, Colorado. The Mesa Verde style spread widely through the Pueblo area. The pottery is not only handsomely decorated, but of an excellent, smooth, hard texture. About A.D. 1200 the Cliff Dwellers left the Mesa Verde region to settle along the Rio Grande and in northern Arizona.
Mesa Verde National Park Museum.

A reconstruction of daily life in a Mesa Verde cliff dwelling. In fair weather the people carried on their activities in the open spaces of the settlement, using their small houses mostly to sleep in. *Mesa Verde National Park.*

democratic. The labor they put into building their kivas is a community effort, undertaken voluntarily.

In the past they were governed by a theocracy, that is, by their priests and religious officials, but the governors' power derived from the consent of the governed. Their lives centered around their religion. When the Spaniards first came among them, they were greatly impressed by their houses, their farms, and their arts. They were also impressed by their magnificent ceremonies.

The Southwestern culture never spread far beyond Arizona, New Mexico, and the southernmost parts of Colorado and Utah. Beyond, in most directions, were high mountains or deserts which could not be farmed with primitive equipment. When your best tools are a pointed stick and a hoe made by tying a deer's shoulder-blade to a handle, you cannot irrigate the Great American Desert. To the eastward lay the High Plains, which, except along well-watered river valleys, were also unsuitable to primitive farming.

The other area where the influence of the growing American civilization reached, the Southeast, was utterly different. Because Columbus thought that the islands he found in the Caribbean were the East Indies of Asia, he called all the peoples he met "Indians," and the name stuck. But as we have seen, the many different groups in the Americas were far from alike. Each one, moreover, had its own name for itself, most of which meant something like "We, the people," or "The real people."

We do not as yet know the southeastern story in as great detail as we do the story of the Southwest. Originally, the people seem to have been hunters of big game, just as they were elsewhere in the hemisphere. Then they relied increasingly on shellfish, fish, small game, berries, and wild-growing foods. Pottery came to them very early—about 4,500 years ago—introduced apparently by coastal sea venturers who may have come across the Gulf of Mexico from the northern part of South America or from Mexico. Many regional variations developed among groups in different parts of the Southeast, and many ideas and new ways of life, including horticulture, continued to come to them from Mexico, as well as from mound-building tribes in the Ohio and Mississippi valleys.

About 1,000 years ago a remarkable culture spread to them from the middle part of the Mississippi Valley. It was a highly ritualistic culture based on intensive farming and with many features derived originally from the great civilizations of Mexico. We call it the Mississippian, or Temple Mound Building Culture, because it was characterized by large ceremonial centers, often fortified, containing huge mounds with religious temples built on their flattened tops.

The Mexican influences can be seen very clearly in this culture. Trait after trait, from weaving feather cloaks to a highly organized aristocracy, comes from the cities of the Mexican Indian civilizations. One of the most striking evidences is the mounds themselves. The Olmecs, Teotihuacans, Toltecs, Mayas, and Aztecs had all built similar flat-topped pyramids on which they had placed their temples and sometimes their palaces. They had built with stone, mortar, and a form of concrete. Pyramids and villages had been arranged in impressive groups that served as religious and civic centers for the farmers and townspeople, and some of the sites had grown into densely populated cities. The people of the Mississippi Valley, who

Reconstruction of life in a section of a Hopi Pueblo village of about A.D. 1700. The women's dresses and the blankets are made of wool from sheep brought in by the Spaniards; otherwise there is no great difference between Hopi life of this period and that of prehistoric times.

U. S. Dept. of Interior.

received these influences perhaps overland via northeastern Mexico, built similar centers, but in a cruder style. The mounds were made of rubble covered with earth. The temples and other buildings were made of wood and thatch. Nonetheless, the form was the same.

Earlier, in the north, principally along the Ohio Valley, but extending to New England and far to the west, peoples of the Adena, and then the Hopewell, cultures had also built mounds, but without temples on top of them. The mound-building idea may have come to them, also, from Mexico, but more likely it had developed independently as early as 1000 B.C. In time, the custom had spread widely, but it had all but died out by A.D. 500, before the new Temple Mound Building Culture emerged along the Mississippi. In the north, however, some of the groups had left behind them "effigy mounds," many of which can still be seen today in Ohio and elsewhere. They were figures of birds, animals, and serpents, made of raised earth, and are particularly vivid when seen from an airplane.

In the Southeast, the people of the Temple Mound Building Culture lived in fairly permanent villages or towns, their houses usually made with pole or wattled walls and thatched roofs, or covered with mats. They were extensive farmers, but the products of agriculture were not their only food. There was plenty of room, and the hunting and fishing were wonderful. So, naturally, farming was balanced by the pursuit of game and fish and the gathering of berries, nuts, and other wild foods. The Temple Mound Builders, with large settlements from North Carolina to Oklahoma, developed some of the finest art, especially in their modeling and carving, that ever existed among Indians of what is now the United States.

The largest mound center was across the Mississippi River from present-day Saint Louis, and other large ones were in Georgia, Tennessee, and Oklahoma. But a typical one of the big ones is the Emerald Mound in Mississippi, which is thirty-five feet high, covers seven acres, and carries six smaller mounds on top. Construction of this kind, without any machinery at all, without even wheelbarrows, calls for a staggering number of man-hours of labor. It requires two conditions. The first is a food supply

Modern Hopi masked dancer representing the Antelope Kachina. He symbolizes the antelope and also, as shown by his bows and arrows, successful hunting of them. The prehistoric Pueblos had very similar masked dancers. The artist probably had to work entirely from memory; as a result, he has made several mistakes in details of the mask.
Courtesy of American Museum of Natural History.

Hopi woman cooking in a room in the village of Awatovi, about A.D. 1700. The hair done up in a whorl on the side of her head shows that she is unmarried; married women did their hair in braids. She is making *piki* bread. A batter of cornmeal and water is spread thinly on a very smooth, hot stone, then rolled up as it cooks. The different colors of corn meal are cooked separately, so that *piki* may be white, yellow, blue, or red.
U. S. Dept. of Interior.

so good that the people can lay in all they need to eat and still have plenty of time for other work; the second is authority to hold them at the hard labor.

The Pueblo Indians of the Southwest put together and built kivas as part of their compact villages. They put in a lot of work on something that every man, at least, would make use of almost daily, as we would build a town hall and a church. The Southeasterners built enormous structures that the common man used only occasionally, although most certainly their religious beliefs told them that they were important. We can be sure that over the laboring people there was an aristocracy with plenty of power. It is not surprising, then, that we find the simple burials of commoners and the very elaborate tombs of rulers, some

Mound Builders gathering corn and squash, a reconstruction based on archeological evidence. In the background is shown a stockade surrounding the town. The roofs of houses show over it. These are fairly large, round houses covered with thatch.
Bettmann Archive.

Mound Builder carved shell gorgets from the Etowah Group of mounds, Georgia. These were worn at the throat or just below it, suspended from a string.
Courtesy of American Museum of Natural History.

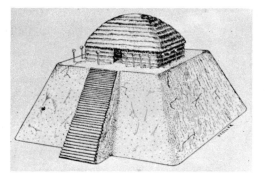

The Castillo, a Maya temple and pyramid in Yucatan, Mexico, built of stone and cement, compared with a reconstruction of a Southeastern temple of poles and thatch placed on

a mound faced with dried mud. The stairway was made of logs.

After Underhill from "Red Man's America."

Painting of a ceremony in a Hopi kiva, consecrating prayer plumes to the rain gods. The altar in the middle, which shows lightning snakes rising from clouds, is made by grinding earth or soft rocks of various colors, which are then poured dry on the ground in a design according to the ceremony to be held. Around the altar are feathered "prayer sticks." Ceremonies like this are of great age, and closely similar to the ones performed in prehistoric times. *Smithsonian Institution.*

Mound Builder bowl carved from diorite, a hard, smooth, green stone, from Moundville, Alabama.
Courtesy of American Museum of Natural History.

An aerial view of an effigy mound, the "Great Serpent Mound," in Adams County, Ohio.
Smithsonian Institution. Photo by Dache M. Reeves.

of whom were so great that servants, or slaves, were killed and buried with them. In the existence of a ruling upper class, perhaps of kings, we see another influence from Mexico.

Many variants of the Temple Mound Building Culture appeared throughout the Southeast, and it reached its climax in the sixteenth century, just before the arrival of the white men. Then there was some sort of mysterious decline and collapse, caused perhaps by epidemics of European diseases which the Spaniards had introduced among distant native peoples and that had spread from tribe to tribe across thousands of miles. Populations dispersed to smaller towns and agricultural villages, and the ceremonial centers, together with the religious and political organizations that had supported them, all but disappeared. The Cherokees, Creeks, and many of the tribes of historic times, however, appear to have been the descendants of groups that had once been builders of the temple mounds.

At least one group of Temple Mound Builders, along with their structures, customs, and organizations, did survive until well after white men came to live among them and write about their distinctive culture. They were the Natchez of the lower Mississippi River, and by the time the French settled in their country in the early 1700's, these Indians were alone among all the native tribes and nations in North America to have an absolute ruler. The king, called "The Sun," was so sacred that he could not defile himself by setting his foot to the ground, so he was carried about on a litter. He wore a feather crown and elaborate feather cloak. Volunteers became his servants, and of their own accord had themselves killed when The Sun died, so that they might accompany him in the after life. He had absolute power over all his people.

The Natchez were divided into two halves, the aristocracy and the common people. The aristocracy was subdi-

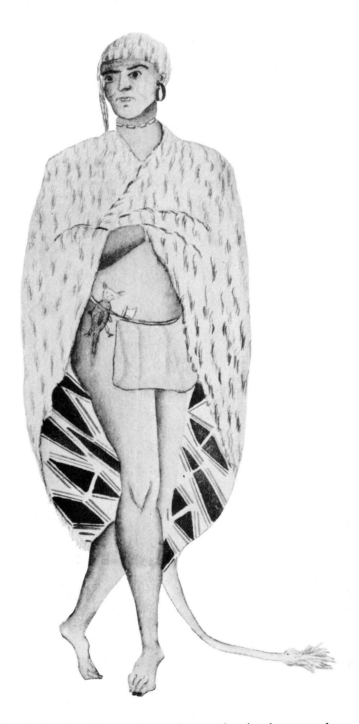

Natchez Indian in winter costume, from a drawing by an early French explorer. The prehistoric Indians of the region must have dressed in much the same way.
Peabody Museum, Harvard University.

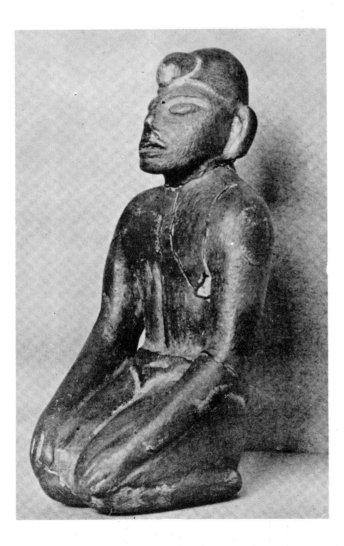

Mound builder carved figurine, from the Turner Group of mounds, Ohio. *Courtesy of American Museum of Natural History.*

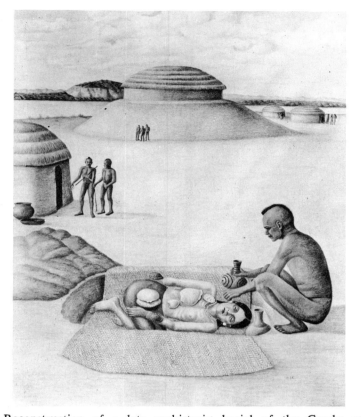

Reconstruction of a late prehistoric burial of the Creeks or Cherokees, Southeastern tribes that were there when the white man came. A man is placing offerings in the shallow grave of a dead woman. In the center background, the local temple stands on a small mound. *University of Tennessee, Miss Madeline Kneberg.*

vided into three classes, Suns, or royalty, Nobles, and Honorables. The common people were lumped together in a single group and called Stinkers.

The catch to this was that the common people could marry as they pleased, but the aristocrats were forbidden to marry within their own half. Therefore, all of them had to marry Stinkers. When a male aristocrat married a common woman, his children were rated one level lower than himself, so that the children of a male Honorable became ordinary Stinkers. When an aristocrat woman married a Stinker man, her children inherited her rank. Thus even The Sun himself was half Stinker on his father's side.

Wherever civilization is developing, the barbarians move inward but the civilized ideas move outward, against the human stream. The high culture of the Southwest was confined by the geography of the country surrounding it, but east and west, and to some extent north, of the Southeast Mississippi Valley high culture lay fertile land. The art of farming spread out from the center as far as conditions made it possible to raise crops. It reached into Canada, westward to the line beyond which rainfall averages less than twenty inches a year, and eastward to the Atlantic coast. To varying degrees, the tribes adopted some of the arts of the high culture, and some of their social organization.

A family with a field planted is not going to walk off and leave it. A family with a ton or so of grain stored up

Model of Natchez daily life in late prehistoric times. The temple on its great mound shows in the background. The king is being carried on his litter in the middle. At the right is a common house, covered with mats. On the left, men are putting corn in a storage bin. *Courtesy of American Museum of Natural History.*

is not going to lug it around just for fun. Wherever farming was being done, the Indians tended to stay put. They moved when they were forced to, or, as most of them used no fertilizer, when the fields became poor.

Most Americans think that, for a long time, Indians had been just as they were when the white man found them. It is a mistaken idea. The Indians were in the middle of the same process of change that covered so large a part of the Old World with civilization. Civilization was spreading. It advanced, fell back, advanced again, always gaining ground with each forward spurt. North America was in much the same position as Europe three thousand years earlier. In it burned a small flame which could in time become a great light. Then the white men landed, wave on wave, with the savage strength that came from steel, gunpowder, and horses, and the flame was put out forever.

II. The Kings of the South

Exploration of North America began with Spanish expeditions along the Gulf Coast from Florida to Texas, and inland northwards into Georgia and Tennessee, between 1521 and 1543. Among them were the famous Ponce de León, seeking the fountain of youth, and De Soto, who was described as "much given to the sport of slaying Indians." They were a rough and high-handed lot, and the Indians they met were competent to give them, in return, a discouragingly rough reception.

Those Indians knew nothing of war bonnets, the dome-shaped wigwams of the New England Indians, or the conical skin tents we call tepees. They were quite unlike the commonly accepted ideas of what Indians looked like.

Some of the tribes found by the first Spanish, French, and English explorers were undoubtedly descended from the Temple Mound Builders. Others had never reached that level of development. Some were to become famous in American history—the Creeks, Chickasaws, Choctaws, and Cherokees—while others, such as the Tumucuas of Florida, the Tunicas on the border of Texas, the Houmas and Chitimachas in southern Louisiana, were soon all but exterminated by the white men and today are extinct, or survive as only small remnants.

These people were not nomadic. Each tribe had its own territory. Since they farmed on a large scale, they lived near their farmlands. Their houses were grouped in large settlements that the early colonists and explorers spoke of as "towns." The heart of each town was a council house and public square.

The houses were solidly built, of wood, bark, thatch, and reeds. In the northern and mountain sections, they were walled; in the extreme south, they often had no walls at all. It all depended upon whether you built a house to keep warm in or to keep cool in. In warm weather, the people wore almost no clothes. Men put on a breech clout. Women wrapped a bit of skirt around their middles. When it turned cool, they wrapped robes around themselves, and the men might wear leggings of buckskin. They had a variety of ways of doing their hair. Women usually wore it long—it is a curious thing that in so many different parts of the world it is the custom for women to let their hair grow long when men trim theirs. Frequently the men shaved their heads, or plucked the hairs, in different patterns. When they did this, they usually left a "scalp lock." Most of the men were warriors, and their scalp locks were a challenge to all enemies to try to collect their scalps.

Then men decorated their bare bodies with tattooing, or "scratching." When a boy was first named, he was "scratched." When he became an apprentice warrior, he was named and "scratched" again, and when he had proven himself by bringing back a scalp, or perhaps a whole head or an enemy's arm or leg, he received a final name and more decorations on his skin.

When we name the famous tribes, we think of them as organized units. They were not. All the Creeks, for instance (who got their name from the English because many of them lived along creeks), spoke one language, held to

Florida Indian warrior of the sixteenth century. The eagle head-dress is a mark of honor indicating great war exploits. He is armed with a wicked, wooden club, and wears an unusually large shell pendant on his chest. Early pictures, such as this woodcut from a book by de Bry, published in 1591, were often worked up in Europe from explorers' sketches and descriptions.

Smithsonian Institution.

one religion, followed one set of customs, but they had no central government originally. Each town was ruled by its own head chief, or mico, and was independent. The people of one language recognized a sort of kinship with each other, usually did not fight each other, and often joined together against other tribes, but this was a temporary confederacy of little states, not a true union.

Early settlers spoke of the head chiefs as "kings," and they were not too far wrong. The chiefs had strong authority and were greatly respected. Some, like the true king of the Natchez, were carried on litters and wore special insignia, such as feather cloaks. Their wives might be similarly honored. They were not hereditary, however. A man attained high rank through demonstrating his superior fitness for it. At the same time that the earliest

Dwelling of the Seminoles of Florida. This house was sketched in the 1880's, but it could as well be a house of the 1580's, except for the steel-headed axe lying against the log in the right foreground. Near one of the house uprights stands a mortar for grinding corn. The double-ended pestle lies beside it. *Smithsonian Institution.*

A shaman or medicine-man, dancing. The artist did not record his tribe, but his name was The Flyer. Medicine men were less important than priests, who were trained to carry on the major parts of the religion.

Courtesy of American Museum of Natural History.

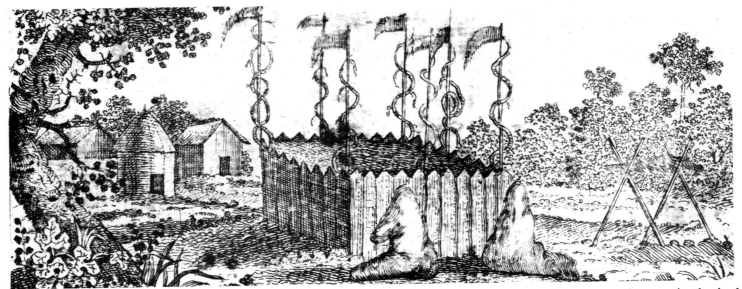

Choctaw (Mississippi) burial ground, with wrapped bodies outside the enclosure. The bodies were left until most of the flesh was gone, when the bones were cleaned by a special, minor priest, and buried in a mound. Choctaw houses can be seen in the background.

Smithsonian Institution.

The wife of a chief of the Timucuas of Florida, of about the middle of the sixteenth century, being carried to an important ceremony. In this drawing the men's bodies are shown without decorations but the royal lady seems to have been tattooed. She may only have been painted. The men's hair is drawn up into a topknot, with a fringe of short hair below like a hat brim.

Courtesy of American Museum of Natural History.

settlers called these chiefs "kings," as they did also some of the chiefs on the Atlantic coast, they were struck by the fundamental democracy among the tribes. These were kings by the will of the people, not by the grace of God.

Reports of this democracy were carried to Europe, especially by the French. There the idea of it was further elaborated, along with the philosophical idea of the child of nature, the Noble Red Man. The influence of the first observations on the Indians can be traced through the French philosophers to the English, and with it went the concept of "government by consent of the governed." This idea was first put into specific words by the British philosopher Locke. Our own Thomas Jefferson, in turn, borrowed Locke's phrasing and used it, slightly changed, in the Declaration of Independence. The evidence is strong that the development of democracy in both Europe and America was affected by sixteenth- and seventeenth-century contacts with the American Indians.

It is not really as surprising as it seems that the white men of those days viewed the Indians with respect. In level of civilization, there was much less difference between a lower-class European of the fifteen and sixteen hundreds and an Indian of one of the more advanced tribes than there would be between such an Indian, if we could find him today, and ourselves. The common European wore more clothes, of course. That was his custom. He was usually illiterate. In his homeland, he worked hard with hand tools to make a living, cooked over an open fire, ate simple food, slept on a hard bed. Even the aristocracy washed less often and were likely to smell more than the average Indian.

The upper-class Europeans who commanded the first expeditions and settlements were highly educated, sophisticated gentlemen. Their material life was rich. The gap between them and the Indians was much greater, but the very fact that they had the education and the training in fine manners and aristocratic behavior that they had, made them appreciative of the people they found in the New World. A Southeastern chief might live, physically, rather like a peasant, but he was a man who carried himself like a nobleman. He had beautiful manners, as did most Indians. He might not know how to read and write, but even so he had been trained in a whole library of traditions, he was a keen thinker, and a pretty good philosopher. All of this appealed to the European leaders.

As to the Indians' warlikeness and cruelty—that was a warlike and cruel age in Europe. The thousands who thronged the public squares in such cities as Paris to see a criminal tortured to death were no better than the hundreds of Indians who admiringly watched a brave enemy

29

This helps to explain why two entirely different myths about Indians exist among most Americans, the myth of the Noble Red Man and the myth of the Murderous Savage. Both are myths; the truth is in between.

As we have seen, the Southeastern chiefs were not hereditary. The high chiefs also were not primarily warriors, although, of course, it was not likely that a man could get to be respected enough to be considered for a chieftainship unless he had proven himself in war. Among the overwhelming majority of Indian tribes all over North America that had any chiefs at all, those who governed the tribes were not war chiefs. They were selected for their wisdom and their general ability. There were war chiefs also, but their business was to lead the fighting, not to govern. In other words, the Indians hit upon the same idea we have in our own government; that the military should be subordinate to a civilian government.

There was plenty else to attend to. There was the farming, for instance. In the spring the men and women prepared the ground and planted, and the songs ran from field to field. Through the growing season the women did most of the work—after all, the fields were theirs—and in the fall they all harvested together. At the time when roasting ears were ready for eating, a great ceremony, the "green corn ceremony," occurred among some of the tribes. Until it was held, no corn could be eaten, no matter how hungry anyone was. Old pottery was broken, the fires

Sixteenth century sketch of a Florida "chief." He may or may not have been a chief; then as now, white men were quick to make chiefs out of Indians. In any case, he must have been a considerable warrior, to judge by the decorations on his body.
Courtesy of American Museum of Natural History.

meet his end in the same way.

Later, most of the observations on the Indian tribes were made by frontiersmen. We admire the frontiersmen for their courage, persistence, and ingenuity, but we cannot deny that they were a rough, impatient, ill-educated lot. Also, they had an emotional need to despise the people among whom they came. They were engaged in driving them out. They had stolen their land, broken the treaties made with them, and intended to steal more land and break more treaties until the varmints were eliminated. To justify their line of conduct they had to claim that the original occupants of the land were beastly savages, that the only good Indian was a dead one. Since the Indians fought back at them with every murderous trick they knew, and since, just like the white men, they frequently killed women and children, they provided the frontiersmen with plenty of evidence for their story.

Tomochichi, head chief of a Creek town, and his nephew, the son of another head chief. Tomochichi was friendly to the original settlers of Georgia and helped them to make a treaty with the Lower Creeks. In 1734 he was taken to England with his wife, nephew, and others, where this portrait was painted. He remained a friend to the English until he died. Both the old man and the boy wear their hair short, with scalp locks hanging down over one ear. *Smithsonian Institution.*

were put out, the towns were cleaned. There was plenty of ritual. Then a new fire was kindled in the temple, and taken from there to all the hearths; everyone feasted, and a fine, fresh, new year started.

This ceremony, with its ritual theme of ending the old and starting anew, strongly suggests more elaborate rites along the same line practiced in Mexico. There, a great destroying of old things, cleaning, and general starting new occurred every fifty-two years, at the close of the sacred period or cycle that they thought of somewhat as we think of a century. Included in it was the quenching of all fires and starting off with new fires—something with much more meaning to the people of that time than to us, since, having neither matches nor flint and steel, lighting fires was a job. As a usual thing, household and temple fires were not let die out, at least hot coals being kept going under the ashes.

The Mexicans had a system of writing and an elaborate calendar. They had a name and number for every day of the year, as we have, and they could easily keep track of fifty-two-year cycles. The people of the Southeast had no writing. It would be natural for them, if they heard of this ceremony of starting all new, to make it annual and to tie it to an important, good event such as the ripening of the corn.

There was one practice in their religion that looks unpleasant to most of us. This was preparing themselves for important rites by taking the "black drink," an emetic that made them violently and quickly sick to their stomachs. Some of their descendants use this drink ceremonially to this day. The idea is that it cleanses them, leaving them purer and more fit for sacred things.

They had a system of clans, with descent traced through the mother. A man belonged to his mother's clan. Usually, a man went to live with his wife's people when he married. Very often, men married women from another town, so that the movement of men to their wives' towns helped to tie a tribe together. In theory, a man could marry several wives, but since he lived surrounded by his first wife's relatives, ordinarily he could do this only if she agreed. As a way of avoiding one of the commonest causes of friction when men must live with their wives' families, some of the Southeastern tribes such as the Creeks had a taboo that is found in many parts of North America. This is called "the mother-in-law taboo." It requires that the husband and his mother-in-law never speak to each other, in many cases never even see each other. Instead, the two may from time to time send each other gifts, as the custom may dictate.

Like most Indians and many peoples throughout the world, these considered marriage primarily an economic and social matter, not a religious one. Marriage ceremonies were simple, and there was often a "trial marriage," during which a couple lived together until the green corn ceremony without being obligated to stay together thereafter. Nonetheless, in case of adultery once a marriage was established, the husband might cut off the tips of his wife's nose and ears, and he might kill her lover—if he were a good enough warrior, or he and his kinsmen combined were strong enough.

Although law was rather simple, there was a definite code. In case of murder, the dead man's relatives were free to kill the murderer. Sometimes, if the murderer was a great chief, a less important man of his clan would be named to be killed—if the victim's people could catch him—in his place. One time a young warrior was thus named as the potential victim in the place of a famous war chief. The young man solved his problem by killing the chief himself. Everyone agreed that what he had done was perfectly fair, and furthermore, since the chief had been a great and strong warrior, that the young man had done something brave and much to his credit.

In addition to clans and the natural division of a tribe into independent towns, another division existed among the Creeks, if not among others. This division started, apparently, from the original occupation of their territory by a people who called themselves Muskogi, and whose dialect was somewhat different from that spoken by later settlers. The Muskogi assumed a certain leadership, and called themselves the "White" People, the others being "Red." Certain towns, dominated or occupied entirely by Muskogi, were called White towns. Wisdom and peacefulness came to be associated with the Whites. They were preferred as kings or town chiefs, while

Austenaco, one of the principal chiefs of the Cherokees, from a portrait made during his visit to London in 1762. The Indians by then wore clothing almost entirely of European materials, but distinctively Indian in cut. Instead of the earlier shell pendants, Austenaco wears a silver gorget below his throat. Most of his hair is shaved off or plucked out, and a small bunch of feathers is tied to his scalp lock. *Smithsonian Institution.*

Reds became "Big Warriors" or war chiefs. Almost every young man went through a period of proving himself in war, otherwise he could never amount to anything. He could not have a man's name, he could not marry. If he really could not stand the gaff there was nothing for him to do but put on women's clothes and live as a woman. Nonetheless, the White clans and White towns were developing toward people and places of peace, balancing a population terrifically concentrated on war.

The White towns were—at least in theory—places of refuge. If a captive doomed to be tortured to death, or someone who because of some offense was eligible to be killed, could escape to a White town, he was supposed to be safe. In practice, the Whites were never as purely peaceful as they were supposed to be in theory; they could not have been and survived. There does seem to have been some intertribal recognition of the nature of these towns, and there are signs that the idea of the Red and White division had begun to spread to other tribes in historic times.

For, if farming and hunting were how one lived, still, as far as the men were concerned, war was what made life worth living. We are likely to think that the less "civilized" people are, the fiercer they are. This is not so. Really, peoples of less complex societies, whose simpler ways of life are most like our idea of "savages," are usually quite mild, although they may fight bravely in self-defense. The fact is that warfare is something of a luxury. You can't do much fighting unless you have a good supply of food behind you. It is the more advanced people, as a rule, who are savage, although in the course of this book we shall see a notable and rare exception, or partial exception, in the Apaches. The relation of ferocity to advanced culture extends right up to the white men, who were (and still are) so civilized that they could maintain large bodies of men whose sole business was fighting and who made no other contribution to the community.

The Southeasterners had a noble religion, a fine organization, lived comfortably, made good pottery, wove a re-markably fine cloth out of thread spun from wild fibres, cultivated wide fields. Much in their lives was gracious and beautiful. But they called war their "beloved occupation." When they were not at war with anyone they said they were idle, as did the more civilized Aztecs. When the British urged the Cherokees to make peace with a certain tribe, they protested that if they did they would have to start a war with another, as otherwise they would not know what to do with themselves. Warfare was spoken of as the greatest of delights, and it was practiced with the utmost cruelty.

They did not wage war as we understand the term. As a rule, they did not seek conquest, try to subjugate other tribes, or drive them out of their territories. In short, they were not fighting to obtain some objective, so there was no need to spoil a war by winning it and thereby bringing it to an end. What they wanted was to run risks and kill people. Had Dale Carnegie lived among these tribes, he would have written a very different book!

The typical mode of fighting was the raid. The war party assembled by a war chief prepared itself by dancing and praying intently. It was usually smaller than the total fighting power of the town it planned to attack. There was a long sneak through the forests, in the course of which a good deal of ritual was observed, then a sudden, murderous attack just before dawn. A favored trick was to set the roofs of the enemy's houses afire with burning arrows, then rush in and kill as the people ran out in disorder.

The Indians were competent archers, using an effective longbow that shot long arrows. (The short bows we usually see shown as Indian came into use after the bowmen acquired horses and began shooting from horseback.) They favored, however, close combat weapons such as spears and clubs. Using these involved more risk, and also meant that the killer was right there to take a scalp or other sample of his victim. Legs and arms could be taken; scalps or heads were better.

Killing women and children was as highly esteemed as

Choctaw eagle dance. The dancers carry eagle tail feathers and weapons in their hands; their bodies are painted white. This sketch was made by Catlin in the 1830's, immediately after the Choctaws had been driven to Oklahoma, but the same dance with the same costumes was probably being performed when the white men first came to America. *Smithsonian Institution.*

Saturiba, a sixteenth-century war chief of the Timucuas, making a speech to a war party before it sets out. Near the end of his talk he took a bowl of water and flung the water in the air, saying. "As I have done with this water, so I pray that you may do with the blood of your enemies." Saturiba wears a sort of crown of feathers stuck into his hair; the seated warriors show an interesting variety of headdresses.

Sauvages Tchaktas matachez en Guerriers qui portent des chevelures.

An early French sketch of Choctaw Indians. The two men are painted for the warpath and carry scalps on their staffs. The seated figure with the feather crown may be a Natchez chief.

Smithsonian Institution.

Early French sketch of the chief of the Tunicas, with the widow and child of the former chief, who was killed by the Natchez. The living chief has his war paint on, and is carrying three Natchez scalps on his staff. *Peabody Museum, Harvard University.*

killing men, since to get to the non-combatants one had to go right into the town. Occasionally women and children were taken prisoner and eventually adopted into the enemy tribe. With most of the Southeasterners adult males were captured for only one reason—to torture them. Warrior prisoners were sometimes spared and adopted, but rarely, except among the Natchez, who kept up their strength by adopting boys and young men into the Stinker half of the tribe.

Live, young adult, male prisoners in good condition were hard to come by. A reasonable man would sooner die fighting than let himself be taken. When a town got one, everyone was delighted. First the returning warriors cleansed themselves from the magical influences of battle, then the captive was tied to a pole in the civic center and carefully and elaborately tortured to death. This dreadful procedure had about it a curious character of a competition. The victim sang his war songs, taunted his captors, did everything he knew to infuriate them and show his superior courage. The torturers, who were mostly the women, did their best to break him down before he died.

A love of fighting for the excitement of it and as a road to glory is found among many peoples. Our own ancestors elaborated it into the rituals of chivalry in the Middle Ages. This torture complex, the deep relish on the part of both men and women in inflicting the most extreme possible pain, is unusual. In other relationships the Indians of the Southeast were not especially cruel or unkind. They were as fond of laughter as anybody, capable of kindness and of love.

A good many attempts have been made to explain the psychology of their extreme cruelty in one special situation, something quite different from barbarous abuse of prisoners by warriors in the heat of anger, but none of them is really satisfactory. One fair one is that the tortur-

ing started as a way by which the women could relieve their feelings over the number of their husbands, sons, and brothers that had been killed by the other tribe, and that then, just as the Romans came to love their bloody spectacles, the people came to love the savage revenge and to refine it so that it became worse and worse.

They called their games, which were inclined to be rough, "the little brother of war," and prepared to play them with fasting and prayer. The most important game, which is still played by some of the surviving tribes such as the Choctaws, was the original of lacrosse. Lacrosse as we play it today, with teams of fixed sides, many rules, and umpires, is still no game for sissies. In its native, crude form, with all the able young men of a town in the play, it provided a splendid way to run risks and break heads, all in a spirit of fun and with no hard feelings.

It is a common observation in the course of history that warlike, aggressive, primitive tribes and nations are people of above-average energy and ability. A good example is the early Romans, who started out pretty much as a group of land pirates and developed into not only conquerors, but engineers, law-makers, and the greatest carriers of civilization that perhaps the world has ever known. It may be that at certain stages of development, certain tribes have more energy than the creative outlets they know of can use up. Given that circumstances require them to do a certain amount of fighting simply to hold their own, they find in warfare the outlet they need. Then when other outlets appear or are discovered, the same energy and ability goes into them.

Choctaw ball-player with the Southeastern form of lacrosse sticks and ceremonial costume, painted in Oklahoma in 1836. The metal studding of his belt, of course, was not available until the white man brought metal to the Indians. *Smithsonian Institution.*

The aboriginal form of lacrosse, as played by the Choctaws shortly after their removal to Oklahoma. One team's bodies are painted white. *Smithsonian Institution.*

Certainly the great tribes of the Southeast responded vigorously to the effects of contact with European civilization. Many of the tribes, such as the Calusas, Apalachees, and Tumucuas, are extinct. The white men were too much for them. Others survive today as mixed-blood remnants, little more than a handful of families, who have kept almost nothing of their old culture or tribal existence except a memory. The great tribes, however, came nearer than have any other group of American Indians to making an adjustment that would have enabled them to survive on their native ground as the full equals of the white men who came pouring around them.

These are the ones that became known later as "The Five Civilized Tribes." They are the Cherokees, Choctaws, Chickasaws, and Creeks, plus the Seminoles, a mixture of Creeks, survivors of certain smaller tribes, and runaway slaves that coalesced into a new tribe in Florida in historic times.

The English were settling on the Atlantic coast. The Spanish established themselves in Florida. The French,

Oglethorpe, the founder of Georgia, presenting Chief Tomochichi of the Creeks and other Indians to the Lord Trustees of the Colony of Georgia in 1734 in London.

Smithsonian Institution.

Stalking Turkey, a Cherokee chief who was brought to England with a delegation of Cherokees in 1762, painted in London. Indian beads, partly shaved head, scalp lock, and feather have been combined with European medals and silver gorget, clothing of European materials, and a fine steel knife to make the portrait more dramatic. Englishmen of those days were colorful dressers, but the Indians outdid them, and chiefs such as this, picturesque, handsome, and noble in their bearing, made a tremendous impression when they walked the streets of London.

Smithsonian Institution.

Sketch of a Cherokee man of 1820. His moccasins and leggings are buckskin, his coat is made out of a trade blanket.

Courtesy of The New-York Historical Society, N. Y. C.

after various tries in Florida and further north, concentrated in Canada and New Orleans and upwards along the Mississippi. All three nations courted the great tribes. Had the Four Tribes, as they were then, been capable of grasping the idea of forgetting their ancient enmities and uniting, they could have controlled absolutely the history of the Southeast. As it was, their friendships or enmities swayed the balance.

The English established an alliance with the Creeks, and relatively good relations with the Cherokees and Chickasaws, the French with the Choctaws (and the Natchez, while they lasted). The people nearest to the Spanish were the bands that were forming the Seminoles, but while there was a good deal of trade and interchange between the two groups, the Seminoles gave the Spanish no positive alliance, which put them at a disadvantage.

The Indian chiefs visited the white men's main settlements and dealt with their governors and councils. Some of them, especially the allies of the English, were taken overseas to meet the white men's kings. Traders and negotiators settled among the tribes and often married into them.

They saw the white men's clothing and possessions, their houses, their cattle, their crafts, their organization, and their use of slaves, and began to copy them. The Indian

costume changed radically. Many of them began building more solid houses. They acquired cattle. They learned the use of the spinning wheel. The Creeks began to tighten their organization into a confederacy intended to unite all the towns of the tribe. They bought slaves. Among them were established the descendants of the traders, with names such as MacIntosh, MacDonald, Ross, and Ridge, who were nonetheless true members of the tribes into which they had been born. They obtained firearms and ploughs, they became better off and stronger than they had ever been.

Small wonder that the Creeks did not hesitate to make a treaty ceding a little land near the coast to the colony of Georgia. The Creeks had no idea that the King of England had already given their entire territory to the settlers, nor that, if it came to a showdown, England could put such armies into the field as they could never defeat.

The English conquered Canada, and most of the French empire in the New World collapsed. The Spanish were weak, soon to quit Florida. The five major tribes in the Southeast found that they had no choice but to deal with England, which they did. The Crown did its best to deal honorably with them. As in its relations with the Iroquois further north, it saw in these Indians not only the owners of land, but an important factor in maintaining their empire against hostile tribes to the west, the threat of the Spanish in the Southwest, the possibility of a renewal of French ambitions. Under English influence, the Creeks tightened their confederacy and dominated the Cherokees and the Choctaws.

Then the colonies revolted. The Creeks did some fighting for England and suffered a defeat. So far as the tribes knew, their friendship with the King was old-established and permanent; they stood by him and he would stand by them. But suddenly Britain had pulled out of all the region south of Canada, the King had forgotten them, and their alliance was dead. Suddenly they confronted a new nation of hardy people who were interested only in the land the Indians occupied. The Americans kept pressing westward, demanding and taking ever more land. All along the line west of the white men's frontier, from the Great Lakes to the Gulf, the Indians began to realize that they were in danger, and that no words, spoken or written, would stop this new, unbelievably powerful tribe.

They had not yet reached the stage of really uniting. In what white men then called "the Northwest," the great Shawnee leader, Tecumseh, had the vision of uniting all the tribes, and to this end traveled everywhere among them. The Cherokees and Choctaws would not make war; the Chickasaws held back. The Creeks were divided; they would not join Tecumseh. Nonetheless, many of the towns

Creek house in 1791. The log walls and roof of shakes or slabs of split wood are copied from standard, white men's frontier construction. *Courtesy of American Museum of Natural History.*

were threatened by white settlers and were soon at war with them. The Creeks had considerable success until, in 1814, Andrew Jackson crushed them.

A little later the Seminoles were twice driven into defensive wars against Americans who wanted their Florida lands. The Seminoles were led by the famous Osceola, and under him put up a terrific resistance. Eventually their main strength was broken, but bands that refused to give

Coosa Tustennuggee, Creek chief, painted in 1825. This is one of a long series of portraits, painted in the early nineteenth century, of Indians who visited Washington. Many of the originals were destroyed by fire, but fortunately a complete set of copies had been made, which now hang in the Peabody Museum of Harvard University. *Peabody Museum, Harvard University.*

John Stedham, or Eolo, a good example of a Creek chief whose father was a white trader, painted in 1825. His costume is an interesting blend of the Indian and white costumes of the period. *Peabody Museum, Harvard University.*

up freedom held out in the swamps and forests of Florida. For a time the United States Army and Navy joined in a simple plan, which was to exterminate all the free Seminoles. They used thousands of men and spent millions of dollars, murdered a lot of Indians—and finally had to give up. To this day in Florida there are bands of Seminoles who claim, truthfully, and proudly, that they never surrendered to the United States.

The Five Tribes realized that they could never stand off the white men by force. The only hope was to learn their arts and become accepted by them as civilized people. The Cherokees and Creeks especially made great efforts to prove themselves to be peaceful, industrious, and progressive, worthy of the full protection of our laws.

There was a Cherokee, Sequoyah, who is commonly rated as a genius. Although the Cherokees had invited

Osceola, the famous chief of the Seminoles, who led them in their final war against the whites and put up one of the stiffest resistances Indians ever made.

Courtesy of American Museum of Natural History.

The campaign to exterminate the Seminoles. This naïve contemporary picture is a work of pure imagination, as may be seen by the fact that the artist has drawn tepees in the left background. It does give some idea of the ferocity with which the Seminole war was conducted. Bloodhounds in fact were used for tracking Indians, but it is doubtful that any performed as in this picture.

Library of Congress.

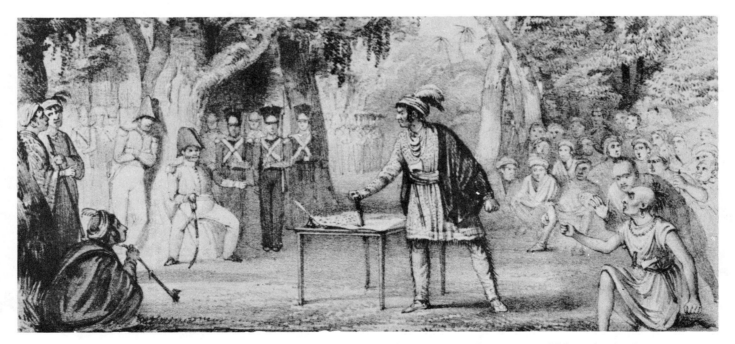

"Osceola's mode of signing a treaty." This somewhat imaginative painting records a dramatic incident in the great chief's refusal to make peace or cede any part of his native land.

Billy Bowlegs, a very able Seminole war-chief, on the warpatn. This painting gives an accurate idea of what Southeastern warriors of the early nineteenth century were like. For purposes of por-traiture, Bowlegs is shown without warpaint. Note tnat the paint on his two followers is not merely decorative, but also serves to some extent to camouflage them.

Courtesy of the City Art Museum, St. Louis.

missionaries to settle among them and open schools, tne schools did not go well. The missionaries were convinced that the Indian tongues could not be written. They taught only in English, according to archaic methods. The teach-ing went slowly, and the Indians were disappointed to find that after a year of study their children could read only a little English.

Sequoyah did not study in the schools, but he nung around them and studied the primers from his own point of view. Then he set to work making marks. He was sus-pected of witchcraft. His cabin was burned, and all his papers with it. He left the Cherokee country with a group of Indians who were seeking a place where they could be at peace, crossed the Mississippi, and settled in Arkansas.

Sequoyah (Sik-wa-yi), inventor of the Cherokee alphabet. He is wearing the silver medal that was presented to him by the Chero-kee legislature in 1824 in honor of his achievement.

Courtesy of American Museum of Natural History.

In 1821 he came back to the main tribe, bringing with him a *written message* from the Arkansas group.

He had invented a form of alphabet, using partly our characters (without regard to the values we give them), partly new ones he made up. The system was clumsy, but neatly adapted to writing his language. At first the Cherokees paid no attention to him. Finally they were convinced.

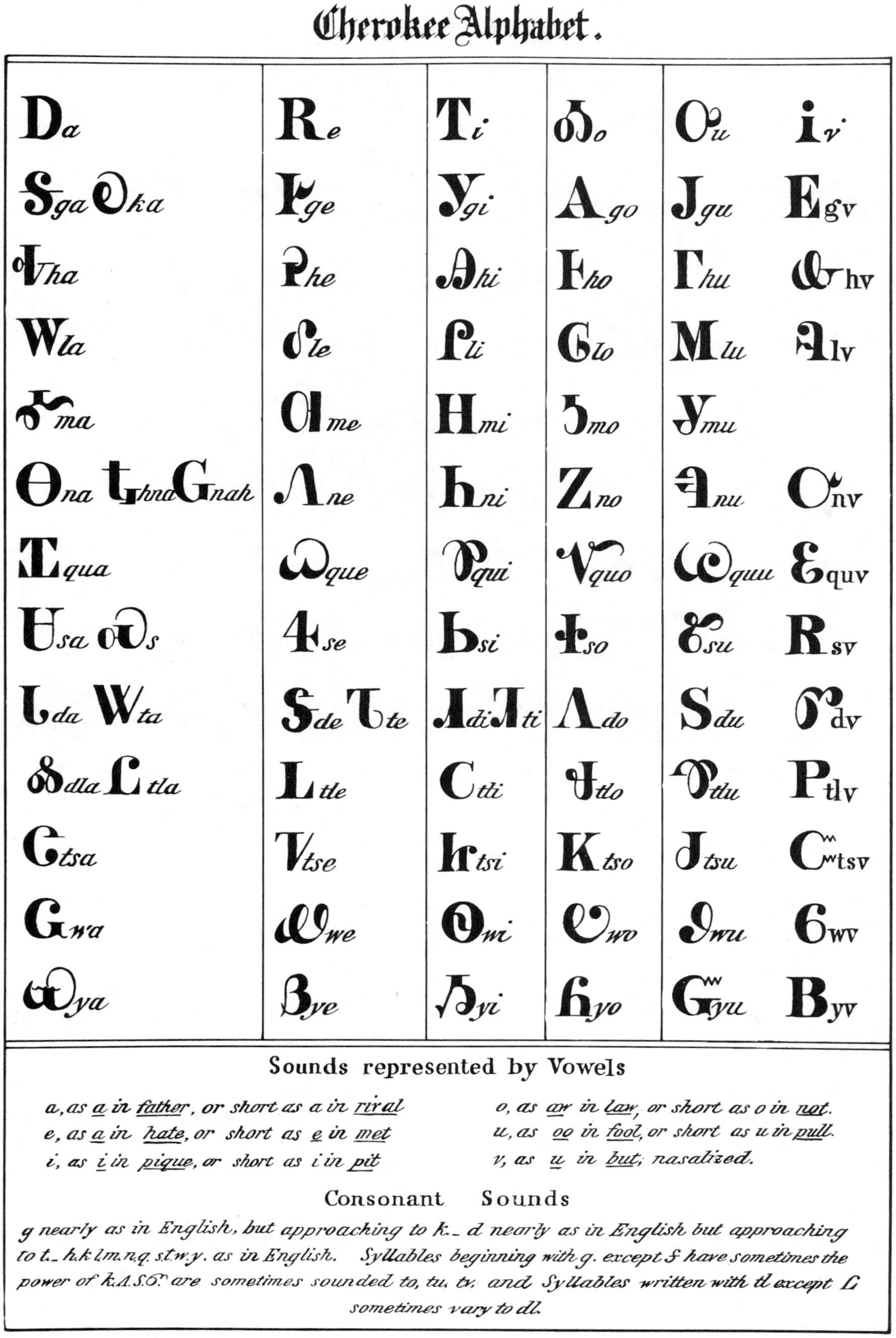

Cherokee Alphabet.

D a	R e	T i	ᴕ o	O u	i v
S ga Ꝺ ka	℉ ge	Ᏹ gi	A go	J gu	E gv
Ꭵ ha	Ꝓ he	Ꭿ hi	Ꮀ ho	Γ hu	Ꮿ hv
W la	Ꮭ le	Ꮭ li	Ꮈ lo	M lu	Ꮘ lv
Ꮫ ma	Ꮅ me	H mi	Ꮽ mo	ᗷ mu	
Ꮎ na Ꮤ hna Ꮕ nah	Λ ne	Ꮒ ni	Z no	Ꮔ nu	Ꮒ nv
Ꮖ qua	Ꮜ que	Ꮗ qui	� quo	Ꮘ quu	Ꮝ quv
Ꮚ sa Ꮕ s	4 se	Ᏸ si	Ꮎ so	Ꮢ su	R sv
Ꮭ da W ta	Ꮆ de Ꮦ te	Ꮝ di Ꭾ ti	Λ do	S du	Ꮼ dv
ᏛᏢ dla Ꮮ tla	L tle	C tti	Ꮺ tlo	Ꮯ tlu	P tlv
Ꮳ tsa	V tse	Ꮮ tsi	K tso	Ꮼ tsu	Ꮯ tsv
Ꮐ wa	Ꮃ we	Ꮝ wi	Ꮗ wv	Ꮽ wu	Ꮛ wv
Ꮽ ya	Ꮴ ye	Ꮝ yi	Ꮵ yo	Ꮕ yu	B yv

Sounds represented by Vowels

a, as *a* in *father*, or short as a in *rival*

e, as *a* in *hate*, or short as *e* in *met*

i, as *i* in *pique*, or short as i in *pit*

o, as *aw* in *law*, or short as o in *not*.

u, as *oo* in *fool*, or short as u in *pull*.

v, as *u* in *but*; nasalized.

Consonant Sounds

g nearly as in English, but approaching to k. d nearly as in English but approaching to t. h k l m n q s t w y. as in English. Syllables beginning with g. except Ꮝ have sometimes the power of k. Ꭿ Λ Ꮝ Ꮎ. are sometimes sounded to, tu, tv. and Syllables written with tl except Ꮮ sometimes vary to dl.

Sequoyah's alphabet, or syllabary, for writing Cherokee.
Smithsonian Institution.

A Portion of the Cherokee Phoenix, July 9, 1828

Part of a first page of the *Cherokee Phoenix,* published by the tribe partly in English, and partly in Cherokee written with Sequoyah's alphabet. *After Foreman.*

What happened then was astonishing. Everyone wanted to read and write. Old men, young warriors, housewives, old women at the spinning wheels, farmers when they rested from ploughing, boys and girls, studied the alphabet. In a matter of months virtually every Cherokee who was not an infant or senile could read and write. Young men went on trips just so they could show off by writing a girl a letter and mailing it, so that they sent her their words from afar.

The Creeks took up the writing. The Bible was printed in both languages, while the Cherokees published a newspaper. Most of the Five Tribes put their laws in writing; the Cherokees adopted a formal constitution with a legislature.

The Five Civilized Tribes, as they were now becoming, did invite white men in to help, but the great progress they made was their own, made on their own initiative. They developed their industries. They became peaceful. They farmed in the white man's manner and ran cattle. In the southern, fertile lowland areas, many of their farms were real plantations, complete with slaves. With the Cherokees in the lead, they were doing something that has seldom been done in all history. They were proving that a relatively primitive people can, on their own initiative, catch up with the Europeans in short order. Progress of this rare

sort cannot be imposed from without, it has to come from within.

As they turned to more intensive farming and, with livestock, became less dependent on hunting, larger populations of these Indians could live decently on smaller areas of land. Had any large number of white Americans of those days honestly believed that Indians were entitled to the same justice as themselves, in a few generations an Indian state might have come peacefully into the Union. White Americans could not let this happen. They wanted the Indians' land. They envied the prosperous farms and plantations. Gold was found inside some of the tribal territories. That settled it.

Between 1832 and 1839, by bribery, by persuasion, by fraud, and above all, by brutal force, the Indians of the Five Civilized Tribes were driven out of their homelands and moved to Oklahoma, a far, strange, unfriendly land. Several chiefs who had been bribed into signing away the old land were killed. Thousands of Indians, men, women, and children, died on the march, "The Trail of Tears." Not a few were shot or bayoneted trying to defend their homes, or as an example to others who were slow to move out.

Under the circumstances, the Indians had to sell their possessions for a song. They had the happy experience of

William McIntosh, head chief of the Lower Creeks, descended from a Scotch trader. He was executed by the Creeks on May 1, 1825, for having signed a treaty ceding Creek lands to the United States without the consent of his people. Both the Creeks and the Cherokees passed laws establishing the death penalty for making such cessions. *Smithsonian Institution.*

Mosholatubbee, or He Who Puts Out and Kills, principal chief of the Choctaw tribe at the time it was removed to Oklahoma.
Smithsonian Institution.

seeing white men moving into their houses as the troops herded them away.

Not all of them went. A fair number of Cherokees hid out in the mountains. These now occupy the Qualla reservation in North Carolina, the land for which was largely purchased with their own money. Some of the Choctaws evaded the troops, and remain scattered on small tracts of land in Mississippi. Nobody even tried to move the unconquered Seminole bands in the Florida wildernesses; they had stung us too often.

In a strange, new land, harassed from time to time by plains tribes of the West and by white outlaws, the Five Civilized Tribes set to work. They tamed the land, planted their farms, built up their herds. They set up competent, modern governments. Once again the printing press got going. They established a public school system. They were back on their feet.

Of course we could not leave them alone. The Five Civilized Tribes were Southerners; they sided with the South in the Civil War. That excused tearing up our treaties and making new, harsher ones. Even that was not enough. The white men were moving West, and some of Oklahoma was fine country. In the end we broke up the Indian Territory, destroyed the self-government system of the Five Civilized Tribes, and put an end to the last vestiges of an experiment in the ability of a group of American Indians, not to be civilized, but to civilize themselves.

Cherokee Indians of the period of the removal of the Cherokees
to Oklahoma.
Courtesy of The New-York Historical Society, N. Y. C.

III. Mothers and Tortures

The influence of the great civilizations of Mexico and Central America reached into the present-day United States along the Gulf Coast and spread upward almost to the Mason-Dixon line. At one time, as we know by the archeological remains, it reached farther, into Ohio.

The situation in North America in, say, 1500, resembled that in Europe at about 1000 B.C. At that time, Western civilization was centered on Egypt. It reached across the Mediterranean into the nearest parts of Europe in decreased form, and as you look farther north, the strength of the Egyptian influences steadily grows less until they disappear. Just so the Mexican influences reaching across the Gulf of Mexico grew weaker to the north, and the level of advancement grew lower.

North of the Cherokees and separated a little from them, the white men found a number of tribes, among the most fascinating people of North America, speaking dialects of the language we call Iroquois. This language is closely related to Cherokee. The Iroquoian tribes were in northern Ohio, Pennsylvania, New York, and held some of the country across the Saint Lawrence River in Canada. They tended to center upon the Great Lakes and the Saint Lawrence. Two of those lakes, Lake Huron and Lake Erie, are named for two of these tribes.

All around the Iroquoian territory were Algonkian-speaking tribes—generally bitter enemies of the Iroquoians. We shall look at them in the next chapter. The Iroquoian tribes, somewhat less civilized than the people of the Southeast yet more advanced than the tribes around them, were warlike and capable of extreme cruelty, but had much in their culture that is poetically beautiful. In them we still can see much that suggests influences of the Mexican civilizations, watered down and changed as we should expect when the ideas had traveled so far and reached a harsher, wintry, northern climate.

Originally the Iroquoian tribes made war pretty freely upon each other, when they were not busy fighting the Algonkians. Like the people of the South, however, the Iroquoian tribes were highly organized and they had a tendency to form confederacies, of which originally the greatest was the one led by the Hurons.

Sometime in the 1400's, five tribes living in what is now New York State organized into a definite league, which the early settlers called the Five Nations. We mean the tribes of this league when we speak of "The Iroquois," and this chapter is mainly about them. The five united tribes are the Seneca, the Cayuga, the Onondaga, the Oneida, and the Mohawk.

Iroquois harvest. The women, working together, gather the ears of corn in elm-bark boxes, shuck them, and drop the ears into a larger box of the same material. In warm fall weather, they wear only their buckskin or doeskin skirts. *Courtesy of American Museum of Natural History.*

Detail of a model showing Iroquois women preparing corn after the harvest. Several are cooking corn in earthenware pots, another grinds it in a wooden mortar with a double-ended pestle, another sifts it through a basket. This model shows, more accurately than the last one, the women's prehistoric warm-weather mode of dressing, with skirts, leggings and moccasins. In the background can be seen a house of the round-roofed type.

Courtesy of American Museum of Natural History.

These tribes, whose territory reached across part of Pennsylvania and the heart of upper New York, occupied a rich and fertile land. They farmed on a large scale, raising fifteen varieties of corn, no less than sixty kinds of beans, and squashes. Wild strawberries, wild greens and herbs, and maple sugar enriched their vegetable diet. The men cleared the fields, cutting down and burning the trees; thereafter, the farming was done by the women. This was not quite as unfair an arrangement as it seems, since the fields and crops belonged to the women.

The men hunted deer, trapped beaver, killed duck, turkey, and wild pigeons, and fished. For the fishing, they dammed the streams, and worked with very large nets made of vines. The women did much of their farming in groups, helping each other and turning work into a sociable occasion. So, too, the men did much of their hunting in parties.

The division of labor between men and women does tend to lay the greatest load of dull work on women, but it is not as lopsided as most people think. Even today, housework is usually considered women's work, and many

a housewife wishes she could escape to the relative ease of her husband's office. To the housework and rearing of the young children, many Indian tribes added the greater part or all of the farming. It was the men's good fortune that their main work was much more interesting. The men's jobs were hunting, which was not always fun—for instance, in deep winter when the family was hungry and the game proved to be scarce—fighting, trade, politics, and government, and a large part of the religion. They took religion seriously, worked hard at it, and wove it into every moment of their lives.

The Iroquois lived in compact villages surrounded by strong, wooden stockades. They built long buildings with rounded roofs, rather like Quonset huts, and the buildings usually referred to as "longhouses," written as a single word, with pitched roofs. Both were covered with elm bark, laid on like clapboards. A longhouse would shelter many families of one clan. There was a row of fires down the middle, with a smoke-hole over each. To the right and left of each fire was a room, which was the indoor home of one family. By all accounts the longhouses were smoky.

Model of family life in one of the front chambers of a Seneca Iroquois longhouse. The baby hangs in a cradleboard, the man is carving a wooden bowl. One form of the aboriginal tomahawk lies at his feet. *Museum of Arts and Sciences, Rochester, N. Y.*

Model of Iroquois village life. The men are putting up the framework of a new longhouse. Note the notched pole at the right, serving as a ladder for climbing into the building with the raised floor. *Museum of Arts and Sciences, Rochester, N. Y.*

Another section of the same model of Iroquois village life. A man is putting the bark covering onto the new house, another carries in a deer. One women is scraping a hide, another sewing, a third carries in a basket of corn, while the one talking to the child shapes pottery. *Museum of Arts and Sciences, Rochester, N. Y.*

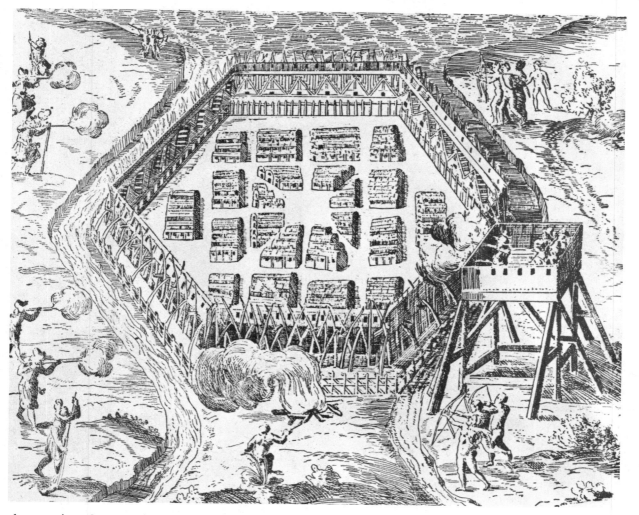

Early French engraving of an attack by Champlain, with French troops and Indian allies, on an Onondaga village in 1615. The village was elaborately fortified with moats and a double stockade. The fire of the white men's guns from the platform they built terrified the Onondagas and the village was soon taken. This was the beginning of the hostility of the Iroquois toward the French, that finally cost the French their empire in North America.

Smithsonian Institution.

noisy, and the dogs were a nuisance, but they were also warm and weatherproof. The houses were built by the men, but belonged to the women.

Elm bark, which was used for the walls and roofs, was important in many ways. The Iroquois were not in good birch-bark country, so elm was what they mostly used, shaping it into utensils, even making canoes out of it. Elm-bark canoes could be easily made, but they were heavy and clumsy. They did have one advantage for war. If you were attacking a stockaded village, you could up-end some canoes against the stockade and climb up the rough bark of their bottoms.

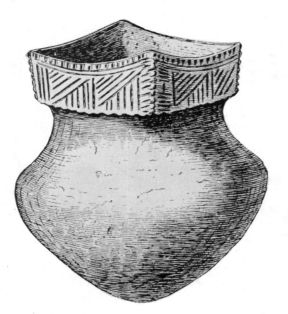

Typical Iroquois pottery, with rounded body and square, decorated neck. *Courtesy of American Museum of Natural History.*

The Iroquois' arts were not nearly as fine as the Southeasterners'. They did make well-smoothed, decorated pottery, better than the Algonkians. They wove an interesting type of sash by a form of weaving that continues to this day. Nowadays the work is done with cotton and wool; originally it must have been done with wild fibers made up into thread. The Iroquois probably did not make any wampum, since they did not live on the coast where clamshells, from which the beads were made, could be had. They must have got it in trade, by raiding, or as tribute, but they developed its use to a high pitch.

Strings of wampum were carried by messengers. Belts or strips of it, in various designs, were often messages or documents in themselves, and records of tribal legends and history were kept on strings of various lengths and arrangements of dark and light beads. Specialists were assigned to memorize the full meaning of a number of strings and belts, which served really as reminders of matters far more elaborate than the strings themselves could record. These men were something on the order of living libraries, able to recite great quantities of important matters as they ran their fingers over the records.

The Iroquois lived in a land of hard, snowy winters. They wore far more clothes than did the people of the South. As a usual thing in the history of mankind, the

Iroquois priest. He is dressed much as all the men dressed in cold weather. Not being a warrior, he has not shaved his head down to the scalp lock.
Courtesy of American Museum of Natural History.

Iroquois warrior in aboriginal costume, carrying a message of wampum. He stands by the bark wall of the longhouse. The wampum is in his left hand. In his right he holds the original form of tomahawk, an efficient club. Often these clubs had a spike of stone or a tooth set in the ball to make them more deadly. All his hair except the scalp lock has been shaved off, and his face is painted. This is not "war paint"; the wampum shows that he is acting as a messenger.

Courtesy of American Museum of Natural History.

Iroquois woman in full, ancient costume, standing at a mortar for pounding corn. There is a large storage basket just behind her.

Courtesy of American Museum of Natural History.

49

Iroquois silverwork—two pairs of earrings. The Iroquois had no knowledge of silver or other metals until the white man brought them; thereafter they developed skill in working metals.
Museum of the American Indian.

When exposed to civilized society, the Iroquois took readily to European costume, always wearing it with touches of their own. This portrait of a Mohawk Iroquois chief was painted in London in the early eighteenth century. He has tied an Iroquois sash around his coat, and holds a wampum belt in his hand. The wolf shown behind him undoubtedly means that he was a member of the Wolf Clan.
Courtesy of American Museum of Natural History.

wearing of clothes starts with the need for warmth and protection. Then people find that clothing can also be a decoration, and start going dressed when they do not need to. After that, being accustomed to seeing everyone covered, the sight of someone uncovered becomes startling, and the idea of modesty is born.

The Iroquois men when fully dressed wore leggings, breech-clouts, and kilts of buckskin, moccasins, and buckskin shirts. In summer this dress might be reduced to breech-clout, kilt, and moccasins. The women wore skirts and leggings in warm weather, full dresses of buckskin when it was cooler.

The combination of leggings, breech-clout, and a kilt of some form to cover the gaps where the leggings and breech-clout fail to meet, occurs over a large part of North America. It is the last step before inventing trousers, which require much more difficult cutting, fitting, and sewing. It is not surprising that the Indians did not take the step over to making trousers, since the easier combination was satisfactory, and sewing through even the softest hides with bone awls or thorns is hard work, as is cutting with stone knives. Trousers and fitted shirts are an Arctic invention; in the far north, the Eskimos had them, as did all the Arctic peoples clear to the Atlantic coast of Europe.

Such nations as the Romans were in touch with people who had been making trousers for hundreds of years, but did not bother to copy them until the betrousered northerners overran them. They preferred to wrap themselves in very fancy blankets, which they called "togas."

The Indians went part way, making the relatively easy legs. Many tribes also learned to tailor shirts and women's dresses neatly, since they found that worth the trouble. Very early they found that when you cut a shirt out of buckskin, you are left with a lot of fragments that are not of much use when buckskin is plentiful. So it occurred to them, instead of cutting these pieces clear off, to make them into fringes.

All Iroquois life was involved with religion. Spirits of all sorts abounded, affecting everything they did. In addition to the ever-present spirits, and the ghosts of the dead who were also present, there were divine beings whom we can well call gods: above all, the Master of Life from whom

50

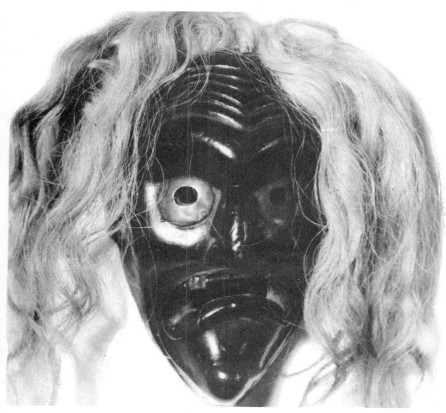

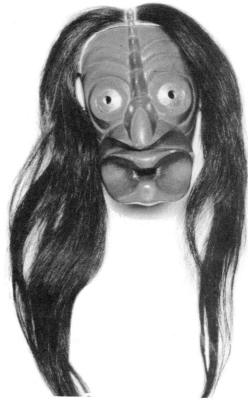

Masks of the False Face Society, worn in the ritual to get rid of the influence of the evil "False Face" spirits. These grotesque, carved faces show an interesting combination of skill, sense of horror, and sense of humor.

Religious dance mask of the Husk Face Society, made of braided corn husks. Masks such as this were important for their symbolism, not their beauty.

came all good things, and his opposite and brother, who was the maker of evil. The good god and the evil one were in constant struggle together.

A human consisted of three parts: his body, what we may call his soul, and his spirit or ghost. When he died, his soul departed for the afterlife, a kind of heaven. It was not the "happy hunting ground." In this book there will be little talk of a "happy hunting ground" or of a "Great Spirit." These are white men's ideas, derived from early information that was misunderstood. Having once got these ideas into their heads, white men inflicted them on tribe after tribe as they went along, regardless of what the tribes' true beliefs might be.

The ghost, as distinct from the spirit, remained near the place of burial and continued to share in the life of the living. A war party might consist of so many live warriors, and a great flock of dead ones coming along to share in the excitement. For the ghosts' benefit, feasts were given in the wintertime, at which the barriers between living and dead were broken down, so that the ghosts shared in the food, the dancing, the games, and the warmth.

There was another form of spirit, the idea of which is difficult for white men to understand, since most white men, except theologians, find it hard to grasp the idea of a powerful spirit that is completely impersonal. This the Iroquois called "orenda." It pervaded all things, and was the sacred or divine essence that related all the elements of this world to each other, including men. A concept along this general line is common among the Indians.

Certain things and men could accumulate more orenda than others. Men got it chiefly through significant dreams. This gave them strength both in daily life and in sacred things. Those who dreamed powerfully enough became shamans, with power to cure sicknesses. Especially important were those who dealt with the False Faces. These were horrible heads without bodies that appeared to people in the forests and bewitched them into sickness. The members of the False Face Society broke the evil spell by a ceremony in which they themselves wore wooden masks carved in the likeness of the False Faces.

Dreams were of great importance; in fact, the Iroquois part way arrived at the ideas of modern psychology. Certain dreams had to be obeyed, and it was dangerous to let a lot of dreams pile up inside one's self without unloading them.

We are likely to find the idea of shamans with magical power among hunting tribes, while among more advanced, agricultural tribes we find fixed, major ceremonies conducted by carefully trained people who are more properly called priests. The Iroquois had both. Their most important ceremony came in the great New Year festival in the month Diagona, the second moon after the winter solstice —that is, in late January or early February.

This was the dead of winter, when the Master of Life might bring back the spring or his enemy might prevent it. The rituals to help the Master went on for days. At the beginning, old fires were scattered and new ones made, which is the same "new fire" idea, certainly of Mexican origin,

Model showing the False Face ceremony being held during the midwinter "New Year Ceremony."

Museum of Arts and Sciences, Rochester, N. Y.

Eagle dance of the Senecas, painted by a Seneca artist. In this picture the costumes clearly show the influence of the white men, being in large part made of woven material. Also notice that the men have given up shaving their heads and instead wear their hair long and gathered in loose braids, a relatively recent practice.

Smithsonian Institution.

that existed in the Southeast. There were many rituals of cleansing, many prayers, and a re-enactment of the gambling contest in which the Master of Life won spring and green growth and all good things from the forces of evil. In the course of the ceremony, there came the unloading of dreams. Some, if they wished, narrated their dreams in public. The Iroquois realized that dreams betrayed one's secret wishes and guilty acts, so most preferred to tell them, under strictest secrecy, to chosen experts, who interpreted them.

At the end, there was a solemn sacrifice of a white dog of a special breed.

This was the time of year when the matrons, the heads of the longhouses, gave new names to adults who had earned them. There was solemn ritual dancing, there was dancing for fun. There were games, clowning, even something like charades.

Note the timing of this festival. It came in the worst of winter. The crops had long been harvested. The men had done their fall hunting and fishing, and after the snow lay deep and the bitter cold was all around, tended to stay put in the crowded houses. Everyone was cooped up. Day in and day out, everyone saw too much of everyone else. Supplies of fresh foods were gone. Shortly the winter should break, the sap begin to rise in the sugar maples. For this feast, the men had to bestir themselves and hunt, disagreeable though that might be, which did them good. Then everyone cut loose in a mixture of fun and solemn piety, with the psychological purging of unloading the dreams thrown in. The result must have been a great relaxing of tensions.

A lot of bunk has been written about "matriarchies," that is, societies ruled by women. So far, we know of no such society in ancient or modern times. The Iroquois did come as close to it as anybody ever did. Like a number of other primitive societies, they gave women a higher position than they ever enjoyed among white men until very recent times.

The fields, the crops, the houses, belonged to the women. This meant that they had the upper hand economically. Descent was traced through the women; a child belonged to its mother's clan. The people all belonged to local clans, such as Wolf, Deer, Turtle, and Snipe. The animal "totem" of the clan was shown over the door of each longhouse, which was occupied by members of one clan plus their husbands. Men went to live with their wives when they married. If the marriage broke up, it was the man who went home to mother, leaving his children behind him.

The Senecas, Cayugas, and Onondagas were further divided into moieties, or halves. One moiety consisted of the Turtle clan plus all clans named after four-footed animals except Deer. The other was made up of the Deer and the clans named after birds. Members of one moiety always married members of the other, a good way to prevent inbreeding in relatively small communities, and the moieties did various services for each other, especially burying each others' dead. They also played against each other in various games, among them a form of lacrosse much like that played by the Southeastern tribes.

Each clan was further divided into "lineages," that is,

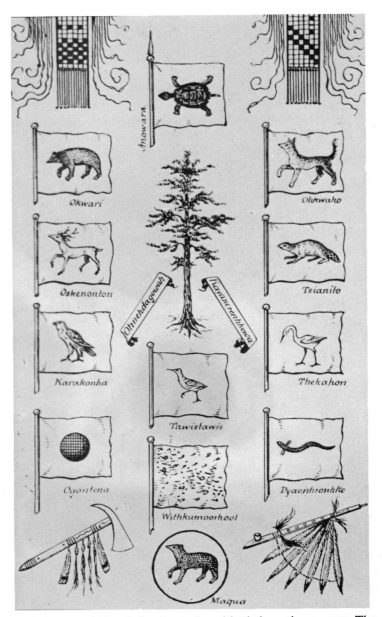

The clan symbols of the Iroquois, with their native names. The pine tree in the middle stands for the League. Strips of wampum are shown at the top as decorations, a late model tomahawk and a tobacco pipe at the bottom.
Museum of Arts and Sciences, Rochester, N. Y.

members descended from a common ancestor. At the head of each lineage was an older woman, the matron. Certain lineages were called "noble"—and still are—and from them the various chiefs or sachems were chosen. The term "sachem," which is Algonkian, is used here for those chiefs who sat in the tribal council and helped to rule the tribe.

When a sachem died, the matron of his lineage selected his successor from among the men of his lineage, then announced her choice to the other women of her longhouse, then to the clan. Undoubtedly the choice was talked over carefully among the women before it was announced, because once it was made public, it was almost always ratified. The matron then got the approval of her moiety, then of the opposite one. When the period of mourning for the dead chief was ended, the candidate was installed and received the deer horns that were his badge of office.

If the new sachem did badly, the matron would warn him three times. If he still did not improve, the fourth time

54

she would "remove the horns" by asking the council to depose him. The council seldom failed to do so. In short, women did not rule, they did not give orders, but they chose the rulers and, by their power of recall, had a good deal of influence over them.

Not long before the first white men came to North America, the Five Nations of the Iroquois organized their famous League, which they called "The Great Peace." The idea seems to have started with a prophet named Deganawida, who had a vision of a great spruce tree with its top reaching through the sky to the land of the Master of Life. The tree was the sisterhood of all tribes, and its roots were the five Iroquois tribes. An eagle perched at its top, keeping watch against any enemy that might come to break the peace.

The idea of the Great Peace was a sort of League of Nations, headed by the Iroquois. It involved three principles, each in turn a pair—health of body and mind, and peace between individuals and between tribes; right conduct and thought, and justice and respect for human rights; preparedness for defense, and maintaining and strengthening the spiritual power called orenda.

Deganawida inspired a somewhat more practical man, Hiawatha, who probably had the main share in setting up the actual workings of the League. There is great contusion about Hiawatha, because Longfellow wrote a poem of that name that many of us had to read in school. Longfellow got hold of some legends of the Chippewas, an Algonkian people who were quite unlike the Iroquois, prettied them up, and centered them upon a fictional hero whom he called Hiawatha. This fictitious character has nothing to do with the real Iroquois statesman.

It was typical of Iroquois daring and Iroquois high-mindedness to conceive of the confederacy as something that should embrace all of the world they knew. It is probable, nonetheless, that the League came into being largely be-

Iroquois costume changed greatly after woven materials and commercial beads became plentiful. This group of models shows Iroquois man, woman, and child of the period from shortly after the Revolution to about 1820. Even the papoose's cradle is decorated with beadwork. The man's costume is cut along the old lines, but there is no fringe, and the general effect is different. The man, who is expounding the meaning of a wampum belt, wears his hair long, in braids. The woman's handsome outfit has evolved considerably more away from the ancient models.

cause of the hard necessity of stopping fighting among the five tribes, so that they might better use their strength against the enemy aliens who surrounded them.

The League was a strong force for a good three hundred years, and it is not dead today. It is often claimed that ideas were drawn from it in the framing of our own Constitution. This cannot be proven, but a number of the main writers of the Constitution were thoroughly familiar with the League. It had in it one idea, at least, that could have been helpful to the founding fathers, who had to work out a strong union of sovereign states that the states would accept. The League dealt with war and foreign relations, but had no power to interfere in the internal affairs of any of the member tribes. If there was a quarrel between tribes, they might ask the League to arbitrate.

The council of the League was made up of fifty sachems from the Five Tribes. These were the same men who were selected by the matrons to govern the individual tribes; thus the power of the women reached to the very top. When a new sachem came onto the League council, he received the name of his predecessor, which was the

A Seneca "squah . . . with his papou," sketched by the French-woman, Baroness Hyde de Neuville, in 1808. This lady, much less elegant than the one in the model, is also dressed entirely in woven materials.

name of one of the fifty original councilors. In addition to these officials, drawn from the "noble" lineages only, there grew up a group of people called "Pine Trees," a title that any outstanding men or women could earn, regardless of his descent. Because one of the easiest ways for a man to become outstanding was as a warrior, the Pine Trees tended to be a group of war leaders. They came to form something like a separate house of the League's congress, but without the vote.

The League council met in the Onondaga country in summer. Only Pine Trees and sachems spoke at the council. Others listened in, and might ask their sachems to speak for them. When a matter had been thoroughly debated, the sachems of each tribe withdrew and held a caucus, as in the end each tribe had one vote. If the vote was not unanimous, the sachems went on discussing until they reached a unanimous agreement.

Most people strengthen important matters with ritual. We have two sets of ritual—religious and legal. Thus, wanting to make marriages strong, we rate marriage as a major religious act and surround it with religious ritual, then we set up an elaborate legal ritual for breaking marriages up. Primitive people make less distinction than do we between law and religion; as in the case of the League of the Iroquois, they will trace what we think of as purely lay institutions to visions and divine inspirations. Just so the Iroquois strengthened the unity of their League with ceremonial, developing some very impressive observances, especially around the installation of a new sachem, preceded by an elaborate ritual of comforting those who mourned his dead predecessor, "beautifying the sky" so that once again the mourners could look at it in peace.

The Iroquois did not make the cult of warfare that the Southeasterners did, but they always had fighting on their hands. War was a young man's road to advancement. Their warfare was mostly a matter of raids by small parties. Sometimes a man would go out alone, to win fame. At least one Iroquois, somewhat in the spirit of a stamp collector paying a great price for a rare specimen, went as far as Wisconsin, passing for days through the territory of enemy tribes, to bring back a unique scalp from a hitherto unknown tribe.

As the League grew strong, raiding was brought under control. Only those tribes with which the council declared a state of war to exist could be attacked. When, after the white men came, the pressures upon all the Indians grew serious, the Iroquois could put armies of five hundred or a thousand men in the field, a scale of operation until then unknown in that part of the world. For long they held the balance of power in the northeast. The French chose to support the Algonkians (whom they first met in Canada) and the Hurons and some of the other Iroquoian tribes. The Dutch, and after them the English, made allies of the Iroquois (the Five Tribes) and armed them. This choice probably determined the fate of North America, as it was a major factor in enabling the English to win the French and Indian War which broke French power on the continent.

At its height, before the Revolution, the Iroquois' Great Peace covered northern New York, Pennsylvania, and much of Ohio. Many tribes paid tribute to them. A number of others, such as the powerful Delawares of the sea coast, displaced by the white men, were given land on which to settle and become subordinate members of the League. The Iroquoian-speaking Tuscaroras moved up from the South to join the League, which thereafter was called "The Six Nations." These additions were thoroughly voluntary. In other cases, the Iroquois would first break a tribe's power by the new method of mass warfare, then bring it in as a subject group, under Iroquois dominance and protected by the Iroquois. So powerful was the League that in some cases, when white men wanted to make a treaty and buy land from a given tribe, they had to get the consent of the League Council. After the Delawares had been taken in, the Iroquois were able to force the Pennsylvania government to stop the sale of liquor to that tribe.

This kind of imperialism takes manpower and costs lives. The Iroquois kept up their strength by their system of adoption, sometimes of all that was left of an Iroquoian tribe that they had broken, more often by adopting individuals. This system, in turn, was part of their unusual, and often fearful, pattern of dealing with prisoners.

The Iroquois were a fairly advanced people. They were loving toward their friends. Their rituals were beautiful, their legends and their prayers full of poetry. Yet they were at times incredibly cruel.

They took as many prisoners as they could, not only strong warriors but also women and children, although young men were preferred. On the way home, these unfortunates were driven as we would not drive animals, and killed if they lagged. When the prisoners reached the village, everyone lined up with clubs and sticks in two lines, between which the victims were made to run. The prisoners were then turned over to the tribal council, which handed them out to the women of families that had lost members. Women prisoners, as a rule, and old men were kept as servants, pretty much as slaves. Children, especially boys, were likely to be adopted into the tribe. So were the captive warriors, and it was the matrons of the family to which they were added who decided whether they should be kept or tortured to death. If they were kept, they became loyal members of their new tribe, and if they were killed, this was done to them as fellow-tribesmen and kinsmen.

This whole group of customs was strange to white men who came to know the Iroquois. A man's native tribe thought none the worse of him for having joined another under such circumstances. There were times when most of the manpower of a tribe might be naturalized "foreigners." The warrior received torture with equal equanimity. When he had become a warrior, he had known that torture was one of the risks he ran. There were no hard feelings involved, fiendish though some of the things the women thought up to do to a victim might be. Like the Southeasterners, the Iroquois captive did his level best to prove that he was too good a man for all their cruelty to break down. This slow killing was thought of as a sacrifice to Aireskoi, spirit of war and hunting and probably also of the sun. One prayer connected with it, and translated by a white man, tells the spirit, or demi-god, ". . . we offer thee this victim whom we burn for thee,

that thou mayest be filled with her flesh and render us ever anew victorious over our enemies."

Notice that this prayer, as recorded, refers to the victim as "her." Women were occasionally tortured when no men could be had. The whole system of slow sacrifices among the Iroquois seems to have been more of a religious necessity and less of an occasion of mere public fun than among the tribes of the Southeast. However that may be, it was carried out on a sizable scale, with dreadful ingenuity. The victim was given water whenever he thirsted, was rested at moments, might even be fed if he could eat, so that he would last. If he was not kept going for a good twenty-four hours, everyone thought it a shame.

The victim, if he had any self-respect at all, acted as if his destiny were a high honor. He feasted with his captors, danced and sang for them. He conversed with his enemies between agonies, and while the torments were being applied, ridiculed and defied them. On one occasion that was observed by white men, an elderly sachem rebuked a number of young men and women who had slipped off into the woods together while the torture was going on, which showed lack of respect for the man who was so bravely entertaining everyone.

During the war between the Five Nations and the Hurons, which ended in the destruction of the latter, an Iroquois prisoner called Saouandanancous was brought in by the Hurons. His hands had been seriously injured. After he had been feasted, the old chief into whose family he had been adopted addressed him with genuine sorrow. He had hoped that the Iroquois would replace his son, but as his hands had been ruined, that could not be. "So take courage," the Huron said, "and prepare to die tonight like a brave man."

He was tenderly cared for and fed all through that day. From the original account, which has been made famous by the historian Parkman, it is clear that many of the Hurons felt real compassion for him and wished there was some way out of destroying him. This did not stop them from killing him by fire in such a manner that it took over twelve hours, always, as one Huron or another applied the particular pain he had been meditating, addressing the man in a kindly way. During one of the intervals when they revived him and let him rest, he gave them news of the Iroquois and of Hurons who had been adopted into that tribe; during another he sang. Once he was dead, he was carved up and the pieces distributed for eating, for the Iroquoians frequently ended their sacrifice with cannibalism.

Again we have to wonder how so dreadful a custom could start and how it could continue. There were no psychologists around then to study the people. Undoubtedly the torture pattern, the feasting of the victim (even on some occasions providing him with a bride for the night before his death), and the cannibalism—not out of love of human flesh, but as a way of absorbing some of a fine man's bravery—came up from the South and originally from Mexico. We ourselves have learned from the accounts of Nazis and of other modern totalitarian countries that cruelty is something of a drug. At first it revolts men, then they get used to it, then they begin to crave it. But the Iroquois practiced their unspeakable cruelty only in a single situation, and even then did not justify it by affecting to hate the victim or think of him as a criminal; instead, they loved and admired him. It is a curious riddle.

The Iroquois and their relatives, the Iroquoians, may have taken this custom for granted; it did not sit so well on white men or on many of the Algonkian tribes. Some of these tribes did engage in torture as the Iroquois did. Mostly it was Iroquois they tortured, when they could get them. The victims must have regarded this as a real social comedown. The practice made the Iroquois hated and feared; it gave them an evil name that was spread out to Indians in general, and made Americans overlook and forget their virtues.

In the French and Indian War the Iroquois tipped the balance of power. In the Revolution, they were loyal to their alliance with Britain, raised Ned all over northern New York and the adjacent parts of Pennsylvania, and tied down hundreds of American fighting men. So long as the colonials were English, they and the Iroquois were friends. In the Revolution the colonials became Americans, and for the first time, and for a brief period, tasted the military power and the horror they had so willingly turned loose against the French and against other Indian tribes. After the Revolution, the British offered the Iroquois a reservation in Canada, to which many of them moved. As many or more preferred to stay in their home country. There is a contention today between the New York and Canadian Iroquois as to which group has the right to call a League council. Some of the decisive wam-

Cornplanter, one of the great Seneca chiefs, painted in 1796. A principal leader of the Iroquois in their warfare against the Americans during the Revolution, afterwards he played an important part in working out the peace treaty with George Washington, under which the League received reservations in the United States and became subject to the new nation.

Courtesy of The New-York Historical Society, N. Y. C.

Massacre of the Johanas Dietz family by Iroquois during the Revolution, as imagined by an artist not long after. At the extreme left a warrior marches off with a collection of scalps on a pole. Behind him three captives are being taken along.

N. Y. Public Library Picture Collection.

pum records went north with those who migrated, some of them were kept at home.

To the annoyance of many New Yorkers, George Washington made a just peace with the tribe. Washington's policy paid off importantly. During the War of 1812, with British backing, the Shawnee chief, Tecumseh, built up a formidable alliance of the tribes between Ohio and the Mississippi River that posed a real threat to the northern United States. This the Iroquois refused to join. Their ancient alliance with Britain had ended, and their word was pledged to the new nation. Had the Iroquois thrown in with Tecumseh, the British troops and Indians combined might well have overrun the whole northern part of the country and brought the war to a very different ending.

During the nineteenth century, the Iroquois were talked into ceding a good deal of their land, and some of them finally were moved to Oklahoma. About nine thousand of them, however, remain in New York, still keeping their identity and still holding to the tradition of the League.

Joseph Brandt, or Thayandanega, a Mohawk, and most famous of the Iroquois chiefs at the time of the Revolution. Educated in English mission schools, he was commissioned a colonel in the British Army. Although he did not become a sachem of the League until 1807, he was the principal leader in holding the Six Nations loyal to their alliance with Britain. After the Revolution, he settled on a grant of land in Canada. He was important enough to have this portrait painted by the famous Englist artist, Romney.
Smithsonian Institution.

Red Jacket, a great Iroquois orator and leader of the tribes against the Americans. He hated all white men with the exception of Washington, who gave him the medal he is seen wearing in this portrait. After the war, he lived on in New York, always fighting for conservatism and the retaining of the old ways. Unfortunately, he was not conservative when it came to liquor, and ended his life as a shabby alcoholic.
Courtesy of The New-York Historical Society, N. Y. C.

IV. The Wigwam People

For many thousands of years, the northern part of the United States from the Atlantic all across to the Rocky Mountains was occupied by tribes of simple hunters speaking languages of the family we call Algonkian. Their territory also extended far into Canada, in the east reaching to Hudson's Bay and covering all the sub-Arctic except the narrow strips of coast held by Eskimos. Among the eastern Algonkians two physical types can be recognized. The older type is longheaded; to them, in prehistoric times, was added a roundheaded group, the two mingling together. The longheads, at least, were very early immigrants to America.

In this chapter we are concerned with the Algonkians east of the Mississippi, and primarily with the ones who lived along the coast. Almost all these tribes, when they were first met by white men, built wigwams, which are dome-shaped frames made of bent poles, covered with bark where bark was plentiful—birchbark wherever good birchbark could be had—or with rushes tied on, or with woven mats, or combinations of these materials. A small

wigwam can be built quickly, but it is not in itself a mobile dwelling.

A few of the Algonkians, even near the coast, also made a dwelling that was a form of tepee. A number of poles are arranged to form a cone, over which, instead of skin, as in the common type of tepee, bark is laid, and held in position by placing more poles on the outside. The framework can be easily taken down and moved from place to place. Such tepees are found mostly among Canadian tribes.

Unless there exists an exceptional concentration of game, hunting tribes are likely to live spread out, in family groups or small bands. A whole tribe seldom assembles. The scattered groups lose touch with each other, their manner of speech is likely to change, they develop into separate tribes. Their organization is loose and informal. Usually you do not find chiefs with any authority, although in any band there will be a man who is listened to by the others because of his wisdom and experience. This was the case with the eastern Algonkians, originally.

Model of a wigwam with one side uncovered to show the framework and pole bed inside. The wigwam shown is of the Chippewas, a tribe living in Wisconsin, but it is typical of aboriginal Algonkian wigwams everywhere.
Courtesy of the American Museum of Natural History.

Tepee-shaped wigwam of the Penobscot Indians of Maine. The main part of the wigwam is covered with birchbark, with a doorway of hide, probably moose hide.
Courtesy of the American Museum of Natural History.

lent of a bible, but shamans or medicine men who usually received their power in dreams and specialized in curing sickness and driving off evil spirits. Among some of the tribes, these shamans developed into remarkable magicians. Tricks such as making the hut dance and shake as if a terrible storm were blowing outside, making animal spirits talk out of the darkness, plunging a knife into empty air and bringing it back covered with blood, compare with the best that magicians and mediums can do today.

All over the world, the type of religious magician that scientists call shamans claim that their knowledge all came through dreams or some such inspiration. It is always clear enough, however, that they have also received considerable instruction. Still, each shaman has a formula of his own, and he is likely to have spent more time learning tricks than in learning doctrine.

The Algonkians of Canada, who still lived in the old manner when white men discovered them, were fairly peaceful. Nobody had taught them that war was glorious, they had no special cause for fighting, and hunting kept the men busy.

History brought about great changes in the life of the Algonkians of the United States. The civilizing influences from Mexico, with their strange blend of corn, cruelty, and advancement, brought many of them a much richer way of life.

Undoubtedly, such arts as farming, pottery, and some simple weaving reached the Algonkians in the ancestral days of the Adena and Hopewell Mound Builders. When the white men came, the Indians of the coastal regions were in touch, all along the line, either with the Iroquois or with the powerful Southeastern tribes. In varying degrees, much more as one went south, less as one moved north, they showed the Southeastern influences.

Much of the Algonkian pottery was coarsely finished, inferior in appearance to that of the Iroquois or the people of the Southeast. Scientists claim that pottery of this type can be traced across the United States, up into Alaska, and all the way through Siberia to Mongolia. The knowledge of it, then, may have come, not from the tribes

Curiously enough, they had a more highly developed sense of the ownership of land than is usual with hunters. Not only did a given tribe claim a certain territory, but often each family had an area of its own within that territory, and resisted trespass.

Religion was also simple. There was a spirit, perhaps a god, who was the Owner of all things—Manitou—but he was inert and did not intervene in men's affairs. There were lesser owners of the various parts of nature. There were no priests trained in ritual and the traditional equiva-

Modern Chippewa wigwams, used as summer residences during the fishing season. These are fairly solid buildings, that can be returned to year after year, and are not intended to be carried around when the people move.
Office of Indian Affairs, Dept. of Interior.

An early Army officer's conception of an Algonkian shaman making medicine. The effectiveness of the brew is derived as much from the shaman's songs, accompanied by shaking the rattle in his left hand, as from the ingredients. The tribe is not specified, but from the long-stemmed pipe to be seen in the lower left hand corner, the shaman probably belongs to one of the tribes that lived west of the Iroquois, who used the traditional "calumet." The artist has drawn the wigwam with part of its wall missing, so as to show the interior scene more clearly. *Library of Congress.*

influenced by Mexico, but from some group of immigrants into the New World who had learned it in Asia. As a usual thing, tribes that live entirely by hunting and fishing do not go in for pottery, since the hunters move often and clay vessels are too easily broken. Exceptions occur, and this may be one of them.

Contacts with the more advanced tribes may have been fruitful, but they were also harassing. The Algonkians were still in the early stages of developing chiefs with real power and other essentials of a strong organization. Mostly they formed small tribes, single villages, with weak ideas of cooperation between villages. The stronger nations pressed upon them, raided them, sometimes collected tribute, kept them in a continuous state of warfare, and taught them, among other things, the custom of torturing prisoners.

This pressure tended to make the small tribes unite. At the time that the English and French began settling among them, they were grouped in a series of loose confederacies, ranging from eight to as many as thirty villages, but most of these lacked the real union of the Iroquois. The strongest were in the south, the Powhatans of Virginia—named for the chief who almost had John Smith beheaded—and the Delawares. Here the Southeastern influence was strongest, customs were largely derived

from the tribes to the westward, and chiefs had real authority.

The people dressed much as did their neighbors. Women wore buckskin skirts and, in cold weather, a loosely fitted, long upper garment. Men wore robes or shirts, and the familiar leggings-and-kilt combination. Women kept their hair long. The men shaved their heads or plucked out their hair, leaving only the traditional scalp lock. It is a curious thought that most of the white men who first explored and settled in America wore their hair long, while the Indians they came among went in for short hair.

The Algonkians who lived right on the coast developed one remarkable craft, the making of wampum from clam shells and certain other thick shells. The tricky thing about wampum is that it is shaped the wrong way. It is a comparatively simple trick, although still not too simple with primitive tools and no metal, to cut shells into flat disks, rub them until they are smoothly round, and bore a hole in the middle, thus making a bead. Necklaces of such shells are common today in the Southwest. They are usually called "wampum," but they are not. To make real wampum, the Indians cut out a longish strip of thick shell, sanded it down until it was a cylinder, then bored a hole the long way of the cylinder. To do this without splitting the bead, whether with a very fine stone drill or a wooden

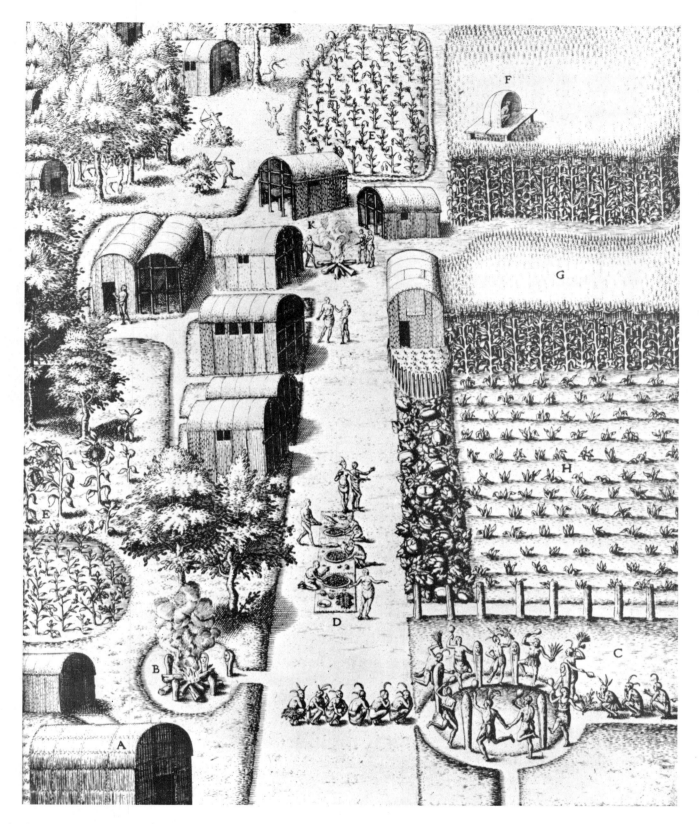

Life in Secota, a Virginia Indian village, when white men first came. The artist, John White, who drew the original picture in 1590, has not portrayed a village, but put in a sample of everything. At the top are hunters in a forest, and on the other side, a man sitting on a covered platform to drive birds away from a ripe cornfield. Below on the right is a field of young corn, to show the method of planting in hills. Fields of pumpkins and tobacco are also shown, various wigwams of the "Quonset hut" shape common among the Iroquois but less usual among the Algonkians, a feast and ceremonial dance going on, and a sort of open-air temple with a fire burning in it. In many ways the culture of the Powhatan Confederacy of Virginia resembled the Southeast more than it did that of other Algonkians more to the north.

From engraving by de Bry.

Another of White's pictures of the Virginia Indians, showing methods of spearing, netting, and trapping fish. The canoe in the foreground is a wooden dugout. *From engraving by de Bry.*

Sixteenth century Virginia Indians, "Theire Sitting at Meate." The way of wearing the hair is well shown. The fringed deerskin robes are without tailoring. This couple appears to be eating hominy, fish, and roast corn. *From engraving by de Bry.*

Model of a prehistoric Southeastern council meeting in a ceremonial earth lodge, reconstructed from archeologists' excavations. **The heavy painting of the bodies in red and white is based in part on early observa-** tions of the historic Indians. The orator wears, in addition to his paint, a decorated breech-clout and carries a fan of white feathers.

Dexter Press, Inc.

A modern Sauk and Fox Indian, who has learned to dress as tourists expect all Indians to dress. The Sauks and Foxes, who call themselves "Mesquakies," moved to Iowa after Black Hawk's futile stand, where they still live on land they bought for themselves. *Dexter Press, Inc.*

Modern deer dance at Santa Clara Pueblo, New Mexico. The dancers represent both the deer and the hunters. The costume, including the knitted leggings, is ancient, except that white, commercial skirts have replaced coarse, cotton shirts of native weave. Each dancer carries a large gourd rattle; the dancers sing, as well as dance, to the accompaniment of the drum. The drummer wears modern Western clothes. *Dexter Press, Inc.*

Hopi Indian in modern Hopi costume, holding a "kachina doll." The dolls are models of the various masked dancers that appear in Hopi rituals, and are usually given to the children as part of their education. *Dexter Press, Inc.*

Mescalero Apache woman in traditional dress, with baby on cradleboard. Buckskin dresses painted yellow were typical of the Southern and Mescalero Apaches.
Dexter Press, Inc.

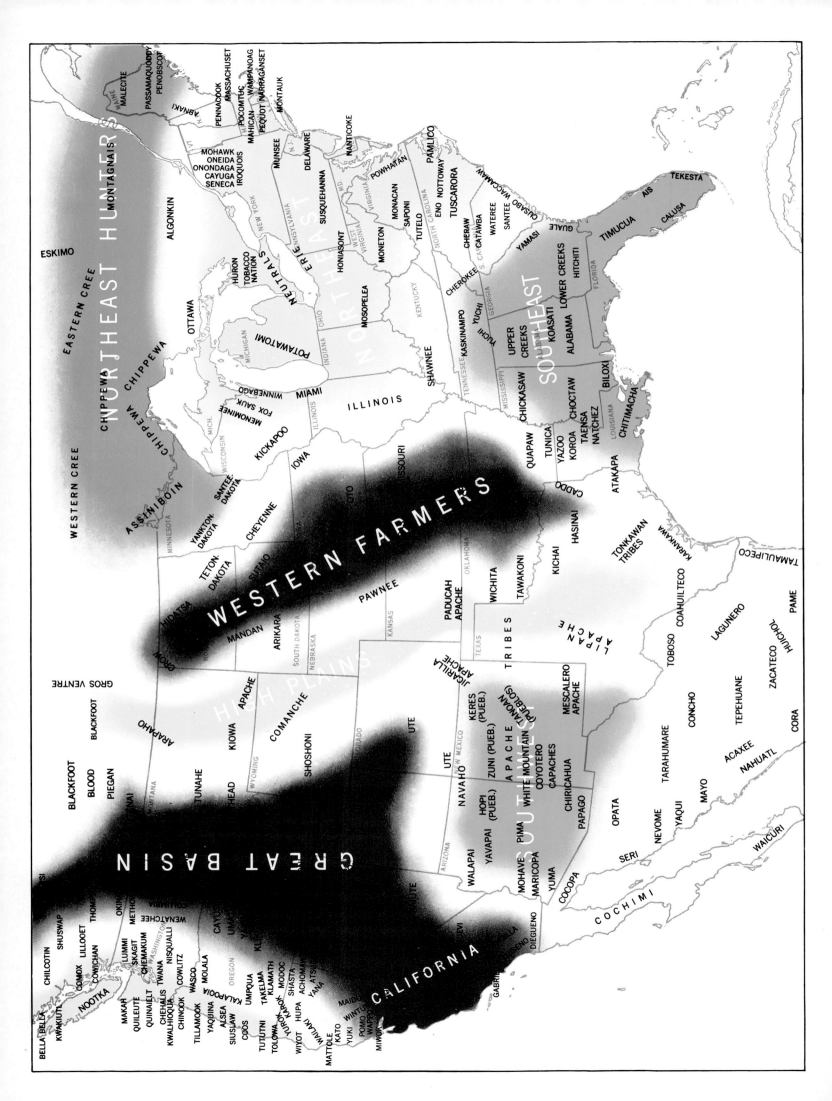

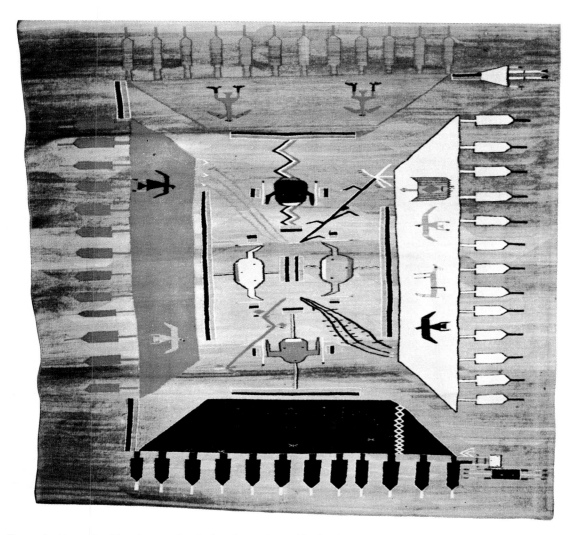

Reproduction of a Navaho sand-painting from the Shooting Chant ceremony, woven in a rug by Klah, a famous medicine man. It shows white morning, blue (grey) noon, red evening, and black night, with the animals associated with the first three and the Milky Way across one end of the night, surrounding four kinds of rainstorm with masks and the four sacred plants. *Museum of Navajo Ceremonial Art, Santa Fe, N. M.*

Map on facing page shows the distribution of Indian tribes in North America in 1650, shortly after the arrival of the white man. Shadings mark the general cultural areas. *Courtesy of Carnegie Institution of Washington, the American Geographical Society of N. Y. and American Heritage.*

"Totem pole" on exhibition at Jasper, Alberta, Canada. The figures carved on these poles represent animal spirits with whom ancestors of the chief erecting the pole had encounters, sympolize other important events, and may include, an animal spirit that turned itself into a human being and founded the lineage. *Dexter Press, Inc.*

Kwakiutl double mask carved out of wood. When the outer part is closed, it represents a raven; when opened, a human head appears inside. The human face and inner sides of the raven mask are painted with bear and raven symbols. The wearer works the mask by pulling strings that run from the outer covering, through the inner mask, and down to the wearer's hand. *Frank Smith Collection, Vancouver; from Art of the Northwest Coast Indians by Bruce Inverarity. Courtesy University of California Press.*

Nootka cradle, carved out of red cedar and painted. The decoration includes a killer whale, head turned backward and tail turned towards the head, and a wolf. The human face inside the bend of the wolf's foreleg is probably only a "filler." *Frank Smith Collection, Vancouver; from Art of the Northwest Coast Indians by Bruce Inverarity. Courtesy University of California Press.*

Present-day Navaho mother and child. *Dexter Press, Inc.*

Characteristic Navaho scene—one woman weaves, another tends a baby, a small boy studies the loom. Little children find the looms irresistible, which is a considerable trial to their mothers. *Dexter Press, Inc.*

Right. Aboriginal dress of Virginia chiefs or important warriors. The costume is little more than a buckskin apron with an ornamental tail hanging behind. The beads of the necklaces are either of shell or of copper. The Indians of the Southeast and their coastal neighbors were able to obtain small amounts of free copper, which they knew how to work. *From engravings by de Bry.*

Below. The ideas received by the Virginia Indians from their more civilized neighbors inland included formal feasts and ceremonies held at fixed times in the year. One of these, seen in 1590, is shown here. According to the artist, the three women in the middle are three of the most beautiful virgins of the tribe. *From engraving by de Bry.*

A Virginia ceremony of the more ancient, shamanistic type, led by a medicine man and held to deal with some particular situation, to insure success in an enterprise, cure sickness, or ward off evil. All the participants are singing, and most are shaking gourd rattles. According to White, this particular performance was in thanksgiving for return from a successful voyage.

From engraving by de Bry.

Moving northward, we come to the Manhattan Indians, who once occupied Manhattan Island, reconstructed in this picture. The wigwams are of the usual, round shape; the people wear more clothing than those who so charmed the artist, White. The man, leaning on an unstrung longbow and holding a tomahawk, has decorated his scalp lock by fastening to it a roach of deer's tail hairs. The woman, dressed much like an Iroquois woman in summer, holds a stone hammer. Her baby is on her back in a pack board, hung from her forehead by a tumpline made by finger-weaving fibers. There is a typical Algonkian clay pot on the fire. *Courtesy of the American Museum of Natural History.*

Algonkian birchbark container. This specimen was made by the Montagnais Indians of Canada, but is typical of other Algonkian work. Note the painted decoration with its curved lines, derived from floral motifs. Even to this day, widely separated tribes of Algonkian speech tend to use curves and floral designs in their beadwork and other decorations.

Courtesy of the American Museum of Natural History.

"Powhatan's mantle," so-called. It is a skin cloak decorated with shells, brought back to England by some early explorer, and now in the Ashmolean Museum. Its exact origin is not known.

Smithsonian Institution.

The uses of birchbark. This model shows Chippewas—note that both men and women wear long, braided hair, like Indians even farther west. The canoes, one of which we see being made, wig-wam, and birchbark containers are typical of the eastern Algonkians also, in those sections where good bark was plentiful.

Courtesy of the American Museum of Natural History.

Not all the Algonkians could go as lightly clad as the ones in Virginia. This model shows Chippewas making maple sugar in the very early spring.

Courtesy of the American Museum of Natural History.

A reconstruction of daily life of the Algonkian Indians of the more northerly part of their territory. The wigwams here are of elm bark. A papoose in a cradleboard hangs from a birch tree; presumably that is his mother grinding corn in the wooden mortar. Note that the woman's skirt is a simple wrap-around, and her blouse has no true sleeves. Various modes of men's dressing are shown, as well as of doing their hair. To the right, partly behind the birch, is a primitive form of loom, on which a woman is making a robe by a process called finger-weaving, a slow, laborious method.

Courtesy of the American Museum of Natural History.

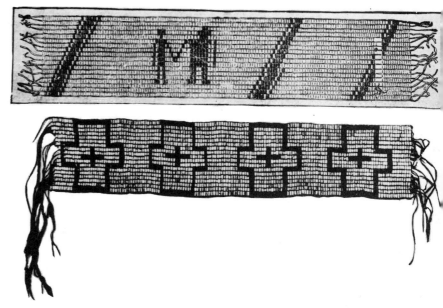

Two wampum belts presented to the English by the Delawares when they made their treaty with William Penn. The four crosses on one are supposed to represent the four tribes or nations involved; on the other, an Indian and a white man (with hat and considerably fatter) stand hand in hand.

Courtesy Museum of the American Indian and
The Historical Society of Pennsylvania.

drill dipped in wet sand, was a remarkable accomplishment. Wampum was correspondingly valuable. Only a small part of each clamshell is purple, hardly more than enough for one bead, while white shell is, and was then, plentiful. Therefore the purple beads were more valuable than the white.

The white men brought metal tools, which made wampum-making much easier, although still no child's play. The quantity increased. Inland tribes, especially the Iroquois, whose use of wampum for records, messages, and the marking of solemn occasions has already been described, bought wampum for high prices in what goods they had to offer. (The Iroquois also took it as tribute, or just helped themselves.)

There was a shortage of currency in both the early English and the Dutch colonies. The colonists began using wampum as currency. Laws were passed fixing its value. Some of the colonists started making it. Then enterprising individuals took wampum to Europe, where it was copied in porcelain and brought back to circulate as counterfeit. The successful counterfeit destroyed the value of the real article. As far as the Indians were concerned, the copies were just as pretty as the original, and just as suitable for decorative purposes, as well as being cheaper. Wampum disappeared, and instead there began the trade in beads with Indians which, for well over a century, made an important export for countries such as Bohemia.

The Algonkians were the people who received the first English and French settlers, who taught them how to plant corn, bake clams, and how to bury a pot of beans at night in a hole in which fire had been made, so that the beans were cooked in the morning. They taught them how to make canoes, to use seaweed for fertilizer, to eat pumpkins and squash, and to smoke tobacco. Today in New England, old-fashioned farmers still plant four grains of corn to a hill. Why four? Europeans usually do things by threes, but Indians go by fours, the number of the four directions.

From them we got such words as sachem, tomahawk, squaw, papoose, quahog, hominy, and succotash. They welcomed the newcomers in friendship, and all along the coast, relations between whites and Indians began with friendly treaties and much help given by the natives to the settlers. But the coastal Algonkians were in a hopeless position.

Behind them, behind the nearer mountains, were the ferocious, far more powerful tribes we have looked at in the last two chapters. And the English had not come just to trade. They came to occupy the land, to work it, to found new and better versions of England. As their numbers increased, they needed ever more land. The Algonkians were between the hammer and the anvil.

The English called Powhatan "king," and recognized his sovereignty by placing on his head a crown sent in the name of the King of England. If the story of John Smith, Pocahontas, and Powhatan is true—as it probably is—it sheds some interesting light. Powhatan ordered the strangely costumed, light-skinned, bearded man *executed,* not tortured. The Indians probably were not going to chop off his head (a European custom), but bash it in. This may mean that this tribe had not fully adopted the Southeastern customs. Then a young woman of high rank claimed him, following the established pattern of women claiming captives. It was less surprising that Pocahontas, an Indian, should have interfered in the proceedings than it would have been had she been an English princess of the same period.

Pocahontas later married John Rolfe, an English gentleman, and went to London to die, probably of tuberculosis. In the end the Powhatans saw the writing on the wall as they were ever more tightly hemmed in. They attacked, the British retaliated, and their confederacy was crushed. In southern New England, King Philip, son of the white men's great friend Massassoit, baptized, educated in the colonists' schools, saw no hope for his people but to drive the white men back. He rose in King Philip's War and gave the English—the "Yinglees," who became the "Yankees"—a very bad fright. The fright was so bad that Roger Williams of Rhode Island, who had lived in peace with the Narragansetts of that state for years, joined the colonists of Massachusetts and Connecticut in an early form of total war. Massacre followed massacre; Indian women and chil-

The Great God who is the power and wisdom that made you and me Incline your hearts to Righteousness Love and peace. This I send to Assure you of my Love, and to desire your Love to my ffriends, and when the Great God brings me among you I Intend to order all things in such manner that we may all live in Love and peace one with another whic̄h I hope the Great God will Incline both me and you to do. I seek nothing but the honoᵉ of his name, and that we who are his workmanship, may do that whic̄h is well pleasing to him. The man whic̄h delivers this unto you, is my Special ffriend Sober wise and Loving, you may believe him. I have already taken Care that none of my people wrong you, by good Laws I have provided for that purpose, nor will I ever allow any of my people to sell Rumme to make your people drunk. If any thing should be out of order, expect when I come, it shall be mended, and I will bring you some things of our Country that are useful and pleasing to you. So I rest In y Love of our god yᵗ made us J am

England 2ᵗ : 2 : 1682

your Loveing freind

WM PENN

I read this to the Indian by an Interpᵗ the 6 mo 1682 Tho: Holme

LET US LOOK TO THE MOST HIGH WHO BLESSED OUR FATHERS WITH PEACE

The other side of the Penn Treaty, the English document with William Penn's signature. This treaty was faithfully kept as long as Penn lived. *Library of Congress.*

78

Cooking succotash—another of John White's pictures. This is the original Indian dish, which included fish as well as corn and beans, and was considerably more savory than the succotash we now make. *From engraving by de Bry.*

An example of the combination of white and Indian cultures—a finely tailored buckskin coat made by the Algonkian Cree of Canada. The decorations are of porcupine quill; the fine sewing involved was made possible by steel needles. The cut of the coat, collar, and epaulets are derived from the Europeans. Here again we see the Algonkian love of floral decoration. This coat dates from the middle 1700's. *Denver Art Museum.*

Pocahontas, or Matsoaks'ats, daughter of Powhatan, as she appeared after she came to London as the wife of John Rolfe. Twenty-one when this portrait was painted in 1616, she soon died, unable to stand the English climate. She was the first, and by far the most pathetic, of all the Indians of noble rank who were brought to London at different times. *Smithsonian Institution.*

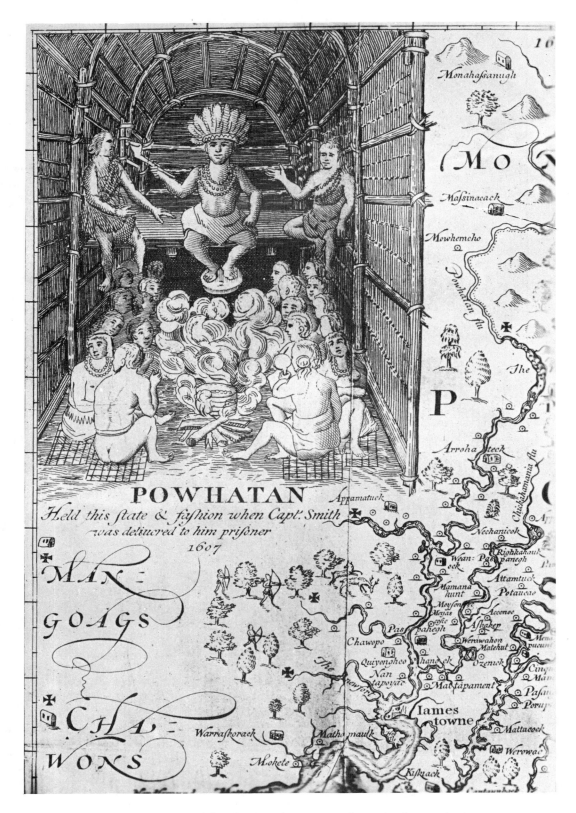

A map of Virginia of 1612, showing Powhatan in the royal wigwam. He wears a crown of feathers. The wigwam is of the same type as those shown in White's pictures. *Smithsonian Institution.*

King Philip, leader of the desperate attempt of the Pequots and other New England Indians to drive out the white men. The drawing from which this lithograph was made was not drawn from life. But it was based on earlier drawings of other Indians, and gives a fair enough idea of how a chief of his period might dress, partly in buckskin, partly in woven goods, with a wampum belt and headdress probably of wampum. *Library of Congress.*

dren were slaughtered by the hundreds or burned alive in their huts along with their men, and the power of the New England Indians was broken. Today the Narragansetts, who once dominated some thirty villages, are few in number, as are the Pequots, while a handful of Mohicans survive in Connecticut.

It was the Dutch who took over what is now New York, settling first on Manhattan Island. There is some question whether their famous purchase of the island for twenty dollars' worth of goods was made from Indians who lived there, or from a band that just happened to be passing through. If the second theory is correct, the equivalent of selling the Brooklyn Bridge goes back a long time.

The Dutch were no easier on the Indians. Like the English, they often enough followed the pattern of attacking an unsuspecting and peaceful village in punishment for an offense committed by some entirely different tribe. After one particularly fine slaughter, when babies were tossed into fires and hacked to death, some eighty Indian heads were deposited in the streets of New Amsterdam, where the governor's wife played football with them.

The alliance that the northern Algonkians made with the French did them no good. It not only put them in conflict with the Iroquois, who were too much for them, but brought the English against them too. Everywhere one turned there was war. Many of the tribes that befriended the white men are extinct; of the others, pitiful remnants remain.

The French-allied Abenakis withdrew to Canada, where many of them still live. In Maine the Passamaquoddies and Penobscots still exist on state-recognized reservations, though in recent years they have been asking for federal recognition. There are some tiny tracts of land in Long Island, also state Indian reservations, occupied by descendants of tribes like the Patchogues and Shinnecocks, once allied in the Montauk Confederacy. In Virginia Mattaponys and Pamunkeys, who trace their ancestry to the Powhatans, are on small reservations in King William County. In North Carolina there are more than 4,500 Eastern Cherokees on a federally recognized reservation, as well as Tuscaroras and Lumbees, some of whom trace their ancestry to the Croatans and other tribes living on the coast when the first whites arrived in the 1500's.

One of the most remarkable stories is that of the Delawares, who were about the most powerful of all the Algonkian tribes. It was with them that William Penn made his famous treaty of peace when he founded Pennsylvania, and so long as Penn lived the treaty was kept. Then, for all their efforts to maintain friendly relations, the Delawares were forced out and took refuge on Iroquois soil, under Iroquois dominance. That was not the end of it. Five times thereafter the white men made treaties with them under which, like it or not, the Delawares sold their land to the white men and moved further west. After the fifth treaty, they bought a tract in Kansas, fenced their farms, built houses and a church, and settled down. Once

81

Lapowinsa, a principal chief of the Lenni Lenape (Delaware) Confederacy, was the victim of the notorious "Walking Purchase" treaty, signed by his people with William Penn in 1686. Under the treaty, the Indians agreed to cede land between the Delaware and Lehigh rivers in eastern Pennsylvania as far north of the region of present-day Bethlehem, Pa., as a man could walk, going and returning, in three days. Penn claimed only as far as a leisurely stroll took him. But in 1737 his successors reopened the treaty and forced the Indians to cede all the land they covered at a run. The portrait of the defrauded chief, who had to sign the new cession, was made by Gustavus Hesselius in 1735.
Pennsylvania Historical Society.

This chapter has dealt mainly with the tribes of the Atlantic coast, but while we are at it we should take a look at the related tribes living west of the Iroquoian area

again they were forced to move, despite most moving appeals that they be allowed to remain on the land they had bought with their own money and on which they were prospering. A sixth treaty was made, and for the seventh time they were moved, to find peace at last in Oklahoma, on far less fertile soil.

What the Indians confronted, and the attitude of many white men, is beautifully and horribly illustrated by the massacre at Gnadenhutten, in Ohio in 1782. Gnadenhutten was a settlement of Christian Delawares under Moravian missionaries. On British advice, in order to avoid trouble, these Indians moved to the Moravian mission at Sandusky. They had planted fields in the old place, so a number of them went back to gather the harvest.

There they were found by a party of about one hundred white men under a Colonel David Williamson. The white men disarmed them, tied them up, then wiped them out with hand weapons—axes, tomahawks, and clubs—thus wasting no valuable ammunition. The Indians prayed and sang hymns. Thirty-five men, twenty-seven women, and thirty-four children were thus disposed of.

Ninigret, a sachem of the Niantics of Connecticut and Rhode Island, who managed to keep his tribe out of King Philip's War, and to avoid having them massacred. This painting is probably a copy of an earlier one which may well have been the earliest direct portrait made of an American Indian other than Pocahontas. Ninigret's simple costume appears to be entirely of buckskin, his "crown" and necklace of shell work, with some bone in the necklace. This is an unusually accurate representation of the summer costume of a chief. *Rhode Island Museum of Art.*

who still kept the older, pre-farming mode of life. Within the United States, the chief of these were the people known as Chippewas or Ojibwas. Both names are not very successful tries at spelling their native name for themselves, which lies somewhere between the two and is not easy for a white man to pronounce.

The Chippewas still live in fragments of their ancient homeland, in Wisconsin and Minnesota, where once they had Lake Superior and Lake Michigan at their disposal. A wigwam people, they were also in touch with tribes farther west, so that their dress was somewhat modified and they had a knowledge of skin tepees. They did very little farming, but fished on a tremendous scale.

People often ask why certain tribes did not learn agriculture when they lived in what today is considered good farming land. Part of the answer is that it is a very different thing to raise crops when you have even such simple machinery as horse-drawn plows and harrows, and metal tools, as against when the most useful tool you have is a pointed stick. The labor is heavy, the results are less certain. Where the growing season is short, the length of time required to get the seed planted may be too great. A reasonable people, when they have plenty of other food, will not go to all that trouble unless they can be sure of good results.

The Chippewas, in addition, had a rich supply of a grain that they did not have to cultivate at all—wild rice. It is still one of their most important crops. Wild rice, incidentally, is not rice. The English explorers gave it that name because the grain is more or less rice-shaped, and like rice it grows in water. The French called it *avoine folle*, "crazy oats."

The Chippewas were in good trapping country, and furnished much of the fur that was traded, at first, through the Hurons to the French and later through the Iroquois to the British. From the French they obtained trade goods and arms, as did the Ottawas and Potawatomis, also Algonkians. Their superior weapons, including muskets, enabled them to push other tribes out of the rich, forested, hunting country and out of access to the magnificent

Portrait of a Chippewa chief. He wears a decoration of small feathers in his scalp lock, and what is probably a piece of beadwork above his forehead, in addition to silver earrings and a silver nose-ring. *Royal Ontario Museum.*

fishing of the Great Lakes and the lesser lakes to the south and west of those. Among others, they forced the Sioux tribes westward, toward the Great Plains, with results that we shall see later.

The tribes of the lake area were as loosely organized as any Algonkians, but they were numerous, they were good fighters, and they were well armed before the white

Chippewas gathering wild rice. The stalks are bent over the canoe and the grain knocked off with small, wooden paddles. *Courtesy of the American Museum of Natural History.*

men began to press upon them. The land they occupied was much less desirable to farmers than the territory to the south of them. Once the white men had broken out of the eastern seaboard, they found what seemed an infinity of room. They took the best, and did not think it necessary to go through the trouble and danger of wiping out tribes that occupied less desirable lands. Hence some of these tribes, such as the Chippewas and Menominees, had better luck than their eastern relatives. Poor though they are today, much though they have suffered at the hands of the white men, they do still occupy reservations carved out of their native land.

Undated French lithograph of a Menominee war dance. Judging by details, such as the deadly-looking, primitive tomahawks, the period is early, but after the Menominees had begun to receive some woven goods. The figure at the right has a metal, trade tomahawk and knife. *Library of Congress.*

Algonkian canoe life, showing *portage,* the system of carrying canoes from one body of water to another, by which very long trips could be made. The great advantage of birchbark canoes is their lightness. Smaller canoes, that will hold two or three people, can be carried even up a steep portage by one man, as is shown near the center of this picture. Down on the shore, to the left, a man is mending a leak in his canoe with tree gum; over towards the right a family has sets its canoe on its side for a shelter and has stopped for a picnic.

Courtesy of the American Museum of Natural History.

V. The Western Farmers

This chapter bites off a big mouthful. It deals with tribes reaching from not far below the Canadian border to the northeastern edge of Texas, mostly west of the Mississippi, but in the north extending east to western Ohio. Often students of Indians classify them as several separate groups; many of them are likely to be grouped with the Plains Indians, while those in the northeast may be treated as a branch of the Woodland Indians such as the Chippewas (or the Chippewas as a branch of them).

We have come to a region where the lines of division according to culture are fuzzy. The peoples of the Southeast form a neat cultural unit. The East Coast Algonkians also formed a fairly neat unit, and so did the Iroquoians. Now, as we move west, we come to people speaking related languages—even languages similar enough so that the speakers can understand each other—yet who live quite differently, and others speaking unrelated languages whose cultures are pretty similar. The different sections fade into each other, so that no matter where you draw a separating line, the line will be somewhat arbitrary.

One of the points this book stresses is that the beginnings of civilization were spreading through North America until the white men, with their civilization, brought the process to a stop. You cannot say that any tribe in the present-day United States was fully civilized, although some were at least semi-civilized, but the things were happening that lead in time to civilization. A steady, rich food supply, fixed towns and villages, political organization, higher religious and intellectual concepts, better crafts, more possessions, and with all this more comfort and more spare time to release men's energy for purposes other than the struggle to stay fed and covered—these are the elements from which civilization grows.

They came into the Mississippi Valley and the Southeast from Mexico along with the corn, and from there they spread, east, north, and west. They spread westward until they came to a natural boundary that stopped farming, and with it stopped the rest. Draw a line starting in eastern Montana at the Canadian border and slanting down to Pierre, the capital of South Dakota, carry it on into Nebraska and there let it bulge to the west about 100 miles, then come back to cross into Kansas east of McCook, Nebraska. In Kansas carry it southward slanting to the east, so that when you draw it through Oklahoma to the Texas border, it cuts off the western third of Oklahoma.

Roughly, east of that line you can count safely on an annual rainfall of twenty inches or better. West of it, the average drops rapidly to fifteen inches or less. That is the country known as the High Plains. *Average* annual rainfall is not a safe thing on which to plan a farming career. There are years when the rain on the High Plains is ample, well above the average, but too many others when it falls as low as four inches, and, as white men today are learning so painfully, farmers are scorched out. The finds made by archeologists show that in prehistoric times, bands of farming Indians did move out into the grass country in periods of extra-heavy rainfall, but when the wet years ended they had sense enough to pull back, and also, room to farm further eastwards. The zone of steady farming ended some distance behind the twenty-inch line, where a year of insufficient moisture was a rarity.

Beginning in the south, the land of the Western farmers started at the northeast corner of Texas with the Caddo tribe, from which the Caddoan family of languages takes its name. From there the Middle Western farming area reached up through Arkansas and the eastern two-thirds of Oklahoma, on up through Kansas east of the rainfall line described above, Missouri, Iowa and eastern Nebraska. One branch of it reached across the Mississippi, eastward, to cover Illinois and Indiana south of the territory of the Woodland hunters, and into Ohio up to the boundaries of Iroquoian country. Another, bending northwestward with the Missouri River, reached up to South Dakota and in early times reached as far westward as eastern Montana.

Up to this chapter, almost all the tribes mentioned were visited by white men of intelligence, education, and curiosity before their way of life had been influenced by white civilization. Now the story changes. Trade goods, metal tools, some weapons, and new ideas spread far ahead of the white men, changing the primitive cultures. As we move westward, the horse, the greatest of all the European contributions to Indian culture, reached the tribes well before the Europeans themselves did. Everywhere, as the white men dislocated and drove out tribes along the coasts, the result was migrations and invasions towards the west, creating confusion, bringing new influences, stirring up the mixture. Many of the first to visit the Western farmers were traders and hunters who were almost or entirely illiterate, who brought about great changes without being able to describe, or caring to describe, what they had first seen. The best descriptions of unchanged tribes that we have are those of French missionary-explorers, and these are all too few. We depend largely on the finds of archeologists to tell us what was in the area as late even as the

1600's. The area is very large, the number of serious archeologists in the United States is all too few. It is no reflection on the scientists to say that what they have proven to date is much too little.

In general we know that all this area used to be occupied by people who did ample farming and also hunted, that most of them hunted the buffalo that were handy to them on the prairies and the High Plains to the west, that they lived in large, settled villages, made pottery, and seemed to be pretty well off. In a number of cases their pottery was finer, they farmed on a larger scale, and moved about less than did their descendants of historic times.

The northeastern, Illinois-Indiana branch of the area, when the white men first had news of it, was occupied by Algonkian tribes such as the Sauk and Fox (who became a single tribe), Illinois, Kickapoos, and Miamis. They were probably fairly recent comers, pushed west by the Iroquoians or south by stronger Woodland tribes, such as Chippewas. Those tribes, in driving others away from the rich hunting and fishing along the Great Lakes, had no idea that they were pushing them into some of the finest farming land in North America. Here, and across the Mississippi in the land occupied by the Siouan Iowas and Missouris, was and still is above all the land where the tall corn grows.

In moving into this section, the Algonkians found a situation somewhat like that of their relatives on the coast —they were in a position to be strongly influenced by the Iroquoians and Southeasterners, and also to be constantly troubled by them. The influences were strengthened in historic times by the arrival of the Delawares and Shawnees, Algonkian tribes of advanced culture. The Delawares, as has already been told, began on the shores of the Atlantic and were then strongly under Southeastern influence. Later, they were under the protection and influence of the Iroquois, before they settled west of Ohio in their long search for a place where they could be out of reach of white men and live in peace.

The Shawnees also came out of the east, although just where their original home was is not clear. Early white writers told of some of them living in Georgia and of others moving north and south through the Appalachian Mountains. They seem to have been a nation that liked to travel. For a time, after they were dispossessed from the east one branch of them went south and lived among the Creeks, with whom they formed a friendship. Finally one branch settled in Ohio, the other in southern Illinois, believing, like the Delawares, that they had found a rich land in which they could live in peace.

The culture of these tribes was in a transition between the old, hunting Woodlands and the Southeast. Early visitors to them tell of their cornfields stretching for miles along the river valleys. They lived in large villages of comfortable, solid wigwams. Out of birchbark country, the wigwams were often covered with mats. They went in for canoes hollowed out of large logs, Southeastern style.

A Hidatsa village of earth lodges on the banks of the Missouri, as painted by George Catlin in 1832. The artist shows Indians bathing in the river and playing along the edge of it, and himself and his companions being ferried across in a "bull-boat." The Mandans and closely related Hidatsas were extraordinarily picturesque, a quality that caused Catlin to draw and paint them in detail, and also drew great attention from the artist Karl Bodmer, who traveled with the German explorer, Prince Maximilian of Wied, in 1832-34. *Smithsonian Institution.*

A Kickapoo wigwam. This example was built by modern Kickapoo Indians in Oklahoma; the young man at the door is a veteran of World War II. The door covering is canvas, instead of hide, and the ladder leaning against the wall is modern; otherwise this is a fine example of a mat-covered wigwam of the type made by many of the Algonkians.
Photo by A. C. Hector.

These were too heavy for portages. They were used on the waters in which they were launched; for journeys beyond their local watersheds, the people went on foot, the men with arms in hand, the women carrying the packs. Good hunting balanced farming, and these people were far enough west to be able, many of them, to go out once a year into buffalo country and try their luck.

West of the Mississippi were many powerful tribes. In addition to the Caddos, tribes of the Caddoan family were the Wichitas in Kansas (the reader will notice how many of these farming tribes have given their names to states or cities), the Pawnees in Nebraska, and the Arikara in North Dakota. All of these unquestionably had moved out of the Southeast; the Caddos themselves could as well be classed Southeastern as Western Farmer.

Elk's Horns, or Masheena, a Kickapoo sub-chief, praying while reading a "prayer stick." This portrait, painted by Catlin in 1831, shows a late phase of costume. The head is not shaved and the shirt is of woven material. The chief wears one of the medallions that the white men handed out so freely in intervals of friendliness.
Smithsonian Institution.

Kickapoo "prayer stick." The marks on such sticks served, like the strands of wampum of the Iroquois, to remind the user of a sequence of prayers, historical or mythical events, or other matters. The highly simplified symbols suggest that the Kickapoos had made important steps towards developing a system of writing.
Smithsonian Institution.

Playing Fox, a chief of the Fox tribe, from the series of portraits of early Indian visitors to Washington. His headdress is an elaboration of the roach idea, with a forepiece almost like a coronet. It is not possible to determine from the painting just what it was made of. *Peabody Museum, Harvard University.*

A Fox warrior, another portrait of the Washington series. He carries an unusually fancy version of the tomahawk. His roach has been developed into a cap, and a curious decoration, probably attached to his waist, projects beyond his left elbow. Although his scarf and loincloth are made of trade materials, the whole quality of his costume is aboriginal.
Peabody Museum, Harvard University.

The rest of the area was occupied by tribes of the Siouan family. That family gets its name from the Sioux, whom we think of as the greatest of all the tepee-dwelling, buffalo-hunting, horseback, nomadic, warrior tribes—but in those days there were no horses in the New World, what we think of today as the Plains Indians did not exist, and the Sioux, later so great, were simply a group of closely related Woodland tribes living west of the Chippewas, some of them doing a little gardening, going into the Great Plains from time to time to see if they could kill a few buffalo.

If a white man had traveled through the Middle West in those days and on up into the Dakotas, he would never have picked the Sioux as most likely to succeed, or chosen those relatively humble people to give the name to a great linguistic family. There were Siouan tribes in the heart of the Southeast, some even on the southern Atlantic and the Gulf coasts, such as the Alibamu from whom Alabama takes its name. West of the Mississippi, from Arkansas north, were, among others, the Ponca, Oto, Osage, Omaha, Missouri, Kansa (for whom Kansas was named), Iowa, Mandan, and Hidatsa. These were people of power; the Mandan in North Dakota counted thirteen villages, as did one branch of the Pawnee in Nebraska. Between their fields, the local hunting, and the buffalo, they lived well. They were energetic people; as we first get to know of them there is about them a quality of exuberance, of people who are going places.

In those times, there was one farming Algonkian tribe of importance west of the Mississippi, the Cheyennes, who then lived somewhat east of central North Dakota. Their way of life seems to have been closer to that of the Mandan and Hidatsa than to the way of any of the other Algonkians.

It was among all these tribes that a visitor in, say, 1600 would have looked for the ones that mattered, the people with a future. If in those days he had been a student of languages and had been tracing the various branches of the Siouan family, he might have noted the existence of those backward, crude Sioux in the northeast, but he would have been likely to have named the family Mandanian, for the powerful and picturesque Mandans, or perhaps Omahanian or Osagian after tribes of clearly advanced culture and marked poetic gifts.

These Western tribes were not merely *influenced* by the Southeast, they were *carriers* of a culture that probably derived from the earlier Mound Builders. Which brings up one of the problems for which we need more material from the archeologists, the history of the Siouans. We find them at the western end of the wooded country along the Canadian border with a hunting culture. We find them on the Gulf Coast with a full Southeastern culture. The Mandan and Hidatsa, at least, have a tradition of having come from the east, up the Missouri River, into North Dakota, and unquestionably brought farming with them. Did the main body of Siouans once occupy the Southeast and Ohio and then get driven out, leaving some behind? Or are those deep in the Southeast invaders?

It is strange that they did not occupy and hold onto the rich lands of Indiana, Illinois, and Ohio. As we see them at the dawn of history, they do not look like a people whom the Algonkians could ever have driven out. Those tribes, not strong enough to stand against the Chippewas, seem to have moved into a vacuum where the farming was even richer. Nor do we know why the Caddoan Arikara, who were such great farmers that the

Houses built by modern-day Caddo Indians at "Indian City," Anadarko, Oklahoma. On the right is a summer dwelling, without walls, similar to Southeastern structures of the Gulf region. The buildings on the left, with their walls of posts and solid clay plastered over wattle, compare well enough with the homes of European peasants at the time America was being colonized.
Photo by A. C. Hector.

Interior of a Caddo house at "Indian City." Objects have been piled on the racks along the walls more for exhibition purposes than for daily use, and the iron pot, of course, would have been unknown until contact with white men. At the left is a buffalo hide, on which a drum made of skin stretched over a large, clay pot stands in front of a basketwork back rest. Ears of multi-colored corn lie on the mats.
Photo by A. C. Hector.

sign for them in the old Indian sign language was the motion of grinding corn, should have trekked all the way to North Dakota. What we don't know, in fact, would fill a book.

In moving so far north, the cornplanters did something that would be a credit to modern agronomical experts. Farther south they raised tall corn that required a long growing season. They developed a short corn that would mature in the shorter time available, and with somewhat less rain, on the northern prairies. But then, one of the miracles of Indian corn is the way it was adapted to so many very different climates. About all white men have done with it since has been to improve the innumerable varieties the Indians developed, and at the present time some of the most advanced breeders of hybrid corn are going back to certain tribes for back-crosses to restore some of the aboriginal hardiness.

The farmers were well established across the Mississippi and out over the well-watered prairies by 1300. The early type of house was the earth lodge, which remained the

Pottery of the Mandan and Hidatsa. The slightly squared necks of the two outside pots with the incised decorations suggest the Iroquois type. *Courtesy of the American Museum of Natural History.*

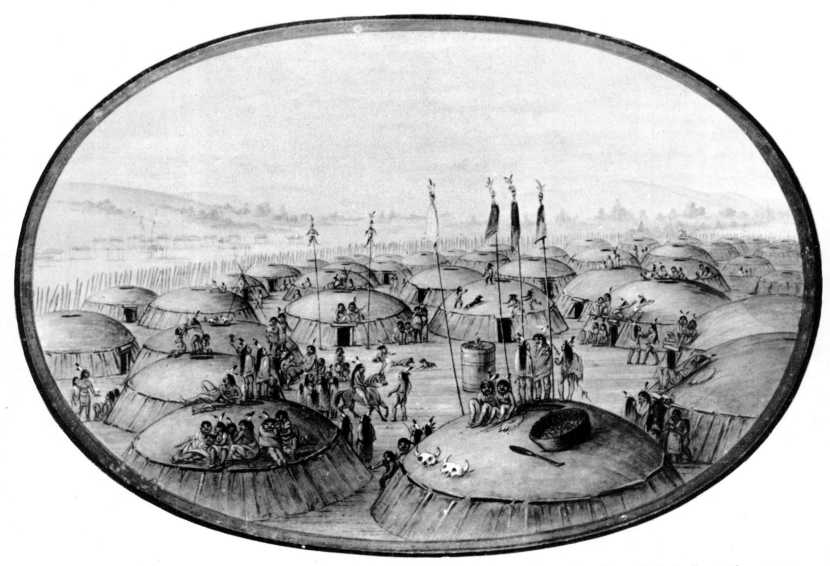

Bird's-eye view of a Mandan village, sketched by Catlin. The bullboat on the roof of the nearest house was placed there for a purpose. When there was heavy rain, the boats were used to cover the smoke holes. A simple palisade of stakes surrounds the village.

Catlin's pictures do not show the vestibule leading to the entrance that is considered typical of earth lodges. Other evidence shows that these tribes also built lodges with vestibules.
Courtesy of the American Museum of Natural History.

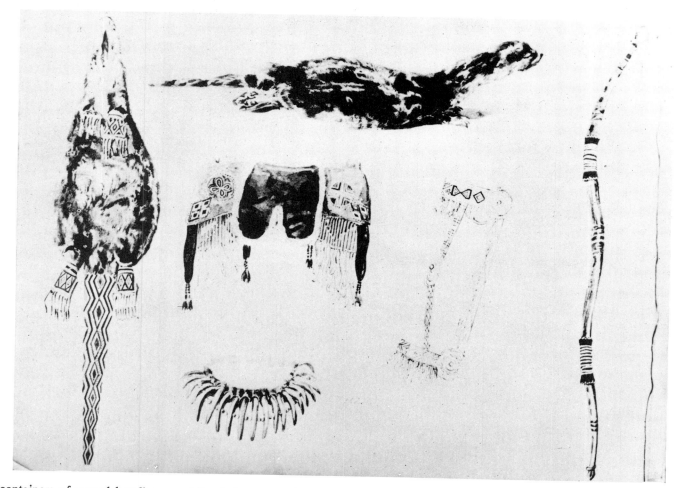

Two containers of sacred bundles, a saddle cloth, two necklaces, and a ceremonial bow, probably Omaha, sketched by Rudolph Friederich Kurz in the 1830's. One of the containers is a whole weasel, and almost surely of magical value in itself.

Smithsonian Institution.

Model of young Mandan woman hoeing corn, period about 1700. The hoe is a buffalo shoulder blade lashed into a wooden handle. The woman's dress is little more than an unfitted, fringed, buckskin robe. A cape-like piece, decorated with shell beads, falls over her right arm like a sleeve. The belt around her waist is covered with porcupine quill work. It may be that this simple costume is a work dress; certainly the Mandans later did much finer tailoring, in which they may have been helped by having steel needles.

Courtesy of the American Museum of Natural History.

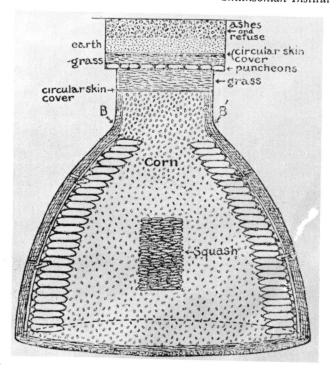

Hidatsa storage pit for crops. The top cover of ashes and refuse was meant to hide the pit from an enemy, if any should come when the tribe was out on a buffalo hunt. These pits were dug as deep as eight feet, and were two to three feet in diameter at the mouth, so that ladders were used for access to the storage part.

Courtesy of the American Museum of Natural History.

"Pawnee women preserving corn," painting by Alvin Jake, modern Pawnee artist. Earth lodges with their vestibule entrances form the background. The women are taking care of corn of the first harvest, when green ears were plucked. Some were eaten fresh, either roasted or boiled; the grain of some, after cooking, was scraped off the cob, dried, and stored. The women are dressed mainly in woven trade materials. *Photo by Bob McCormack.*

Pawnee earth lodge, built by present-day Pawnees at "Indian City," Anadarko, Oklahoma. The outer surface of the lodge is covered with small brush and grass.
Photo by A. C. Hector.

standard dwelling for tribes from Nebraska north. This was a solid structure of rafters carried on a strong central framework, the wall and roof rafters (the walls sloped inward and were part wall and part roof) were covered with willow branches, over that grass, then sod, and finally a layer of earth. The whole might have grass laid over it, sometimes tied in bundles. Many lodges, as among the Mandans, were strong and large enough for people to gather on the roofs in good weather.

Often the floors of these lodges were dug out to a shallow depth, which increased the height to the ceiling and provided a bench going around the outer edge; in a good-size Pawnee lodge, a hundred people could comfortably find seats on this bench. A square opening was left in the roof, under which the fire was placed—the system commonly used by the English, among others, until after the Norman conquest. A form of vestibule was built extending from the entrance to the main part of the lodge. The height of the ceilings run around eleven feet; floor measurements of forty to forty-five feet square were common, and lodges built for ceremonial purposes were considerably bigger.

The layout of smoke hole and door, with no windows, suggests a stuffy, airless dwelling, and probably in the dead of winter, when the door was tightly closed with hides, the air got pretty thick as well as warm, but so long

Interior of the Pawnee lodge at "Indian City." At this point, the earthen bench formed by digging out the floor is widened to make an altar, on which are a buffalo skull, painted drum, two dance rattles, and other objects. A sacred bundle hangs above the altar. Corn is drying upper left, and on the upper right a cradleboard is hanging. *Photo by A. C. Hector.*

as even a slight draft was allowed in the doorway the ventilation system was good. A constant current moved through the vestibule to the fire, where, being warmed, it rose through the smoke hole. The outgoing warm air drew in more fresh air.

The essential layout of a dwelling partly dug into the ground, with a vestibule entrance and a central smoke hole, is extremely old and widespread. It is the pattern of the Eskimo igloo, of the kiva of the Southwest, and occurs in Siberia.

Often the villages were fortified, either with stockades of poles or with earthen ramparts as much as six feet high. Many villages were placed on bluffs overlooking rivers, in such locations that they could be approached only from one direction. Fortifications occur among the prehistoric villages excavated by archaeologists, but the use of them probably increased after these Indians obtained horses, which resulted in something of an increase in raiding.

Another basic type of dwelling probably came up from

A Mandan earthen lodge, photographed around the turn of the century. In this we see a reduced form of the vestibule that was so greatly extended in the Pawnee type. A bull-boat rests beside the door, handy for use on the water or to cover the smoke hole.
Courtesy of the American Museum of Natural History.

Interior of the lodge of a Mandan chief in the 1830's, another of the pictures made on Prince Maximilian's expedition. Even favored horses were stabled inside the lodges. The men, unadorned in the privacy of the home, are taking turns smoking a common pipe. Assorted gear hangs from the poles, including, on the right, a buffalo dance headdress, shields, and spears, and on the left a woman's burden basket, worn on the back with a tumpline over the head just above the forehead, and a paddle. The horsetail hairdo on the man on the right is reminiscent of the scalp lock so common a little further east.

Courtesy of the American Museum of Natural History.

A Mandan village on the Missouri River in North Dakota, sketched on Prince Maximilian's expedition. Bull-boats are clearly shown in the foreground. They were made by stretching buffalo hides over a frame of light wood.

Courtesy of the American Museum of Natural History.

Grass houses of the Wichita tribe; modern reproductions at "Indian City." The one of which part is seen on the right is un-finished. Similar houses were also made by the Caddo.

Photo by A. C. Hector.

Interior of a Wichita grass house at "Indian City." Racks along the wall form benches at the lower level, beds at the higher. The small stump in the left foreground provides a step for climbing into the upper berth. On the part covered with a buffalo robe are a cradleboard or baby carrier, gourd ladles, and a parfleche, a form of valise made by folding rawhide. *Photo by A. C. Hector.*

Lithograph of a Wichita village seen in 1852. Planted fields are just in front of the houses. Illustrations of this kind were often worked up by eastern illustrators from crude sketches and descriptions, plus a dash of imagination. In this case, the illustrator has given the lodges round, clearly defined smoke holes. Actually, the poles of the framework intersected at the top, and smoke seeped through the grass covering. *Smithsonian Institution.*

the prehistoric Southeast, as it is commonest among Caddoan tribes. This is the grass lodge. Poles were planted in a circle in the ground and bent together at the top. The result was a curved cone, not a round dome as in a wigwam. Lighter poles were lashed horizontally around this framework, and on these was tied a thick thatch of grass. The finished product looked rather like an enormous, shaggy beehive. These also were roomy and solid.

The Osages, a Siouan tribe living in southern Missouri and northern Arkansas, built oval or rectangular houses with straight walls and curved roofs, which they covered with mats or with skins. (Being within striking distance of the buffalo, they had a goodly supply of heavy skins.) These buildings ran from 30 to 100 feet in length, 15 to 20 feet in width, and averaged 10 feet high. There is a suggestion here of the Iroquoian longhouse, but we have no knowledge as yet of any contact between the two peoples.

The white men never did exploit the idea of automatic, controlled ventilation through a single entrance and a smoke hole. Our tents, typically, are closed at the top. Since early times we have had the A-tent and the pyramid tent; in the Middle Ages, knights and nobles had handsome, large, round tents with pointed roofs. You could not make a wood fire in any of them without making yourself perfectly miserable. Our campfires are built outside.

From Siberia into Alaska, and on down to the land of the Western farmers, there was a tent that used the prin-

ciple. A framework of three or of four poles, lashed together near the top or hooked together by interlocking crotches, was set up, with the lower ends well apart. More poles were laid against this, their bottom ends forming a circle. Over the whole, skins were stretched in such a way as to leave an opening at the top—the same principle as in the Abenaki wigwam described in the last chapter. This was the primitive form of the tepee. You could, and still can, have a fire in the middle of it without being smoked out; it would keep you warm in winter.

The tepee was probably invented in the Arctic to keep out cold, but it is also a good tent in hot weather, when our tents, under direct sun, become intolerable. The arrangement allows lifting a section of the tent at the bottom, and again the principle of air movement comes into play. Air heated by the sun striking through the sides rises through the smoke hole; cooler air continuously flows in along the ground.

Because of the number of poles required, tepees are cumbersome things to carry around, but they are quickly set up and quickly struck. The writer of this book has spent many hours in them, and will testify that they are the most comfortable of all makes of tent.

The farming tribes used their tepees mostly when they went out after the buffalo, which usually was an annual affair when the great herds, in their migration, came nearest to their territory. The buffalo hunt was a difficult business. A man on foot, armed with a stone-tipped lance and stone-tipped arrows, ran real danger when he went to

Sketch of an Omaha village, 1850, by Rudolph Friederich Kurz. Part of an earth lodge shows at the extreme left, another is in the background. In the center are the tepees used for hunting. These are the larger, elaborated tepees that came in after these Indians obtained horses. In the upper right hand corner is a pencil sketch of a scout disguised as a wolf. This was a common device for scouts who wanted to spy on an enemy village, so that, if seen lurking, they might be mistaken for animals.

Smithsonian Institution.

The Mandan buffalo dance, as seen on Prince Maximilian's expedition. Rituals such as this, in which the dancers portray both the game and the hunters, are common all over the world. They were known at least 12,000 years ago in Europe. Through them, the participants expect to obtain power over the game.

· *Courtesy of the American Museum of Natural History.*

Mandan dressed and painted for the buffalo dance.
Courtesy of the American Museum of Natural History.

kill one of those big, aggressive, thick-hided beasts—the more so since they were almost always in herds, the bulls quick to attack in defense of their females and young.

The tepees then were small, because the poles had to be dragged along by dogs. The people went out on foot, always with one eye peeled for some other tribe with which they might not be on friendly terms and that might be after the same herd.

Much of their hunting was done by stampeding the animals; for instance, by setting fire to the grass, and driving them either over a cliff or past a line of archers who picked off as many as they could. Their kill was limited by what they could use on the spot plus what they could dry, or "jerk," and carry back for later use; and the amount they could carry back was what the women could take on their backs, including the hides, or what could be added—not much—to the burdens already dragged by the dogs. They had no wheels, no wagons. They made a contraption known as a travois. Two tepee poles were tied to the shoulders of a dog, the free ends dragging on the ground, and across these the load was placed. In winter, the northern tribes had toboggans, on which much more could be hauled, but in winter the buffalo were in the south.

Women must have looked forward to the big hunt with some dread, much though they wanted the meat, the warm robes, and useful skins. At home, their position was better, for they were the mistresses of the fields. They raised the corn, squashes, and beans, and the crops were theirs. Tobacco, a sacred plant, was often raised by the men. Farming gave the women a lot of work to do, but it did leave them some leisure, and it gave them authority. Also, it was a demonstration of woman's mystic power, the gift of fertility, of creating life.

Throughout the area we find the signs of relationship with the Southeast. Most tribes had clans, some of which counted descent through the mother, some through the father. Many were divided into halves or moieties, like the Iroquois, the Creeks, and the Natchez; some grouped their clans into several different larger groups instead of only two. The common thing, as usual, was to regard all members of a clan, even though they came from different villages and were total strangers to each other, as relatives, who helped each other and, as relatives, could not marry. Such clans are called "exogamous," meaning "outward marrying." Some were "endogamous," that is, although all fellow-clansmen felt bound to one another, they also married only within the clan.

Chieftainships were well defined. Among some tribes, chiefs were appointed for life, among some they were partly hereditary. Many tribes, especially in the northeastern group, had both war and peace chiefs, the peace chiefs being the real governors, the war chiefs leaders of war parties. When Tecumseh formed the great Algonkian alliance against the United States, he stressed the fact that "the chiefs," meaning the peaceful governors, were no longer in charge.

Young men went in search of visions, usually going off by themselves and praying for a supernatural visitor. The vision a man might receive was an indication of the extent to which he had what the Iroquois called orenda,

Engraving from a sketch by Bodmer, on Maximilian's expedition, of Mandan toboggans drawn over the ice by dogs. The women are thoroughly bundled up against the cold of a Dakota winter.

A family might own twenty or more dogs, which were a nuisance inside the lodge, but were made to earn their keep.

Smithsonian Institution.

Engraving from a painting by Bodmer of a dance of the Mandan Female White Buffalo Society, a women's ceremonial organization. White, or albino buffaloes were greatly revered and believed to have power over the species as a whole. The women wear headdresses of white buffalo skin, the principal woman also has a white buffalo robe with the fur left on. The others wear robes of dressed skins ornamented by painting and porcupine quill embroidery. The dance was solemn, involving very little motion—more a rhythmic prayer than a dance, intended to lure the buffalo within reach. *Courtesy of the American Museum of Natural History.*

special strength from the all-pervading, unseeable god the Algonkians called by names related to Manitou, the Siouans by names similar to Wakonda. Very strong visions led a man to become a shaman, in which case he read the future, gave news of people at a distance, and diagnosed sicknesses but often left their treatment to specialists in actual medicine. The medical treatment ranged from setting bones and administering healing herbs to such tricks as sucking stones, thorns, and small animals out of the patient's body.

These shamans did spectacular tricks. There were large-scale ceremonies also, that could be conducted only by men with something on the line of priestly training. Among many tribes the shamans, who received this training, were on the way to being priests; among others there were true priests. The Pawnee shamans trained their disciples after the manner of priests. There was also a true priesthood which was strictly hereditary; among these, five, of whom the highest was associated with the evening star, were in fact more powerful than the chiefs. The Pawnees had a definite sun worship and related star cult, including an annual Morning Star Ceremony. At this ceremony, a captured maiden was sacrificed. The captive might have been taken at any time of the year. She was well treated, and told nothing of her fate. Three days before the great day, she was stripped of her clothing, painted all over, and treated as a sacred person. Every attempt was made to keep her from divining what was coming.

Before the morning star rose on the fourth morning, she was led to a raised scaffold. It was considered a lucky sign if, in her innocence, the girl mounted the scaffold without resistance. Then she was tied. Priests symbolized torture of her, but did not actually hurt her. Then a man shot her through the body from in front, just as the morning star rose, and at the same moment another struck her over the head with a club. Death was instantaneous. Her heart was cut out as a sacrifice to the star, and every male in the tribe shot an arrow into her body, older relatives doing this in the name of boys too young to draw a bow themselves.

At the beginning of the nineteenth century, a young Pawnee warrior of high reputation rebelled against this rite. At the critical moment he cut the girl free from the scaffold, threw her on his horse, and ran off with her. He set her free near her own tribe. When he returned, he was not punished, but admired for his courage. The people seem to have been relieved to drop a cruel practice, and it ended there.

The symbolized torture clearly derives from the Southeast, with great improvement. Treating the victim as holy, holding the rite when a certain star appears at a certain time of year, cutting out the heart, and many other details, seem pure Aztec—except that the Aztecs would have sacrificed a man. Certainly the Pawnees show up as a lot more likeable than many of the tribes further east.

Partly through the visions of inspired individuals, partly by ways now lost in the mists of antiquity, among these tribes there sprang up a collection of sacred objects, such as the sacred arrows of the Cheyennes, or more often, what are called "medicine bundles" or "sacred bundles."

Both names are poor. So many Indian things were named by white men in ignorance, contempt, or both. They saw that Indians combined healing with religion—as did we until not so long ago—so they called all Indian religious practitioners "medicine men," regardless. They saw that the Indians wrapped objects that they considered sacred in various kinds of packages, often beautifully decorated. When white men were allowed to see what those objects were, they did not think much of them, any more than an Indian would think much of some of our sacred symbols. They saw that these packages, or their contents, were sometimes used to heal the sick, just as, in the 1500's, Cabeza de Vaca treated sick Indians by touching them with a cross, so they called them "medicine bundles." This is much as if Indians, seeing Christians pray for health, were to call our cross "medicine sticks," and about as accurate.

The best name we have for these packages is "sacred bundles," and it will have to do. Many were personal property, handed down from father to son, or buried with the owner. Others became clan or tribal property. They were the centers of major rituals. Among the Algonkians, other than the Cheyennes, bundles usually were clan property, so the great ceremonies relating to farming were performed by clans. The owner of the bundle was instructed by the man from whom he inherited it in the prayers and rites that went with it. He alone could lead them; thus he was a priest.

The northern tribes, both east and west of the Mississippi, gave reverence to the calumet or sacred pipe. Pipes were carried in special dances, they served as passports for messengers, and were used in many rituals. A pipe dressed with red feathers signified war; one with white feathers meant peace.

The bowl of a true calumet was made from a stone, catlinite, found in Minnesota in the country of the non-farming Sioux. This stone is soft and easy to work when first dug out of the ground, then it hardens. The bowls were fitted with long stems which were decorated with great elaboration. Some pipes could be smoked for pleasure, in which case the tobacco that was raised with special ritual by the men was not used. Others were smoked only on ceremonial occasions. Many tribes permitted smoking only by persons who had attained some rank. Often young men were forbidden to smoke because smoking would damage their wind. This special reverence for smoking and tobacco, and for the pipes themselves, seems to be a pattern that developed spontaneously among the Middle Western farmers and does not derive from the cultures further east.

In the Southeast, war achievement was the common man's road to fame and rank. With them it was a murderous business of killing everyone possible and bringing home the gory samples as evidence, with the alternative of capturing a strong man to torture. Among the Western farmers, except in the southern part where Southeastern influence was strongest, torture was not a requirement, and nowhere was it as hideous as farther east. The main thing was for a man to prove his courage, and these tribes came to the logical conclusion that the greatest courage a man could show was to lay his bare hand upon an armed enemy, preferably one who was surrounded by his comrades. Killing from ambush was not honored; killing of any kind, in fact, was secondary to proving bravery, except on those rare occasions when two tribes found it necessary to engage in serious war with each other. There is a vast difference between sporadic fighting for the sake of glory and wars of conquest such as those with which the Iroquois astounded their neighbors and in which the white man specializes.

Scalps were taken as a regular thing, but they were not essential, and a man was not judged by the number of his scalps. Before starting on a war party, to get into the spirit of the thing and acquire power, or after it, to celebrate a victory, the men danced. The dance after a successful raid is generally called a "scalp dance," since any scalps taken were featured. In these dances, each warrior dramatized in stylized form what he would do or had done, bending low to track the enemy, leaping to the attack, going through motions of combat. The footwork was light and fast, in time to fast, cheerful songs almost always pretty and often beautiful, and to the rapid beat of a high-toned drum. It was a fine means of showing off. Similar dances were performed for pure fun. As each individual danced as he pleased, no rehearsal was necessary; one needed only to know how to dance, and know the tune. It is from these performances that the "war dances" evolved that are now part of the common, commercial stock of Indians all over the United States.

Boasting was an important part of the war complex. On appropriate occasions, warriors stood up before the public in turns to recite their brave deeds. The performance was far from modest, but it had to be accurate; everyone kept careful track, and knew just what any man had a right to claim. If he claimed any act that was not his due, he would be hooted down and disgraced. White frontiersmen were quick to adopt this trait. They mixed it with whiskey and imagination, to produce the famous "brags" of the early frontier.

Fighting was a good deal of a sporting proposition, carried on by individual initiative. Hunting was a more serious business. Hunting parties were often carefully organized, and under many circumstances hunters were not allowed to go out except by permission of the chiefs, in order that no hasty individual might frighten the game. This control was especially tight in regard to the buffalo hunts. It could also, as among the Illinois, apply to the return of hunters, so that all the kill could be pooled and properly distributed.

The Illinois had a peculiar social institution that is found among no other tribe in North America. As a regular thing, handsome adolescent boys were trained as homosexuals and became concubines of the men. Apparently, these same boys later grew up to be effective warriors and husbands, but they would, understandably, themselves also turn to boys for their indulgences. The situation reminds us of the ancient Greeks.

Widely across the United States the Indians had an interesting attitude towards male homosexuals, leading to the institution known by the French term, berdache. It was recognized that certain persons were born in male bodies, who yet were incapable of living the virile life of a male Indian. Innately, they were women. At the age at which a normal youth began the full activities of man and warrior, these special individuals gave up. They formally donned women's clothes, and from that time forth worked, and were classed, as women. When a youth made this choice, it was a source of real sorrow to his parents, but once the matter had been well talked out, no obstacle was put in his way.

The custom provided a useful place for persons who otherwise would have been hopelessly misfitted. The fact that in a tribe there might be one or two, or perhaps half a dozen berdaches, also probably provided an outlet for homosexuals of a different, more vigorous type who would otherwise have become anti-social, as they are in our

An Osage warrior of the early nineteenth century. It is difficult to make out what the decoration above his forehead is. His head is shaven, eastern style, and the comb of his natural hair heightened by a roach.

Courtesy of The New-York Historical Society, N. Y. C.

society. No parallel arrangement existed for women. For whatever reasons, the women seem always to have been able to adapt themselves to a reasonably fruitful life within their own sex. Some tribes credited *berdaches* with magical powers, some merely looked upon them with contemptuous pity, among some they became the finest workers in the women's crafts.

Among the Middle Westerners we begin to find Indians who look like what nowadays most people expect Indians to look like. The comb of natural hair, made by shaving all the head except for the strip along the crown, was elaborated with an artificial roach of deer's tail hairs, dyed red, to which feathers might be added to signify that the wearer had won certain combat honors. Tribes that did not shave their heads, but wore their hair long (much less trouble, and much warmer in winter), could tie on these handsome, made roaches, too. Among some tribes, feathers were tied directly in the hair, standing up, lying flat, or hanging down, as badges of war achievement. Early portrayals of Omahas and some of the northernmost tribes even show "war bonnets," quite like those now so famous.

Buckskin clothing was elaborate, and often decorated with porcupine quill embroidery, later replaced by beads.

An early illustration of the famous "war bonnet," from a sketch by Kurz in 1851. The man in the feathered bonnet with the handsome, painted robe is an ordinary Omaha warrior of the period, the plainly dressed man at the left, receiving his report, with a quiver across his back, is Young Elk, a major chief of the tribe. It was not at all unusual for chiefs to dress simply except on those occasions when it was necessary for them to wear their regalia. A true chief was not supposed to be interested in his own welfare or material advancement.
Smithsonian Institution.

The general effect was similar to that which the Plains Indians later made so famous, which is not surprising, since much of Plains Indian culture derived from these farmers.

In the eighteenth century, horses that had run loose from the Spanish herds in New Mexico and increased fantastically on the good grazing of the Plains, reached the Middle Westerners, who soon learned to ride. With horses, both war and hunting became easier and more fun. The big hunts were ever so much more comfortable, the women's part in them greatly lightened (it was a break for the dogs, too). There developed a tendency to stay on the hunt longer, live a somewhat shorter part of the year in the villages, and depend a little less upon the crops. As the horses came from the West, trade goods began coming from the East. While it lasted, the way of life was richer than it had ever been.

The land occupied by the Middle Westerners included the areas that white men, seeking for farms, would most covet. It was impossible for their few thousands to stand against the might of the growing United States.

It is curious how the history of the two main groups of Algonkians runs parallel. The Western Algonkians found themselves between the British and the French. They tended to ally themselves with the French, which, when Canada fell, turned out to be a mistake. Then they put their faith in the British, who proceeded to lose, first the Revolution, then the War of 1812. The Indians were left at the mercy of the Americans, against whom the kings of France and Britain had defended them, and they found little mercy.

It was among these tribes that the two most ambitious attempts to form large confederacies against the whites occurred. The first was organized by Pontiac in the middle of the eighteenth century, threatened for a while, then died out. The second, and much more menacing, was led by Tecumseh, a Shawnee, against the Americans at the time of the War of 1812. Tecumseh was one of the noblest of all Indian leaders, a statesman and great orator,

A Mandan chief wearing his best, painted on Prince Maximilian's expedition. A cover with an eagle feather on it has been drawn over his lance; the next ornament below that is a scalp. The horned headdress is a variant on the war bonnet, and was the more common type in early times. The long-skirted shirt, leggings, and moccasins are richly decorated with porcupine quill, fringes, and bits of fur. Another scalp hangs from the right side of his chest. Like the Omaha chief, he has allowed a bit of beard to grow under his chin. *Courtesy of the American Museum of Natural History.*

Engraving from a painting by Bodmer of a Hidatsa "dog dancer," 1834. The Dog Society was an important organization of young men pledged to bravery in war and used for police duties. Note the highly decorated bow and equally ornamented leggings.

Smithsonian Institution.

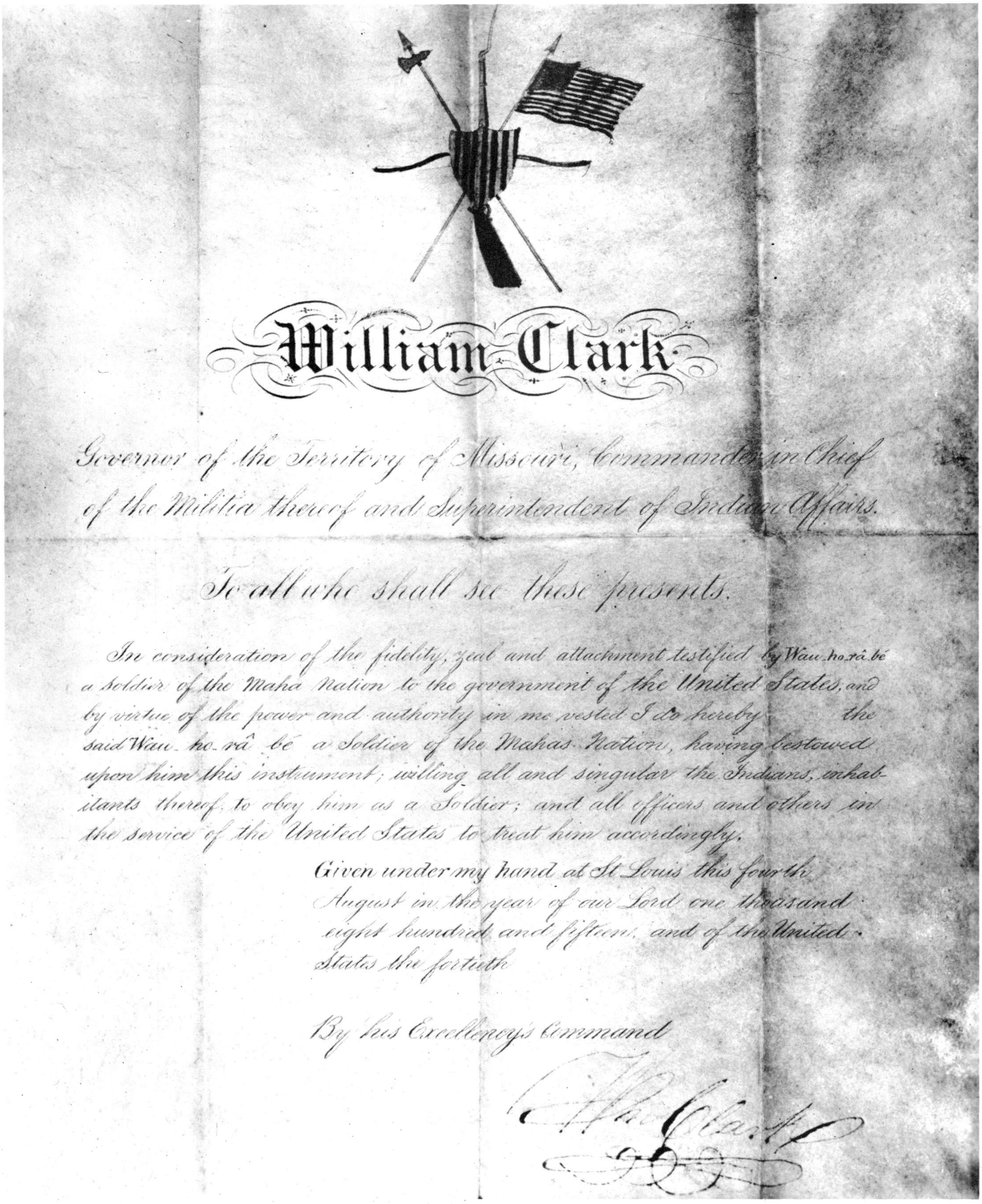

William Clark

Governor of the Territory of Missouri, Commander in Chief of the Militia thereof and Superintendent of Indian Affairs.

To all who shall see these presents.

In consideration of the fidelity, zeal and attachment testified by Wau-ho-râ-bé a soldier of the Maha Nation to the government of the United States, and by virtue of the power and authority in me vested I do hereby   the said Wau-ho-râ-bé a Soldier of the Mahas Nation, having bestowed upon him this instrument; willing all and singular the Indians, inhabitants thereof, to obey him as a Soldier; and all officers and others in the service of the United States to treat him accordingly.

Given under my hand at St Louis this fourth August in the year of our Lord one thousand eight hundred and fifteen, and of the United States the fortieth

By his Excellency's Command

Wm Clark

Combination passport and certificate of authority issued by William Clark, governor of Missouri Territory, to an Omaha named Wau-ho-ra-be in 1815. First contacts between Indian tribes and white men were almost always friendly, the friendliness lasting until the white men in that district felt strong enough to do without it. *Smithsonian Institution.*

104

Contact with the white men—Hidatsas at a fur traders' post in 1834, from a drawing by Bodmer. The white man with his hand inside his coat is Prince Maximilian of Wied; the taller man at the extreme right is the artist himself. *Smithsonian Institution.*

a stern war leader, and yet a man of mercy who would not let prisoners be killed. More than one white family, seeing his warriors overrunning their land, put themselves in his hands and found safety. He personally travelled from Illinois to the towns of the Creeks in the deep South, to the Osages, and to the Chippewas. The grand alliance he tried to form involved forgetting too many old feuds, becoming friendly with too many entirely alien peoples, for the tribes he dealt with. His confederacy was never strong enough, and when he himself was killed in a rear guard action in the British retreat from Detroit, the whole thing ended.

The Algonkians were debauched with liquor, first by the French, then by the English, then by the Americans, who used a barrel of whiskey as the standard prelude to another profitable treaty. The kings, and to a lesser extent the republican government in Washington, tried to keep the treaties, but the frontiersmen would have none of it. Seldom were peaceful Indians so freely shot down in cold blood, promises so regularly broken, the doctrine that the only good Indian is a dead one so heartlessly put into practice. The deer and turkeys were killed off, the good farming lands taken. Weakened by drunkenness, poverty-stricken, hungry, broken, the tribes could no longer exist. Black Hawk of the Sauk and Foxes made a futile effort to hold onto land that was honestly his, in the pathetic, so-called "Black Hawk's War," and with that the resistance ended. Those tribes that survive at all, survive for the most part on bleak little holdings in Oklahoma.

The tribes west of the Mississippi fared somewhat better, although far from well. Smallpox was one of the white men's most important contributions to Indian life all over the continent. As the disease had never existed in the New World, at times when it caught hold its ravages were terrible. The western epidemic of 1837 raised havoc with many tribes. It broke the powerful Mandan and Hidatsa, reducing the Mandans from 1,600 souls to 150, and doing about as well by their neighbors.

The white men flowed around the farming Indians, surrounded them, engulfed them. By then we had adopted the policy of concentrating as many Indians as possible in the "Indian Territory," which later became Oklahoma. Most of the tribes named in this chapter wound up there, regardless of original treaties, of whether they put up a stiff fight or, like the Pawnees, decided that their day was done and that the only course was to keep the peace and try to learn from their conquerors. In those days people knew little about petroleum and cared less. There was no use for many minerals that are now valuable, nor did the geologists of those times know how to find the desired minerals hidden in the ground the way they do now. The purpose of crowding Indians into Indian Territory was to place them on land that nobody wanted. Not until the United States began to fill up from coast to coast did white men hunger after that poorer soil. It did happen that in the end a few tribes found themselves sitting on mineral wealth. The greatest joke the white man ever played on himself was when he put the Osages, by force of arms, on undesirable land under which was hidden one of the richest oil deposits in North America.

The remnants of the Mandan, Hidatsa, and Arikara tribes are in North Dakota. They have made a partial comeback since the great smallpox epidemic, numbering now about 1,700 for all three tribes, or less than a fifth of their population at the height of their power. Their present holdings are not in territory suited to farming, and as their principal reservation, at Fort Berthold, was recently flooded down the middle by one of the new dams across the Missouri, destroying their low-lying land, it is difficult to see where they will turn next.

VI. The Old Settlers

In 1540, Coronado, marching north from Mexico City, passed first through the outer part of the Aztec empire: cities and towns in which the common people lived no more poorly than did the common people of Spain. He went on into ever drier country, by villages of settled farmers sited where there was water, then to a desert stretch lying along what is now the U.S.-Mexican border where he encountered small bands of poor and primitive desert rovers. Finally, in the drainage of the upper Rio Grande, he came again to towns and villages, the houses arranged as compactly as in a medieval town, the fields stretching along the bottom lands and often rich with irrigation, the people well organized under strong governments, dressed in garments of cotton and in skins, adorned with shell and turquoise.

He had entered the eastern portion of what today we call the Southwest. Following a fable, he turned east and went on, across the High Plains, where he found people living in skin tents who followed "the wild cows," and finally, when he came to the grass lodges of the Wichitas, gave up in despair and turned back.

He had traveled the length of the second branch of the river of knowledge and advancement out of Mexico, left it to cross the land of the Plains hunters, then, without knowing or caring, reached the western extension of higher culture coming from the Gulf Coast. The tribes along the Rio Grande the Spanish called "Pueblos," as we do today. The word means "village" or "town."

The land of the New Mexico and Arizona semi-civilized tribes is not one that anyone would pick for the place of the greatest dedication to agriculture in North America. It, the true Southwest, is sharply unlike the flat country of Texas and Oklahoma to the east, the howling deserts and the coastal ranges of California to the west. It is a land of low rainfall, the greater part of it having less than the average of twenty inches a year which, as we saw in the last chapter, marked the limit beyond which the Western farmers did not go.

Its lowest parts, in the south, are 2,000 feet or better above sea level except along the banks of the southern part of the Colorado River; much of it lies above 5,000 feet, and in the north its highest peaks top 13,000. It is a rugged country, seamed with canyons, studded with the cliff-sided, flat-topped hills the Spanish call "mesas," meaning "tables," as do we after them. It is strung with mountain ranges, the upper slopes of which are green and well watered, but too high, with too short a growing season for farming. Rivers are few and sparse; water-

A land you would not pick for a center of farming—Monument Valley in the northern part of the Navaho Reservation, at the north edge of the Southwest.

Courtesy of the American Museum of Natural History.

106

Irrigated land at Taos Pueblo. The buildings of the Pueblo itself show in the background, far left and right.
Smithsonian Institution.

Pima country, in southern Arizona. With irrigation, the Pimas made desert land like this blossom, but the Papagos have had to do the best they could without irrigation.
Smithsonian Institution.

A desert dry farm. The site chosen is in a canyon, at a place where, when it does rain, water flowing down the canyon will flood the corn. The stalks will be little higher than this when the corn is mature. *Smithsonian Institution.*

courses, called "washes" or "arroyos," in which water floods violently after a rain but which at other times are dry, are common. Over large parts of it, the midsummers are frying hot, the winters fierce with cutting, icy winds and driving snow.

This is the country where men make their principal living by farming unirrigated land with an average annual rainfall of *thirteen inches,* showing a skill at dry farming and an achievement in developing specialized varieties of corn and other plants that we, with all our technology, have never equaled.

Above I wrote "where *men* make their principal living by farming." The word stressed is important, for if we want to bring out the vast difference between what these people took from the civilizations to the south and what the Southeasterners took, two things stand out above all. First, the men did the farming. These people borrowed and developed six colors of corn, a number of kinds of beans, squashes, tobacco, and cotton. They learned formal rituals, often performed by masked figures, the making of

really fine pottery, weaving and embroidery, possibly the idea of building their solid houses. Their basketry craft may have come from the north. Also, in a country where the hunting was comparatively poor and big game hard to come by, they looked upon farming as primary. The dry farms call for endless labor. Where irrigation developed, as it did wherever there was the water for it, it brought with it much heavy work. So farming became a man's occupation. The women stayed home, with leisure to devote to elaborating and beautifying their basketry, and above all their pottery.

It is interesting that in the Southwest we find a tendency for the best basketry to be made by the tribes who had the least crops or else by those just outside the Southwest proper (the outstanding exception to this generalization is the Pima tribe). If you watch the making of fine basketry, you will see that it is laborious, slow, exasperating. Tiny stitch after stitch has to be made with a stiff strand in tight, stiff material. A simple basket takes an inordinately long time to make. In modern times, basketry of the really fine type, the kind of weaving that holds water, is the first craft to disappear.

Pottery, on the other hand, is quick and satisfying. The bowl or jar grows under the potter's hand while you watch. The motions are smooth and comparatively un-cramped. Once she has assembled her clays, ground and mixed in the silica-bearing earth, prepared her paints, a skillful potter can make half a dozen pieces in a day without too great effort—more if they are small—set them to dry, and have a baking tomorrow. It is skilled work, but it is much more pleasant and immediately rewarding than that of the basket maker.

Pottery is heavy and breaks easily. Basketry is light and hard to break. Pots are unsuitable ware for camping people who move often, fine for those who stay put. It is reasonable that the tiresome, fine basketry should be made by poor wanderers, first for their own use, then to trade to the richer farmers for the good foods they raise and their varied manufactures.

The second sharp difference from the Southeast was the entire absence of human sacrifice or torture and a general dislike of war. Setting aside the Athapascan invaders and certain tribes along the Colorado River, whom we shall come to later, a man got mighty little advancement out of being a warrior. The big battle was against the environment—to maintain a way of life of considerable richness, which required an assured food supply and plenty of time free from the day-to-day struggle for food in an unfavorable climate. War was a distraction, a diversion of energy to a sterile purpose that was badly needed for a productive one. It meant the loss of strong backs and arms that could ill be spared from the labor.

It could mean, also, the loss of knowledge as important as physical strength. It is a general saying that civilized man seeks to control and alter his environment, while primitive man adapts himself to it. On the whole this is correct, even though the first man to light a fire to keep himself warm and the first to wrap himself in skins to keep out the cold were beginning the control of environment. Now, if the Southwesterners had merely adapted themselves to their surroundings, they would have moved out, or they would have given up the endless struggle to raise crops and become wanderers, hunting anything they could get, no matter how small, gathering wild seeds, berries, and roots where they might chance upon them. Instead, as the Southwest came to its present condition of dryness, they fought back. They developed their amazing dry farming systems, exploiting the last drops of moisture in soil we should describe as waterless. They really altered the country when they took up, probably under Mexican influence, a system for placing on the level, cultivable land the rain that fell in the high mountains, which is what irrigation amounts to—a method of capturing distant rain.

Against the odds they faced, the greatest physical strength, the most intelligent methods, were not enough by themselves. In such a battle, men need divine help. Whatever the religions may originally have been, they came to center upon rain, the crops, and hence, as a corollary to these, the welfare of the people. Among most of the settled tribes, the religion was formalized, with fixed rituals coming at specified times of the year. They were based upon an elaborate series of myths, a veritable unwritten bible, which had to be thoroughly understood. The prayers had to be memorized, along with details of costume, motions, dance steps, offerings.

This kind of thing calls for trained priests. Obviously, it is immaterial whether the priest be, or have been, a warrior. Having taken scalps is no qualification, possibly the reverse. To maintain the priesthood, there must always be young men in training. Among some tribes, only a young man of a certain descent could succeed a certain priest. In the last few years, the death or conversion to Christianity of certain Hopi Indians, with no others available of the required descent, has put an end to several important ceremonies.

Hopi Antelope Priest in 1897. For certain ceremonies, the participants wear only the ancient clothing. This man's simple outfit with the cotton kilt is much the same as what his prehistoric forebears wore in warm weather, except for the silver necklace over the shell one, and that the embroidery on the kilt is done with wool. *Smithsonian Institution.*

Among other tribes, a younger man could enter upon the training if he was accepted by the priest or the society that handled a certain ritual. Not every man was accepted. Usually there would be one whose training was carried to the point where he could be the next priest of that particular ceremony, and through this succession he might even be in line eventually to become governor of the tribe.

Even today, among some of the Pueblo tribes, it would be difficult to make up a strong war party without including at least some young men of the group described. Kill them off, and the loss to the people would be—or certainly would have been in earlier times—like the loss of the only younger scientist who understood the theory of relativity or was trained in the latest experiments that promise a cure for cancer. Early in World War II, two young Hopis refused to register for the draft. They were the only men eligible to succeed two important priests, and the priests and their councilors ruled that the youths could have nothing whatsoever to do with this warlike measure. They were not allowed to register and then become conscientious objectors, which could have been arranged. They refused to register, and they went to jail for it. Nothing like that could have happened among any of the Indians we have looked at up to now.

Now, if you have rich possessions and stores of food, and if you are surrounded by people who have few possessions and poor food, no matter how much you dislike it you are going to have to fight. This was true in the Southwest. There were war organizations and rituals; some tribes had war societies and war priests or bow priests. Many of them fought well. The Papagos and Pimas, in southern Arizona, were noted for their success against the Apaches, and all of these Indians could be prickly customers on occasion, even the Hopis whose very name, "Hopi," means peaceful.

Necessary fighting was often surrounded by heavy ritual. Scalps might be taken, or in place of them, a few strands of hair. Sometimes only certain men, of near-priestly standing, took scalps. These trophies were likely to be regarded with considerable fear and had to be purified, prayed over, fed, to be kept harmless. The warrior who had killed someone had to go through elaborate purifications before he could rejoin his people. To do well in battle thus was a nuisance. The Pimas and Papagos required sixteen days of purification for a killer, which greatly limited their otherwise important value as allies to our troops against the Apaches; the Papagos designated only a few men out of a war party, men with special power from their visions, who should do the killing if all went well. Much of the sacred aspect of war was rationalized to fit the eternal quest for rain and fertility. Victory will capture the rain, the prayers say; the strength taken from the enemy will bring water.

Although it was, and is, dry, the Southwest offered better chances for farming than the territory surrounding it, even better hunting than much of that territory. Many different groups of people settled in it, as is shown by the languages still spoken there.

In recent years, detailed, long research by scholars tends to show that many families of Indian languages that we once thought stood alone, in fact are related to others. In this book, there has been little mention of these greater families. Some of the relationships are not fully proven. Others are pretty sure, but even so, the differences between the related families are so wide—as wide as the difference between English and Sanskrit, or wider—that the speakers must have separated in most remote times, even perhaps before they crossed over from Siberia into the New World in some cases. When the relationships are so remote, they are of little or no help in understanding the history of a region such as the Southwest, and it is more useful to stick to the well-proven, more closely related groups of languages.

In the area we find several tribes speaking languages of the big, Uto-Aztecan family. The name comes from the fact that both the Utes of Utah and Colorado and the Aztecs of Mexico belong to it. The chief of these tribes are the Hopis in northern Arizona and the Pimans, that is the Pimas and Papagos, in the southern part of the same state and northern Mexico. Over along the Colorado River are the Yumans, a totally different linguistic group. Among the Pueblos, in addition to the Uto-Aztecan Hopis, we find no less than three separate families speaking a number of languages: the Zuñi, near the Arizona border, and, further east and in the Rio Grande valley, the Keresans and the Tanoans. Of these, the only ones having any proven near relation with any speech outside the area are the Tanoans, whose family relates to Kiowa, spoken by a great Plains tribe. Scattered all over New Mexico and Arizona are the warlike tribes speaking Athapascan languages, the Navahos and Apaches, comparatively recent invaders.

Nowhere in America does a visitor have a greater feeling of antiquity than in the Southwest. When you go to England, you may look at Roman ruins, but you won't run into any centurions or gentlemen in togas; you know of the Norman conquest and view the Norman castles, but you find no one speaking the Norman tongue or stalking around in chain mail. In the Southwest, it is probable that the Pimas and Papagos descend, at least in part, from the ancient Hohokam people, who, in turn, derive from the yet older Cochise culture. The Pueblos, or some of them, beyond doubt once inhabited the ruins that stare so picturesquely from the cliffs of the north, and to this day they practice rituals that were familiar to their ancestors a thousand years ago. Everywhere the ancient arts, costumes, ways of speech, crafts, houses, are preserved well enough to be recognizable. Here is antiquity on the hoof. Even the recent invaders, the Athapascans, have been in the country for nigh on to a thousand years, while the first white men, the Spaniards, came here in the late fifteen hundreds. Both keep their own tongue.

The old settled, farming tribes of the Southwest fall into three groups: the Pimans of southern Arizona, the Yumans along the Colorado River on the Arizona-California border, and the Pueblos. The Pueblos include the Hopis in northern Arizona; the Zuñis, Acomas, and Lagunas forming a connecting link across western New Mexico between the Hopis and the Rio Grande; and, at the time the Spanish came, a string of settlements, many of two or three thousand population, on the Rio Grande and some of its tributaries from near the Colorado border almost to El Paso.

The Pimas themselves, from whom the Pimans take their name, lived along the Gila River, the only important stream in southern Arizona. They irrigated on a large scale, digging ditches many miles long with their primitive tools, raising the usual crops and cotton. South of them, extending into Mexico, were their close relatives the Papagos, the "bean people," so called because in their extremely desert country they could raise beans better than anything else.

The present Papago reservation embraces a goodly part of their original territory. It is the hardest-looking piece of land in which one can imagine anyone farming. Actually, under the circumstances, they could—and can—try to farm, but they could never put their whole reliance on their crops. The various edible forms of cactus, such seeds and berries as could be found, and the poor hunting of the area rounded out their diet. Even so, in early times they went to work for parts of the year for their richer cousins on the river, as now they work for the big cotton farms outside their desert.

Living in country that is warm for most of the year, the Pimans wore little clothing. They built flat-roofed houses of poles—often digging out the ground inside—walled

with cactus rods or brush and sometimes plastered with the clay called "adobe," which dries extremely hard. The Papagos, because of the nature of the country, could live only in small villages widely scattered, coming together from time to time for their most important ceremonies, one of which included dancers with masks. The Pimas lived in larger concentrations, since it took so much less area to feed a family.

They made fine basketry and pottery of good quality. In the pottery we encounter a strongly Mexican tradition that runs all through the Southwest. Most eastern pottery was made by working a lump of clay into shape, and if it was decorated, the decoration consisted of patterns molded or cut into the outer surface. The surfaces tended to be rather rough. Southwestern pottery is built up with coils of clay, like the "snakes" children like to make with modelling clay, then smoothed out. The surface is polished

Papago woman making bread. She has moved her gear to the sunny side of the house to accommodate the photographer. The round, flat loaf or *tortilla* is patted into shape in her hands, then cooked on the clay griddle in front of her. Her clothing, of course, is entirely of trade materials. *Smithsonian Institution*.

Returning Piman warriors signal a successful war party with a column of smoke. The signal is answered by two columns of smoke from the village. *Smithsonian Institution*.

Papago mortar and pestle for crushing mesquite beans, one of the important wild foods of the tribe. *Smithsonian Institution*.

carefully, then over it is painted a slip of very fine clay, on which designs may be painted.

The Pimans, in their religion, paid a great deal of attention to visions which gave power, in which we see the old, shamanistic pattern. Their principal religious officials, however, worked their way up through a course of training and their major ceremonies required priestly control. Once a year the Papagos fermented a kind of wine from the agave cactus and held a ceremony in which large quantities were drunk to symbolize the soaking of the ground with rain. The result was that everyone went on a pleasant, mild binge, accompanied by music, dancing, prayer, and happy feelings. Ritual intoxication is also a trait we find well developed in Mexico and on further south, but is unusual in North America.

Social organization was simple. There were clans, with descent traced through the father, but they ceased to have

Papago woman with carrying basket, in which she has another basket and two pottery jars. The carrying basket ends at the front in a sort of harness to go over her head. *Smithsonian Institution.*

Pima baskets, tightly enough woven to hold water.
University of Arizona.

Papago summer shelter, made of cactus rods. The house proper, of adobe, can be seen behind it. *U. S. Indian Service.*

Papago granary basket, for storing grain. This very thick basket is virtually mouse- and weatherproof. The house is built of adobe bricks, introduced by the Spanish. *Smithsonian Institution.*

Papago pottery maker. The large jar in the foreground is drying, preliminary to baking. American Indian pottery is made entirely without the potter's wheel. *Smithsonian Institution*.

Yuma Indians and a white visitor in 1862. The cloaks belted around the Indians are made of strips of fur, probably rabbit, woven together. *Smithsonian Institution*.

any function long ago. A village, or group of villages, was governed by a council of elders, presided over by the "big man," who was primarily a priest and whose civil authority lay in his reputation for wisdom.

West of the Pimans, on the banks of the Colorado River, were the Yumans, the Yumas and Mohaves, people whom you can look at as borderline Southwesterners, or as Californians who happened to have become involved in farming. Most unlike the Pimans, they seemed to farm because they couldn't help it. Their territory included narrow areas of flatlands along the river that were flooded at regular intervals. These were extremely fertile. Without the labor of irrigation or much of any effort, crops grew on them. So the Yumans planted—or rather their women did, which sets them apart from most of the rest of the Southwest. Also, their ceremonies were little concerned with agriculture, nor did they have important rites for success in hunting.

The farming land, owned by clans or families which counted descent through the father, was jealously guarded. Trespass meant a fight. Men often went naked, the women nearly so, and both sexes were elaborately tattooed. Their houses were like the Pimans', but usually larger. Pottery

Modern Yuma woman and baby. *U. S. Indian Service.*

Mohave men, photographed probably by Ben Wittick, a pioneer Southwestern photographer, in the 1870's or '80's.
Smithsonian Institution.

Mohave woman, also probably photographed by Wittick. When early Indians were dragged into a studio and placed before a camera, they seldom could manage a lively expression.
Smithsonian Institution.

Yuma house, 1926. The deep shelter in front provides a cool place for daily life. *U. S. Indian Service.*

Mohaves building a house, a much humbler affair than the Yumas' but solid—note the heavy poles of the framework. Probably also photographed by Wittick in the '70's or '80's.

Smithsonian Institution.

Yuma shoulder-cloak of beads, for women's wear.

University of Arizona.

Yuma woman painting pottery. *U. S. Indian Service.*

was fairly good, basketry simple, arts in general not highly developed.

Visions or dreams were of great importance, the prime sources of power. It was almost impossible to assume any function, from fighting to oratory, unless one had had an appropriate vision. Each tribe or district had a civil leader, often hereditary, whose authority was purely advisory. As important as he were Brave Man, who led in war, and the Scalp Keeper. Both of these officials received their power from dreams. Scalp-taking was important, and the people danced each month for the accumulated collection.

The interest of the Yumas and Mohaves centered on war, which they seemed thoroughly to have enjoyed. The best fighting was with people of their own general group, who played the game the way they did. Then the fighting was formal, with the warriors of both sides drawn up in formation, ceremonious challenges, and duels between men of importance on both sides before the fight was open to the public. Captives, often taken, were brought home, purified, and then either killed or kept as slaves.

Death took on great importance. The Yumans cre-

mated their dead—an unusual custom in North America—on enormous piles of logs laid up with great care. Through the night while the pyre burned the dead one's clan danced. Afterwards, the deceased's house was usually burned. Once a year, relatives of those who had died fairly recently assembled for a feast and ritual lasting for four days, with many songs and speeches and, at the end, a sham battle.

The Yumans were the principal users of a weapon in which they took great pride, and with which they were extremely skillful. This was a short club shaped almost exactly like a potato masher except that the handle ended in a spike. You could bash a man's head in nicely with the thick end, or, reversing your stroke, stab him with the spike. This instrument called for a close in-fighting that might have made a Creek or a Choctaw think twice.

In yet another way the Southwest turns the Southeast topsy-turvy. In the Southeast, the nearest approach to civilization was among the tribes closest to Mexico; in the Southwest, it was among those farthest from it—the Pueblos, who, along with the Navahos, are what most of us think of when we think of that part of the country. It was

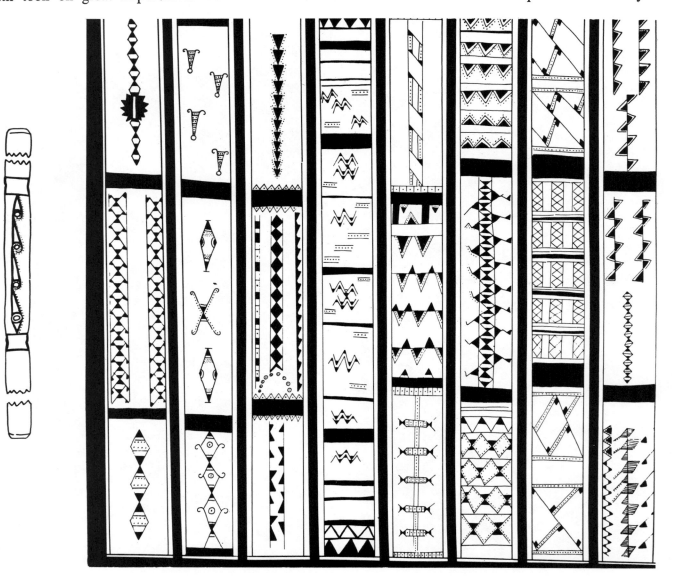

Yuma designs for decorating flutes. The way the design is put on the instrument is shown on the shortened sketch of a flute on the left. Flutes were by no means universal among Indian tribes.
University of Arizona.

116

not a question of *how much* Mexican influence the Pueblos received, but of what they did with it.

The modern Pueblo Indians are in large part directly descended from the ancient Pueblo people described in Chapter I. Some may be descended from other groups, such as the Hohokam, who moved to the north; some are probably the heirs of simpler people settled along the Rio Grande, who adopted Pueblo ways when those Indians moved there from the older locations farther north and west. The main line, however, is continuous, both in racial type and culture.

As already noted, they lived in compact towns. In the west, the houses were built of stone cemented with adobe clay. In the east, most houses were built entirely of adobe. They did not know how to make square bricks by pouring the mud into forms, but patted the adobe into "turtle-backs," lumps shaped distinctly like a turtle, and laid these up with a lavish plastering of the same material between courses. Roofs were flat, with a covering of the same hard-dried adobe over the top for insulation and to keep out rain. Even so, under heavy rain or if snow was allowed to pile up and melt, these roofs leaked.

Houses were often several stories high, and for defensive

A two-story house in the Hopi village of Shungopovi. Large, modern windows have been installed in the lower story. Some meat is hanging on a line to dry over the window at the right.
U. S. Indian Service. Photo by Milton Snow.

The Hopi Pueblo of Walpi, in Arizona. It was built up on top of the rock tip of the mesa in early historic times, after the Navahos became menacing. Under the strip of sheer cliff are the sheep pens. In the distance can be seen the arid, sandy land the Hopis farm. The tiny dots on a light streak of sand in the left background are, believe it or not, peach trees.
Courtesy of American Museum of Natural History.

purposes might be built without any doors on the ground floor. Ladders, which could be pulled up in time of trouble, led to the upper levels. In each village, usually in a central open space, were the kivas, the ceremonial chambers that also served as men's gathering places.

The men farmed, hunted, wove, embroidered, and made jewelry of turquoise, shell, and bright stone. The women did a good deal of the building and all the plastering, cooked, and made pottery and basketry. The men ran the government and controlled the ceremonies, but the women had an important place in the religion, and had a lot more to say about civil matters than appeared on the surface. A man has to live with his wife, and while it is he who has the say in government, it can become uncomfortable for him at home if he says the wrong thing.

There is a strongly held theory that there is an innate connection between agriculture and the tracing of descent through the mother. The argument in part is that the women did the farming, hence owned the fields, hence the most important inheritance was through the women. As we have seen, the Pimans, whose men were farmers, and the Yumans, who left that dull work to the women, both traced descent through the men. The western Pueblos traced it through the women, with a very strong clan sys-

tem, strongest of all among the Hopis, but it was the men who worked the fields. Everything went by the clans, or by certain lineages within the clans. The fields were clan property, subdivided into family property belonging to the female head of the house. Rituals, ceremonial properties such as masks, priesthoods, the chieftainships of the villages, went by clans.

When we consider the Hopis, we find that "priest" and "chief" are almost interchangeable terms. The Hopi word is *mongwi*, which they usually translate "chief," but every *mongwi*, even the Town Chief, is primarily a religious official. A given chieftainship belongs to the main lineage of a particular clan. The head of that clan is the "clan mother." The old lady has no formal authority, but when she speaks her piece, everyone listens. Someone descended from her will inherit that particular chieftainship, and with it the ceremonial properties that belong to it. That man will marry a woman of another clan, to which his children will belong. One of his nephews or great-nephews, his sister's or his niece's child, will succeed him.

The father is a guest in his wife's mother's house. He tends to his sons' education, plays with them, helps them along. But they are not members of his clan. It is the chief member of their clan, their mother's brother, who will

Part of the Pueblo of Taos in New Mexico. The photograph is taken from the roof of an outlying building. The central mass rises to four stories. The dome-shaped objects on the ground are ovens, which were introduced by the Spanish along with wheat. The Pueblo Indians make extremely good bread.

Smithsonian Institution.

118

Hopi weaver. He is working on a woman's dress. The outer edges, which are finished, are in a herringbone weave; the central part, on which he is now working, has a diamond weave. The simple trousers he wears, split up the side almost to the knee, were introduced by the Spanish. *U. S. Indian Service.*

Interior of a modern Hopi basketmaker's home. The Hopis make large numbers of handsome baskets, but the work is not as fine as that of the Pimas or Apaches.

U. S. Indian Service. Photo by Milton Snow.

Inside the kiva. For purposes of a ritual drama, a screen with symbolic decorations has been set up, with serpents that can be manipulated from behind. On either side of the screen stand men wearing the masks of Goyemshi or "Mud Heads," a special class of sacred beings. The third masked figure represents a female kachina. *Smithsonian Institution.*

A Zuñi woman making pottery. This manner of sitting upright with the legs straight out is peculiar to Pueblo woman. On the rug beside her (a Navaho saddle blanket) are her pot of pigment and the water-worn stones she uses for smoothing the pot before slipping it. The stone slab at extreme right is for grinding corn.
Museum of the American Indian.

Diorama showing Hopi life (at Walpi) as it was from about 1700 to the middle of the 1800's. Meat, probably mutton, is hanging to dry. Strands of chile, introduced by the Spanish from Mexico, hang against a wall. An old man in the background is spinning, a younger one is weaving a blanket, and near him a woman is changing the baby in its cradleboard. In the left foreground, a woman making pottery is picking up another coil of clay to add to the pot she is shaping. At the extreme right, beside the woman tending the baby, is one of the jars with which, until recently, women carried water up from the springs at the bottom of the mesa. In the background a man can be seen riding one burro and driving another.
Courtesy of American Museum of National History.

Acoma Pueblo jar. The decoration is black and a rich, earth red on creamy white.

Courtesy of American Museum of Natural History.

Pueblo jar. Identified by the Denver Art Museum as from Acoma, but the design of a bird under an arch is more like Zia work.

Denver Art Museum.

Modern Zuñi woman with a basket of flour on her head. The base of her costume is the same dress as that of the early Hopis, to which much has been added, such as the imported shawl and the embroidered apron. Note the moccasins with the high legs made of much buckskin wrapped around. A good pair of these moccasins requires the skin of a whole buck, and is evidence either that her husband is a good hunter, or can afford an expensive article.

U. S. Indian Service.

Unmarried Hopi girl, wearing the "squash blossom" hairdress worn in that tribe by girls. The photo, by Wittick, probably in the 1880's, shows the usual effects of subjecting an innocent subject to long posing. Note the calico blouse under the dress. The traditional wool costume is hot and scratchy; as soon as Pueblo women could get softer materials to put under it, they did.
Smithsonian Institution

Hopi married woman of the 1890's, with the married women's hairdress. *Smithsonian Institution.*

Modern Zuñi girls in their very best attire. This general manner of dressing is typical of Pueblo women today on important occasions. *U. S. Dept. of the Interior.*

discipline them, while their father will discipline his nephews. As a result, among the Hopis a lot of Freudian theory goes out the window; the situations Freud described just don't exist.

The Hopis and all the other Pueblos are monogamous, in contrast to the majority of Indian tribes, who permitted two or more wives although many Indians took only one. Their monogamy was rather like that of modern white Americans; a man might marry only one woman at a time, but divorce and remarriage were not too difficult.

As we move eastward from the Hopis, clans become weaker and the mother-descent fades, until along the Rio Grande, among the Tanoans, we find clans feeble or non-existent, inheritance through the father, houses and land belonging to the men. Yet all of these are farmers.

With the exception of the village of Moenkopi, founded in recent times, none of the Hopi villages has water for irrigation. In fact, they are placed in the next most discouraging country for farming after the Papago. Yet by farming they have lived in that country for a thousand years, as they do today. They are the supreme dry farmers of the world, and probably the hardest working. Their corn is scrubby and tough, the stalks hardly three feet high, but it yields fine, big ears. They have almost given up raising cotton now, since commercial cotton is so easy to come by, but their beans, squash, and tobacco thrive and to their ancient crops they have added such others as peaches and peanuts.

Conditions were much easier along the Rio Grande, where there was irrigation. The Pueblos there, especially the northern ones, were in contact with the hunting tribes to the east, which meant both trade and trouble. They had less inhibitions against warfare, although their fighting was essentially defensive, and their war organizations were more elaborate. Their country being too cold for cotton, they did less weaving, and got their cotton garments, the men's kilts, the women's robes, from their relatives to the westward. They also wore more buckskin. Most Pueblo men wore their long hair done up in a queue at the back, to be let down during ceremonials, when the long, hanging mass represented rain. The northern Pueblos, however, adopted to varying degrees the two braids we associate with the Plains Indians.

All the Pueblos possessed elaborate, formal ceremonies based upon a great body of sacred myths. Most of their dances, which are dramatized prayers, are strictly disciplined. Every step, every gesture, is exactly rehearsed. There is little room for the individual star; what counts is the perfect performance in union by all concerned. The music consists of human voices accompanied by drums, the songs arranged in complex variations of rhythms according to the sequences of the particular dance. The quality of their performances is not at all wild, and is much more than merely picturesque. Visitors today throng to see certain of the major public ones, not only the tourists who happen to be there at the time, but artists, musicians, dancers from all over the United States and from foreign countries.

With the probable exception of Taos, at the extreme north, all the Pueblos followed what is called the "kachina cult." The kachinas are not gods; they are divine beings

who act as intermediaries between man and god. They are present among the people, invisible, loving, beneficent, during half the year. In that half of the year, they may be made visible according to instructions they themselves gave to mankind in ancient times, if men who have been properly trained and initiated put on the masks that represent

The governor of San Ildefonso Pueblo, on the Rio Grande, in 1900. It is difficult to make much of his costume, as he has wrapped himself elaborately in a trade blanket. Governors and lieutenant-governors of Pueblos were established by the Spanish, who also granted them definite right of self-government. The United States is pledged to observe these rights and uphold them, under the Treaty of Guadalupe Hidalgo by which Mexico ceded the Southwest to the United States. *Smithsonian Institution*.

Painting of the *Anakchina* or Longhaired Kachina dance, by Bert Poneoma, a modern Hopi. The men's bodies are painted black and yellow. Their masks represent the blue of the sky and colors of the four directions. Two other small kachinas, danced by boys, act as "side dancers." The two small figures in the middle are *kachinmanas,* or kachina maidens, usually danced by boys. Over their foreheads and falling from their chins are orange-colored fringes of hair, representing rainfall as it is seen at dawn or at sunset. *U. S. Dept. of the Interior.*

Hopi kachina dolls. These figurines, carved out of cottonwood, represent the various masked kachinas. The kachina dancers present them to children as part of their education.
Courtesy of American Museum of Natural History.

The Hopi Snake Ceremony, popularly miscalled the Snake Dance, as it was performed before the days of tourists, from a miniature model. This is a very quiet, intense ritual by means of which snakes, who represent lightning, are blessed and then released to carry the prayers of the priests via the underworld up to heaven.

Courtesy of American Museum of Natural History.

[Tur]tle Dance, painted by Pablita Velarde of Santa Clara Pueblo [on] the Rio Grande. In addition to the line of dancers painted and [dr]essed in the ancient manner, with rattles in their hands, two [ma]sked kachina dancers take part, along with a couple of *koshare*, [or] sacred clowns, their bodies painted in stripes. Koshares are [me]mbers of a special society. They represent spirits of great power whose clowning is part of their mysterious nature. A third clown can be seen on the roof of the kiva near the ladder that leads down inside. The priest who is supervising the ceremony, right foreground, wears beaded leggings of Plains type, which are common among the eastern Pueblos.

Philbrook Art Center.

them and dance with the required, exact, and very solemn ritual. Then indeed the kachinas are present. It is not that the masked dancers *are* kachinas, or are thought to be, but that the real kachinas are there with them.

Unlike the masks of the Iroquois, in these there is no attempt to depict real faces, however grotesque. The masks are covered with symbols that express the powers of the kachinas or the good things for which, through them, the people pray—rain, crops, sunlight, fertility.

As noted in Chapter I, about nine hundred years ago wandering bands from the far north came into the Southwest. They spoke languages of the Athapascan family, and seem to have drifted south through great stretches of unoccupied or thinly occupied territory, some of them picking up a few ideas from the primitive tribes of the Great Basin inside the Rocky Mountains, others from the Western farmers, until they landed in the Southwest. These people the Spanish called "Apaches." One tribe of them, called the "Apaches de Nabajú," lived in close contact with the Pueblos. (Spanish *j* is pronounced *h*.) Later the "Apache" part of the name was dropped and they became known as Navahos, one of the most famous of all tribes today.

The various tribes that developed from these bands took over varying degrees of the Southwestern farmers' culture,

and also caused the farmers endless trouble. The Navahos learned farming thoroughly, as well as weaving. They copied Pueblo rituals, but always with strong modifications of their own, and merged their own, northern myths with the rich Pueblo mythology to produce a body of poetic, sacred tales of extraordinary quality.

In the Navaho adaptation we see most clearly one of the strong characteristics of these Athapascans. Whatever they took, from the farming Indians and later from the Spanish, they took only in the form that suited their way of life. The Pueblos lived in compact groups in which everyone knew everyone else's business, and each individual was kept exactly in line by the force of unremitting public opinion. Each group was tightly organized, every individual exactly placed, all under the government of the priestly chiefs. The power of those chiefs would have been tyrannical, had it not been that they, too, were bound by the rigid, unwritten constitution of their customs, enforced by the same public opinion.

The Navahos wanted no such life. They liked individuality and elbow room, and placed their dwellings accordingly. They took over a lot of Pueblo ritual, but fitted it always to their own basic religion. Their primary concern was to keep themselves in harmony with God and all His creation. The clearest symptom of having got out of

The Hopi Tashaf Kachina Dance, painted by Fred Kabotie, one of the most famous of modern Indian painters. The long line of masked figures, chanting and slowly dancing in unison, their rattles creating a steady beat like the drumming of rain, makes a most impressive affair. Four clowns are gathered at the front of the line. Note the four unmarried girls sitting on the lower roof at the right, with squash-blossom hairdress. They wear white cotton shawls, edged with bright red and black, a traditional manner of dress.

Philbrook Art Center.

harmony was illness, hence their ceremonies always centered upon healing a patient, although the effect of the ceremony was much greater than the single cure. The Pueblos made sacred, stylized pictures with dry pigments on the floors of their kivas for certain rites. The Navahos took over this idea, elaborated it enormously into the famous "sand paintings," of which there are hundreds, and tied it into their healing-harmony pattern.

The general idea of obtaining well-being and success through being in a somewhat mystic harmony with the forces of nature, and hence with the universal spirit that embraces all, is widespread among the North American Indians. It has been stated in lofty terms by some Sioux religious leaders. It is most clear to the outside observer in the ceremonies of the Southwest, which are calculated not only to put the participants into the desired relationship, but also to affect the onlookers so that they, too, are brought in. Anyone who watches a ceremony with sympathy and respect is considered to be helping. The Navahos have developed this idea, which involves the concept of omnipresent, impersonal God, to a high point in the doctrine of *hozhoni,* a word for which no satisfactory English translation has been found. It involves happiness, right feeling, right thinking, correct performance of ritual, and

Navaho woman at Bosque Redondo, with baby in cradleboard on her back. *Laboratory of Anthropology, Inc., Santa Fe, N. M.*

A Signal Corps photograph of a Navaho woman during the period of captivity at Bosque Redondo. These Signal Corps photos were posed for under some duress, which shows in the expressions. The woman wears the old, woolen costume, and her moccasins include the high buckskin wrapping found among the Pueblos. Note the contrast between the fine weaving of her dress and the coarse, purely utilitarian blanket on which she leans.
Laboratory of Anthropology, Inc., Santa Fe, N. M.

Young Navaho warrior at Bosque Redondo. He wears crude leggings of buckskin above his moccasins, reaching short of his knees. His quiver is of lion skin.
Laboratory of Anthropology, Inc., Santa Fe, N. M.

Modern Navaho wood-carvings of figures from the Yeibichai rite of the Night Way Ceremony. At the left stands the priest holding a basket of a type sometimes made by Navahos, more often traded from the Paiutes. His costume is typical of the period from 1900 until recently. In the center is the masked figure of Talking God, also known as Yeibichai, or "Grandfather of the Gods." At the right is one of the masked dancers who take part in the rite.

Navaho warrior at Bosque Redondo or Fort Sumner.
Laboratory of Anthropology, Inc., Santa Fe, N. M.

Drawings of a Navaho arrow-swallower. The arrow-swallowing is one of a series of *alili,* or special performances, put on during the last night of the Mountain Way Ceremony.

Smithsonian Institution.

128

a condition of union with the divine force throughout the world.

The Navahos became great farmers, and later great herders. They could have lived comfortably in peace. But they continued to be warriors and raiders, adding to the products of their own industry what they could take by stealth or by force.

They learned weaving from the Pueblos, probably from captives whom they enslaved, but left it to their women to do. After the Spanish introduced wool, they became the

A

B

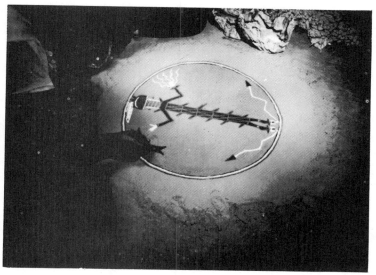

C

D

E

The making of a small sand-painting; in this case in a rite to heal a child. *A*. The priest or singer and a helper prepare the background. *B*. The singer begins the figure. *C*. He has completed the figure, which shows the great, benevolent war god, Slayer of Enemy Gods, standing on lightning and with lightning in his hand. *D*. He puts on the last touches. *E*. The picture finished, he sings his prayers and shakes his rattle. The mother sits opposite him, holding the child.

Courtesy of American Museum of Natural History.

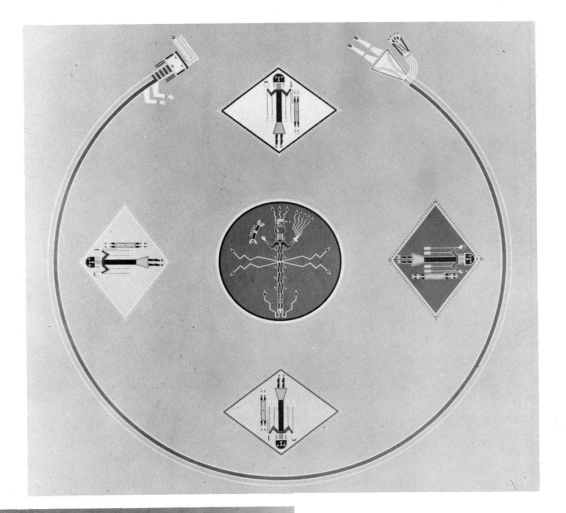

Navaho sand-painting from the fourth day of the Night Way Ceremony. In the center is Slayer of Enemy Gods against a blue sun. The spikes along his body represent his flint armor. In the four directions are white, blue, yellow and pink stars, each with a fire god in it. The whole is surrounded and protected by the rainbow. *Museum of Navajo Ceremonial Art, Santa Fe, N. M.*

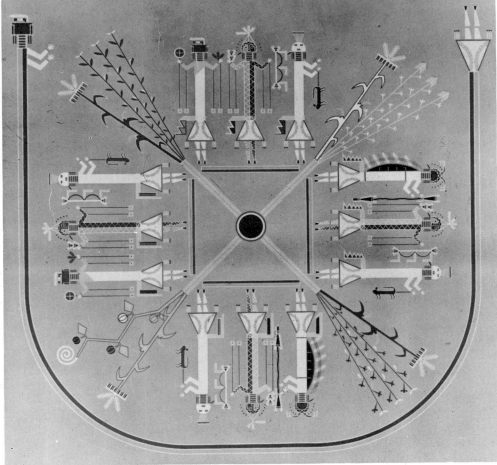

Another sand-painting from the Night Way. In the center is a sacred, never-failing lake, from which grow corn of four colors, squash, beans, and other plants. Four rainbow bars surround the lake, on which stand gods who are invited to be present at the ceremony, carrying a variety of sacred objects. The protecting Rainbow Girl wears the mask of a Yeibichai dancer, painted blue. *Museum of Navajo Ceremonial Art, Santa Fe, N. M.*

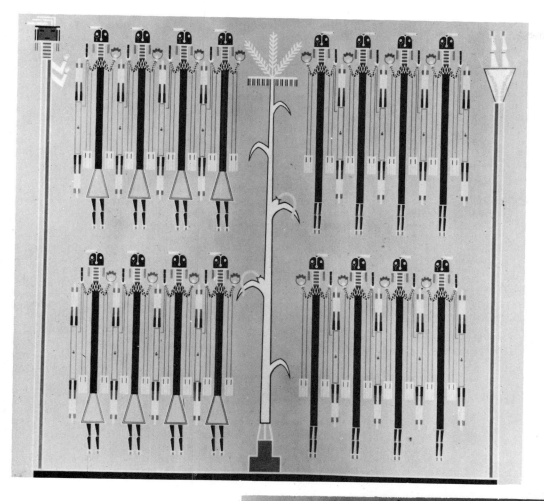

The last sand-painting of the Night Way Ceremony. It shows sixteen Black Fire Gods, eight on each side of a cornstalk. The zigzag lines on their arms and shoulders are the Milky Way; the dotted Y on their masks, the Pleiades. Each carries a stick for making fire in one hand, strings of blue corn cakes, "traveler's bread," in the other. The black line at the bottom symbolizes water, the white line on top of it is foam. Again, the painting is protected by Rainbow Girl. *Museum of Navajo Ceremonial Art, Santa Fe, N. M.*

Sand-painting of the whirling rainbows, used in a rite held in summer to bring rain and ensure crops. Here we have a whole series of Rainbow Girls or Goddesses, in addition to the one protecting the whole. At the east side, two Dontso, the flies who act as messengers of the gods, guard the opening that is not protected by the enclosing Rainbow Girl. *Museum of Navajo Ceremonial Art, Santa Fe, N. M.*

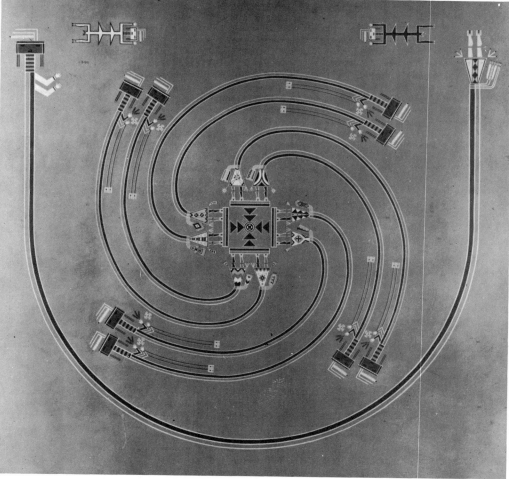

Navaho woman weaving.
Courtesy of American Museum of National History.

Navaho woman spinning. *Museum of the American Indian.*

Navajo women weaving and spinning, painted by Harrison Begay, modern Navajo artist. This picture well shows the present Navajo women's costume, with cotton skirt and velveteen blouse, and the manner of doing the hair. *Philbrook Art Center.*

Navaho silversmith and his simple equipment. *Museum of the American Indian.*

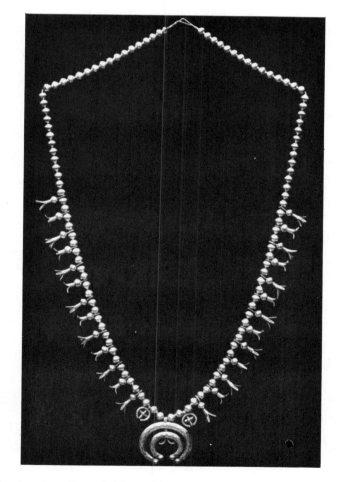

Navaho silver "squash-blossom" necklace. The design was brought by the Spanish, who learned it from the Moors. The floral elements, among the Moors, represented pomegranates, and the crescent at the bottom was to ward off the evil eye. The Navahos call the crescent "big snake," which is their name for the constallation Draco. *Museum of the American Indian.*

Navaho silver bracelets. The upper one is hammered. The main part of the lower one, which has a turquoise set in it, is cast, with the twisted element added afterwards.

Courtesy of American Museum of Natural History.

The old type of Navaho hogan, with a basic, tepee-like framework.
U. S. Dept. of Interior. Photo by Milton Snow.

Recent type of hogan with stone walls. *U. S. Indian Service.*

outstanding weavers of North America. Their designs are totally unlike those that their original teachers still weave. Much later, they learned silversmithing from the Spanish, and became the silverworkers of the Southwest. Latterly, various Pueblo tribes have taken over the craft as well, altering it as they did so.

The Navahos also copied the strong mother clans of the western Pueblos, but without such items as the clan mother. A man is a permanent guest in his wife's home—unless she decides to divorce him. In the Pueblos, the home was openly dominated by the old mother. Among the Navahos, the new couple builds a separate dwelling, and it is forbidden for a man and his mother-in-law to see or speak to each other.

The Navaho dwelling is a *hogan* (pronounced hoe-GAHN). Its original form was a framework of heavy poles laid up like a tepee, with a small vestibule at the entrance —suggesting a cross between a tepee and an earth lodge. It had a tepee-like smoke hole and was covered with a heavy layer of earth. Later this was elaborated into an eight-sided building with a domed, cribbed roof, and in recent times has been further elaborated, as in laying up stone walls. It would not, however, occur to Navahos to save effort by building a series of rooms in a single unit in which many families would live in close contact.

Originally the Navahos must have dressed much like other Apaches. Their hair hung loose over their shoulders, they wore buckskin with simple ornamentation or none. With Pueblo contact, they took over items of Pueblo woven clothing, such as a short, poncho-like shirt, then the Spanish-derived dress that is still the holiday attire of Pueblo men. The women partly copied the blue and black woven robe of the Pueblo women, but the Pueblo form is a single piece, worn over one shoulder and under the other; the Navaho is two pieces, usually joined over both shoulders, and with their usual exuberance, into their dresses the women wove strips of brilliant red. This women's costume disappeared during the last half of the nineteenth century, to be replaced by the velveteen blouses and very

These next pictures show the evolution of Navaho costume since 1868. In this one we see a leading Navaho warrior, known then as "Bullet," in captivity at Bosque Redondo. He wears tight-fitting cloth breeches tucked into knee-high buckskin leggings, both ornamented with silver buttons.

Laboratory of Anthropology, Inc., Santa Fe, N. M.

134

Bullet has become Manuelito, the principal chief of the Navahos. This picture was taken when he visited Washington in 1874. He wears Pueblo-style trousers, a handsome Navaho blanket, and has a lion-skin quiver and a rifle in a buckskin case ornamented with eagle feathers. His turquoise and shell jewelry is of Pueblo manufacture. *Smithsonian Institution.*

Manuelito's favorite wife, who accompanied him to Washington. Note the handsome silver "concho" belt of large plaques.

Smithsonian Institution.

An elderly Navaho of about 1890. His lower garments are the same as Manuelito wore in 1868, but he has added a shirt, and wears also the blanket with broad, red, white, and black stripes, with touches of blue, that was the correct thing for men's wear. These blankets are incorrectly called "chief blankets."

Smithsonian Institution.

Jicarilla Apache beadwork, which compares well with Plains work.
Courtesy of American Museum of Natural History.

Diorama of Apache life as it might have been seen earlier in this century on the San Carlos Reservation of Arizona. The San Carlos Apaches consist of parts of several tribes who were settled on that reservation. A woman rocks a baby in a cradleboard, another covers a basketry water bottle with pitch, in the shade of the summer shelter. In the background a woman is thatching a **wickeyup.**

Courtesy of American Museum of Natural History.

Navaho woman grinding corn, at an exhibit in Chicago in 1940. Her blanket, which hangs from the pole on the right, is from Pendleton, Oregon. Navahos have almost entirely stopped wearing their own weave, which they make to sell. The method of grinding, with a small stone rubbed over a large one, is entirely unlike that of the eastern Indians. It is found throughout the Southwest, and probably derives from Mexico.
U. S. Dept. of the Interior.

Young Jicarilla Apache man, about 1900.
Courtesy of American Museum of Natural History.

full, swinging calico skirts that are standard for Navaho women to this day. Both sexes took to doing up their hair at the back in the Pueblo-style queue.

Navaho culture, as a matter of fact, is a curious blend that would take a book to analyze—if we were able to sort out all the items. There are elements from the original, northern Athapascan culture, from the early Plains, the Pueblos, and others from the tribes of the Great Basin behind the Rockies. Thus, they occasionally made pottery that is distinctly eastern, while their baskets are very difficut to tell from those of the wandering tribes of southern Utah. Their so-called "medicine men" are lone operators, like shamans, but in fact they are priests, meticulously trained in certain myths and ceremonies, after the Pueblo model.

Along the eastern border of New Mexico, the Apache tribes—the Jicarilla Apaches in the north, the Mescaleros in the south, the now all but extinct Lipans roaming western Texas and into Mexico—were a bridge between the

Plains and the Southwest. The Jicarillas look most like Plains Indians, with their tepees, their braided hair, their buckskin clothing handsomely adorned with fine beadwork. Many of their ways reflect the Plains, but in early times they raised corn, beans, and squash, and their principal ceremony combines sand-paintings, a Navaho-Pueblo-type masked dance, a Basin-type dance of men and women together, and the old Athapascan pattern of the ceremony performed at night, by bonfires, within an enclosure of green branches.

The Mescaleros show little Pueblo influence, and had little interest in farming. Based in mountains where the hunting was good, with access to buffalo country, they were hunters and raiders. They used both the tepee and the "wickeyup," a dwelling made of branches and grass laid on over a framework of poles, sometimes with a rounded roof, sometimes a pointed one. In their best form, these wickeyups sometimes make one think of the Wichita grass houses, sometimes suggest wigwams, and sometimes are clearly tepees with a different covering.

The wickeyup was the typical home of the other Apaches, the tribes that sifted down through the Pueblo country into the heart of the Southwest and on into northern Mexico. When there was peace and the people were to stay put for a reasonable time, they built them elaborately —large, comfortable residences. In time of war they were no more than shelters hastily thrown together. An Apache band could break camp and be gone in a matter of minutes.

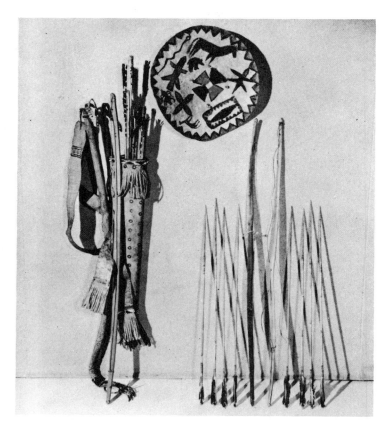

Mescalero bows and arrows, quiver, and shield.
Courtesy of American Museum of Natural History.

Mescalero Apache objects —seed and bead necklace, beaded awl case, and pouches. *Courtesy of American Museum of Natural History.*

Apache woman grinding corn. Her mill is considerably cruder than the Navaho type. *U. S. Dept. of Interior.*

Well-built Apache wickeyup at "Indian City," Anadarko, Oklahoma. *Photo by A. C. Hector.*

Apache shelter in wartime—camp of Geronimo, the famous Chiricahua patriot, in Mexico in 1886, at the time of his capture.

The wickeyup in the center is little more than a bird's nest upside down. *Smithsonian Institution.*

Apache woman and children, probably at San Carlos, with samples of their basketry. The women adopted this style of dressing in the latter half of the nineteenth century. *U.S. Dept. of Interior.*

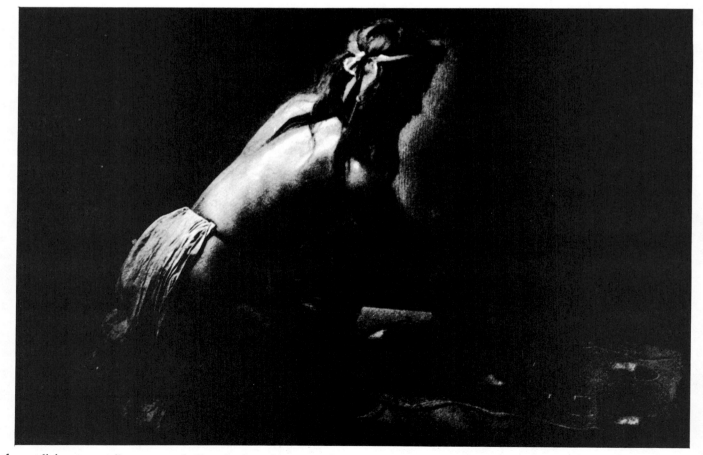

Apache medicine man, tribe not stated. Since he is making a sand-painting, he is probably Jicarilla. As is common among Indians, his hair is undone and he is stripped to the most primitive, ancient costume for purposes of his ceremony.

Courtesy of American Museum of Natural History.

Some of the Western Apache women planted little gardens. The bands roamed about, gathering a great variety of edible seeds and wild plants, hunting, and watching for chances for a raid. Government was democratic. There were families from which chiefs were expected to come—as did the great Cochise of the Chiricahuas—but if a man of no special family had sufficient ability, others began following him, and soon he was in fact a chief. The shifting organization and the movement of the people themselves make it difficult to arrive at a satisfactory listing of Western Apache tribes. A "tribe" was a number of Apaches speaking one dialect, having the same customs and religious practices, recognizing a certain likeness, rather than unity, among themselves. Under strong leaders, tribes cohered, such as the Chiricahuas under Cochise or the Mimbrenos under Mangas Coloradas.

For the Apaches and Navahos, war was a business. Properly speaking, it was not war, but armed robbery accompanied by acts of brutality. The purpose was to obtain booty and, occasionally, slaves. Obviously, it was a dangerous occupation, but it was foolish to run needless risks. The point was to get the booty and come home without loss, if it could be managed. For this the young men were rigorously trained in boyhood, with such toughening items

"Apache Fire Dance," a part of the Mountain Spirit ceremony, by Al Momaday, Chiricahua Apache painter. *Philbrook Art Center.*

Apache Mountain Spirit or *Gan* dancers. Ignorant whites often call them "Devil Dancers," which is incorrect and insulting. They represent benevolent minor gods. The ceremony is known to most of the southern Apache tribes, now on the Mescalero, Fort Apache, and San Carlos reservations. These dancers were students at the federal Indian School at Albuquerque, New Mexico.

U. S. Dept. of Interior.

Measuring cloth to be issued to the Indians at San Carlos, 1887. The long-haired man with chevrons on his sleeve is a sergeant of Apache scouts enlisted in the U. S. Cavalry.

Smithsonian Institution.

as running several miles in the hottest weather with a mouthful of water and spitting out the water at the end to show that they had not swallowed it, and such combat training as standing and dodging arrows that others shot at the recruit.

They became as hardy as human beings can be, skilled in combat, incredibly observant, and gifted at concealment to a degree that seems like magic. All of these qualities stood them in good stead after the white men came to press upon them, as when Cochise, for instance, with less than two hundred warriors, held the U.S. Army at bay for over ten years and forced us in the end to make a peace with an unconquered enemy.

Actual Spanish settlement of the Southwest came in the 1590's, almost entirely in the Pueblo area along the Rio Grande. Missionaries and small military expeditions reached eastward to the Hopis. Unlike the English, the Spanish were not land-hungry colonizers; they came in relatively small numbers, to conquer, Christianize, and exploit the natives. They did not, therefore, seek to drive the Pueblos off their land, but wanted to keep them on it, a source of labor and taxes. The Athapascans, free-moving, eluded the Spanish grasp, while it was not until later that the priests reached to the Pimans.

The Spanish hand lay heavy. The old religion was forbidden, forced labor was close to slavery, taxes drew off the corn and the woven goods, and there were the churches and priests to support. Ninety years after the first Spanish town was founded, the Pueblos achieved what none of the eastern tribes had been able to manage—perfect, con-

Apache hunters, photographed (and posed) in the 1870's.

Smithsonian Institution.

Geronimo, his son, and two of his followers, in 1886, shortly before their surrender to General Crook. When Cochise made peace with the U. S., Geronimo refused to agree to it, and with a small band went off to the mountains of Mexico. He and his group terrorized the ranchers on both sides of the border for fourteen years. He was finally captured by the use of large numbers of Chiricahua scouts. *Smithsonian Institution.*

Apache woman of Geronimo's band. The tip of her nose has been cut off—the common punishment for infidelity.
U. S. Dept. of Interior.

Chiricahua man, in the period of transition to white men's costume. Native costume is all but extinct among the Apache men, except the Jicarillas. *U. S. Dept. of Interior.*

certed action. Under the leadership of Popé, a man of ceremonial standing from the Pueblo of San Juan, on one day they all rose, from the villages on the Rio Grande to the Hopis 250 miles and more westward. Mission priests were killed, and the Indians fell upon outlying Spanish ranches. The Navahos and some of the other Apaches gladly joined in.

Santa Fe was besieged, and in a short time the Spanish were forced to abandon it. Their retreat did not end until they reached El Paso, "The Ford," the crossing of the Rio Grande into Mexico. That was in 1680; it was not until 1693 that De Vargas was able to lead his troops once more into Santa Fe.

Until the Pueblo Rebellion, the Spanish had kept close watch on their horses. Indians had been forbidden to own the animals, and the herds were guarded. During the twelve-odd years after the Rebellion the animals ran wild and multiplied, and the Navahos and Apaches discovered their usefulness. After the Spanish returned, there was constant stealing of their horses. It was thus that one of the most important of the white man's weapons passed into Indian hands and, increasing fantastically in the natural horse country of the Plains and the prairies east of them, changed the whole Western Indian picture, as will be told later.

The Pueblos along the Rio Grande submitted again to Spain. They became Christian, but also kept up their old religion, more and more boldly as Spanish military power in this far corner of a dying empire grew weaker. It was due to the forbidding of their ceremonies that the Indians made them secret, so that today no white man may see a Pueblo masked dance.

Zuñi, to the west, rejected the Spaniards and their priests. Courageous friars established a mission again at the Hopi village of Awatovi. At the invitation of certain of the Awatovi priests, the men of the other Hopi villages attacked the town in the night, killed the missionaries and destroyed the place. The residents of Awatovi scattered among the other Pueblos of the tribe. The Hopis and Zuñis, therefore, never adopted the "double-barreled" religion of the more eastern people, in whose villages church and kiva stand in sight of each other. Nor did they hold their masks secret, and a well-behaved visitor may witness among them today the sacred rites that have come down through centuries.

The Spanish may have caused the Pueblos a lot of grief, but they also brought iron and steel tools, wagons, draft animals, wheat, fruit trees, sheep, and cattle, all of which greatly enriched the native farming pattern. They taught the Indians the ancient Mediterranean-Asiatic art of making adobe bricks in molds, which enabled them to build larger houses.

Meantime the Navahos and Apaches were growing bolder, and to the eastward appeared tribes of whom no one had ever heard before, the Kiowas and Comanches, mounted raiders from the Plains. From the early 1700's until the American annexation of the Southwest in 1846, the Pueblos and the Spanish stood back to back, fighting off the wild tribes that endlessly harried. Spain all but forgot its distant colony. One king sent to Santa Fe an order describing how the troops should trim their mustaches, but he sent no pay for those troops, no muskets, no gunpowder. During that period, one New Mexico Pueblo after another was abandoned, leaving nineteen, of which eighteen survive today. There was no peace until, after the annexation, forty years of warfare subdued all but a few small bands of hold-out Apaches and the Plains tribes had been broken.

The North American Indians seldom achieved war as we understand it, which is unremitting hostility against another people. This was true in the Southwest. Just as earlier they had traded with the Athapascans, so, later, the Pueblos alternated between fighting and trading with the mounted Comanches. The horsemen wanted their corn, the Pueblos wanted the buffalo meat and hides.

The Spanish, to their shame, abetted the trade because they wanted slaves. It is a question whether the slave-taking pattern that existed to some extent in the Southwest was not introduced by the Christians. Taos was the trading center. There the Comanches brought, among other things, captives taken from heaven knew where, to exchange for corn, wheat, woven goods, and firearms. When the Spanish bought a girl, the Comanches made it a rule to rape her before handing her over. Then they would say, "Here she is; she's spoiled now."

This may have been a way of expressing their opinion of the people with whom they dealt, the preachers of crops and peace who still were glad to buy the human products of habitual war.

In historic times the Navahos and Apaches also took slaves. Children and women usually wound up as members of the tribe. Among the Navahos, there are a number of clans in excellent standing that trace their origin to the women captured from various tribes.

The church and the kiva in sight of each other; San Ildefonso Pueblo in 1879. The church shows at the back of the village. A short distance in front of it can be seen a round building with stairs leading up one side. which is one of the kivas. Irrigated fields are in the foreground; in the background is the light streak of the Rio Grande. *Smithsonian Institution.*

San Xavier del Bac, the principal mission to the Pimans, built in the first part of the eighteenth century by Papago labor under the supervision of the priests. It is still an important center of local Indian worship.

The Spanish came in small numbers; so at first did the North Americans, who are known in the Southwest as "Anglo-Americans." Much of the land the Indians occupied was unattractive to white men (unless there were known to be minerals in it), some of it was downright repulsive. As a result most of the Southwestern tribes got large reservations of their own land, and were allowed to keep them. By the time the pressure to obtain Indian land became strong, the national conscience had changed and the old custom of tearing up the treaties found white, as well as Indian, opposition.

There were breaches of faith, of course. Many of the Pueblos lost chunks of their land, for which later they were compensated. The Chiricahuas, after being at peace for a generation, were forcibly uprooted from the reservation they had honorably won for themselves under Cochise. There were other, similar instances, but it remains true that the Indians of the Southwest today hold the largest unbroken tracts of land remaining to any tribes, fewer of their tribes have become extinct, most make a tolerable living, and they have been able also to retain more of the old cultures than can be found anywhere else in the United States.

Perhaps the worst deal of all happened to the Pimas. Without being conquered, they became mildly Christian, and from the priests learned to plant wheat. They raised wheat so successfully that the grain they supplied to the American troops was vital to their success in that part of the Southwest. They also served the white men well as scouts against the Apaches. They accepted a reservation of their own land for themselves willingly enough. Then the white men moved in around them, took up the water, emptied the river, and by pumping the wells, lowered the underground water beyond the Indians' reach. The Pimas watched their ditches fail and their fields turn dry. Then the great Coolidge Dam was built. The terms of its construction included a provision for furnishing water to the Pimas. Then they found themselves up against a new set of problems. They were used to small-scale farming, each man on his own plot; they had no capital—in fact they were desperately hard up—and the use of the new water involved pumping and the payment of fixed charges, none of which they could manage. The pattern of farming around them is that of the large-scale, mechanized, industrial farm, with which they cannot compete. They are still struggling desperately but gamely to work out the problem and become once more what they were until the white men came—prosperous, hard-working, self-sufficient people on their own land.

The Navahos have had the strangest history. In 1868 the great frontiersman, Kit Carson, led troops against them to end their days as raiders of others. The greater part of the tribe, about eight thousand in all, surrendered, and went on "the long walk" from their homeland along the Arizona–New Mexico border to Bosque Redondo in eastern New Mexico, where wild theorists thought that many people could become happy and prosperous on forty square miles of inferior land with insufficient water. The crops they planted failed. They went hungry. The Comanches raided them. After four years, by which time their condition had become a public scandal and even the hard-boiled newspapers of New Mexico were taking up for them, they were returned to a reservation in their own country, issued two head of sheep apiece, and given tools. There they were joined by an estimated four thousand who had never been rounded up.

One thing was certain—their experience had converted them to peace. They fell to work to restore themselves as farmers, herdsmen, and craftsmen. Their flocks increased rapidly, and so did they. The land in which they lived was so rugged, much of it so desert, and so remote, that no one wanted it, so their reservation was enlarged many times, to about the size of West Virginia. On some of this vast area today it takes forty acres to maintain one cow for a year; on great parts of it nothing can be raised. It is pure rock.

Most of them were hostile to white man's culture and hence to schooling. The reservation was enormous and almost without roads. No one knew how many Navahos

Navaho sheep corralled for dipping. Once a year all sheep are made to swim through a vat of a mixture that destroys lice and ticks in the wool. *U. S. Indian Service.*

Chee Dodge, the next great Navaho leader after Manuelito and the first of a series of remarkable chairmen of the Navaho tribal council, examining Navaho crafts exhibits.
U. S. Indian Service. Photo by Milton Snow.

Trailer and Quonset hut school on the Navaho reservation in the 1950s. Schools like this were put up by Commissioner of Indian Affairs Glenn Emmons in 1954-56 to meet the tribe's urgent de-

mand for education for all its children.

U. S. Indian Service. Photo by Milton Snow.

there were; estimates in the late 1920's ran around twenty-five thousand. Few schools were built, only a fraction of the tribe even learned to speak English. Still they increased, and still, egged on by all the officials who dealt with them, they increased their flocks. The number of their sheep and horses far exceeded what the arid land could carry, and the land began to deteriorate rapidly. Where there had been brooks, there were deep-cut arroyos, and with the cutting out of the watercourses the watertable dropped, taking the fertility out of the high ground. With the grass eaten off, the violent thunderstorms washed off the top soil, which ended in the Colorado River where today it is helping shorten the life of Boulder Dam. I myself know canyons where, not long ago, a stream at surface level ran for miles with cornfields strung along on either side of it. Now the stream is an arroyo of irregular flow, fifty feet below the old level. What is left of the high ground on either side is dry, useless for farming.

In 1933 the government awoke and decreed a drastic reduction of stock, with grazing thereafter only according to carrying capacity. It had to be done, but it was done clumsily and too hastily, and however it was done, well or badly, it shattered the Navaho economy and changed the life of the tribe. The Navahos took years to get over the shock of it. They were eating well, they were independent, they were doing all right—then everything was turned upside down.

When ration books were issued in World War II, we began to discover how many Navahos there were—over sixty thousand of them! Today the best estimate is double

that—125,000—a great body of people increasing rapidly, on a tract of land that can support, at best, twenty-five thousand. In such a situation, poverty continues widespread and agonizing.

The Navahos took a long look at their own problem and decided that what they needed above everything was education—a school seat for every child, no matter if all the adults went hungry. That was back in the 1950's, and the government responded by building many day and boarding schools, so that soon it could be said that there was a school seat somewhere for almost every Navaho child. But this created many problems. The ignorance of untrained white teachers about the Indians' cultural and historic background; the classroom use of English, rather than Navaho, by the Indian children who were unfamiliar with English; the lack of proper teaching materials, relevant to the lives of the Navaho youths; and, above all, the removal of children, many of them very young, from their homes to far distant boarding schools all made matters worse. Finally, the Navahos themselves began to make moves to take over the education of their own children. A "demonstration school" at Rough Rock on the reservation, in which Navaho parents had considerable say over the curriculum and teaching methods, was a success. It was followed by the opening of the Navahos' own Community College, with an Indian enrollment of more than 600, and the taking over by the Navahos of one of the schools previously run for the Indians by the Bureau of Indian Affairs. The last development set the stage for further similar moves not only by the Navahos, but by other tribes in all parts of the country.

These actions by the Navahos reflected advances on many fronts which the tribe was making on its own through its tribal council and other elected officials. The council consists of seventy-four delegates, representing ninety-six chapters, or smaller "neighborhood" groupings that make up the large reservation. The council, as an effective governing body, has created various tribal economic development units. By great good fortune, much of the Navaho country turns out to have oil, uranium, gas, coal, and other natural resources on it, so that the tribe in recent years has received many millions of dollars for permits and leases from large corporations that wish to use these resources. It has not been an unmixed blessing, though. The council has used the money for more efficient government, for an antituberculosis program, for the development of enterprises and industries that will bring long-term income and create steady jobs for Navahos, for scholarships for the young people, and for many other benefits for all the tribe; but it has also meant opening parts of the reservation to some of the worst of the white man's developments—coal strip mines, polluting power plants, unsightly transmission lines, and industrialized centers—and many of the Navaho people have resented and opposed these actions of the tribal council which have threatened the health, beauty, and peace of the reservation. How it will all come out no one knows. But one thing is certain. Large reservations, like that of the Navahos, are being confronted increasingly with the pressures and changes wrought by the modern technological world, forcing the Indians to make decisions that are unprecedented for them and are often hard to make, but which will affect the fate of their reservation and themselves.

VII. The Great Open Spaces

In carrying this story from the farmers west of the Mississippi to those of the Southwest, we jumped a great gap, the vast area of the High Plains between the slopes of the Rocky Mountains on the west to the twenty-inch rainfall line on the east, from north of the Canadian border, down almost to the Rio Grande in western Texas. Here was one of the greatest grazing areas the world ever knew, the home of the buffalo, the range where the Spanish horses run wild multiplied beyond belief. It looks like the objective of a pincers movement of higher culture from both the Southeast and the Southwest, but those pincers never closed. The land defied farming—until our modern machinery arrived to break the tough, thin sod, with disastrous results.

As has already been pointed out, the buffalo country was not inviting as a permanent place of residence to people without horses or metal, so long as they could live well on farming and on hunting easier animals. The stone heads of spears and arrows, if they strike a hard bone at the wrong angle, can break, with disastrous results. A wounded bull can be a long time dying, and, until he drops, fast on his feet and deadly. Early buffalo hunting was no tame sport.

The Plains were not empty, of course. With such a food supply, there were bound to be people, but this was not a preferred area, and it was sparsely occupied. In 1540 and thereafter, the Spanish explorers spoke of "Querechos," "Teyas," and "Paducahs" in the Plains. They lived in skin tents, used dogs as beasts of burden, and hunted. The Spanish saw one Indian put an arrow through a buffalo, and remarked that that would have been good work with a musket. These were probably Apaches, ancestors in part of the later Western Apaches of the Southwest.

Whoever they were, they were not many, not strong enough later to hold their territory against the tribes that came in, nor, in the early days, to keep the French and their Pawnee allies from coming across to raid the Spanish settlements in the Southwest.

As has already been told, the horses the Spanish brought into New Mexico ran wild and spread eastward. The Spanish also brought horses into California. At times their outposts on the West Coast reached well to the north. From there also, horses escaped, and multiplied in Oregon. There were wild horses increasing on the Plains, and in the northwest, inland from the sea, various tribes captured horses and took to raising them. The Cayuse tribe became such outstanding horse raisers and traders that "cayuse" became a cowboy word for horse later on.

Blackfoot pony and three types of dogs, sketched by Kurz in 1852. The very simple saddle over what seems to be a buffalo-skin saddle blanket is typical of Plains men's saddles. The bridle is no more than a long thong tied around the horse's lower jaw. The dogs are big, solid, working types.

Smithsonian Institution.

Painting of a "Plains Indian Village Scene." This does not show the encampment of any particular tribe, but is a composite, including men riding out for the start of a buffalo hunt. The buffalo have come closer to the village than would be likely. Meat can be seen drying on a rack, a hide stretched out for tanning, another, on a frame, being scraped down. Beyond that hide lie bundles of goods wrapped in decorated hides, as they were packed for carrying on travois. Behind the horseman in the foreground, on the ground, lies a woman's saddle with high pommel and cantle, a form derived from Spanish models.

Courtesy of American Museum of Natural History.

The Indians of the northwestern mountains traded horses to the east. One by one, in the 1700's, the tribes surrounding the buffalo country learned to ride. At the same time, tribes in the east were in a turmoil, pressing westward, and others near the Mississippi and in the lake country were obtaining arms, including guns through trade. The Chippewas, who dominated the rich fishing and trapping country described in Chapter V, became well armed through trade. About 1770 they destroyed the main Cheyenne settlement in North Dakota, and even earlier they had begun pushing the Dakotas themselves, the group of related tribes we call "Sioux," out of the wooded country into the open spaces.

As late as 1724 some tribes of western farmers were described as traveling with only dogs to haul their goods. In the 1760's, the more easterly Sioux were still primarily canoe Indians; by 1796 they had abandoned the use of canoes and taken completely to horses. That is a conven-ient date for the beginning of the era of the horseback culture of the High Plains.

The Sioux were mounted. So were the Cheyennes, who abandoned their farms and moved west. The Algonkian Blackfeet on the Canadian border to the west, the Crows, relatives of the Mandans and Hidatsas, the Uto-Aztecan Comanches coming down out of the Rockies, all turned to the new life centered upon the buffalo, made possible by the horses and by the white men's goods—metal tools and weapons, increasing numbers of guns, and along with them blankets and beads—that came by trade through tribes in the northeast.

In Montana there was a tribe speaking a language closely related to the Tanoan of the Pueblos, the Kiowas. Once they had horses, they moved to the Panhandle country of Oklahoma and Texas, where they became neighbors of the Comanches, with whom they joined in industriously raiding the Spanish and Pueblo settlements.

"Traveling," by Keahbone, modern Kiowa artist. The arrangement of two poles to make a travois and placement of the load on it are clearly shown. The woman wears the costume of the period after the introduction of beadwork, with which her baby's cradleboard is richly decorated. She would probably have been riding on the more elaborate saddle shown in the last illustration.

Philbrook Art Center.

Except for two small groups, the weaker Athapascan tribes were driven out. In the north, the Sarsi attached themselves to the Blackfeet, in time acquiring a good deal of that tribe's culture. In the south, the Kiowa Apaches, as their name implies, joined the Kiowas, becoming something in the nature of poor relations. The Kiowa Apache speech is closely related to that of the Western Apaches of the Southwest; their culture is essentially Plains.

Those who had farmed, such as the Cheyennes, forgot about it, or continued only the ceremonial planting of small plots of tobacco. Even the Western farmers greatly stepped up their pursuit of the buffalo. For horsemen, hunting the big beasts became an exciting and profitable game. With horses, too, the weight of hides necessary to make really big tepees could easily be carried, long tepee-poles to match could be dragged, and the animals could

carry plenty of belongings with them as the people moved.

During part of the year, when the buffalo were in their territory, each tribe lived richly. There was more than enough to eat, there was leisure for art. They painted their tepees and adorned them with medallions of beadwork. They decorated everything that would take a decoration, the men by painting, the women with the lavish porcupine quill embroidery, and shortly with the rich beadwork that produced some of the handsomest costumes the world has ever seen.

During that time when the buffalo were out of their territory, which for most tribes was the winter, the pickings were not so good. They stored as much meat as they could by jerking it—slicing it thin and sun-drying it. They made pemmican by pounding up dried meat, mixing it with dried, crushed berries, putting it in sacks and pouring

Blackfeet Indians traveling, from a model in the Blackfoot Museum at Browning, Montana. Women rode the loaded horses while the men roved on either side and ahead, both to hunt and to guard the party. The travois poles, which are also tepee poles, project far beyond the horses' heads.

U. S. Dept. of Interior.

Model of a small camp of Blackfoot Indians, in the Blackfoot Museum. Two of the tepees are painted, and a man is in the course of painting the one at the right. The owner's shield and other paraphernalia hang on a tripod in front of the polka-dotted tepee at the left. Women are working on buffalo skins, cooking, and hanging meat to dry. *U. S. Dept. of Interior.*

A Comanche village in Texas, as seen by Catlin in 1834, while the artist was traveling with the First U. S. Dragoons (heavy cavalry). *Smithsonian Institution.*

Modern, decorated Cheyenne canvas tepee. A design of calumets down the middle of the back divides two groups of pictures of war exploits. The two poles outside the tepee control the "ears." *Courtesy of American Museum of Natural History.*

Blackfoot tepee with model figures inside. The two flaps on either side of the smoke hole, called "ears," are clearly shown here. These flaps were a Plains improvement on the more general type found from Siberia to the Atlantic, permitting adjustments according to the direction of the wind or closing the hole almost completely if desired. *Courtesy of American Museum of Natural History.*

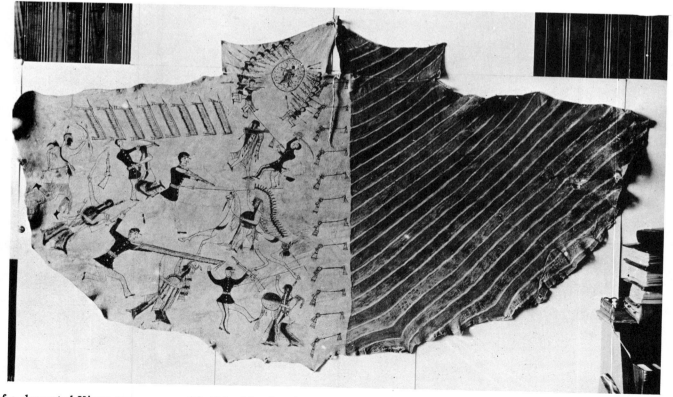

Model of a decorated Kiowa tepee cover of buffalo skin. One half carries a striped design, the other a lively picture of battle with U. S. Troops. *Smithsonian Institution.*

melted fat and marrow over the whole. It was nutritious, but a pretty nasty dish, according to white men who tried it, until you got used to it. Those tribes that controlled mountain country moved into it for the deer hunting. The others hunted what they could find on the Plains. Most of them, in the lean months, had to break up into small groups, as there was not enough food to be found in one place to feed the whole tribe. The Cheyennes tried staying together through one winter, and nearly died of it.

In due course the buffalo came back. They always came back. It was a mystery; the great animals disappeared and in season returned in their thousands, predictably, as certain as spring itself. Inevitably, many religious beliefs clustered around them. By then the tribe was assembled again—hundreds, perhaps a thousand or more, of the gleaming, tall tents grouped in a great semi-circle. At night, if a bright fire was burning in any of them, they glowed like lanterns. (Much of the time, on the treeless Plains, they were limited to small fires of dried buffalo dung.)

Then one day scouts came in with the news that the buffalo were coming. The ordinarily lax discipline of the tribe immediately became strict. The police took over—in some tribes, the members of the Dog Society—selected young warriors. An over-eager hunter might frighten the great herd away. All must act together, swooping upon the herd, if possible, in such a way as to get the animals milling before each man moved in for the kill. A hunter who went ahead on his own might be whipped, or his tepee and all his belongings might be burned. The men mounted their "buffalo horses," fast animals with plenty of

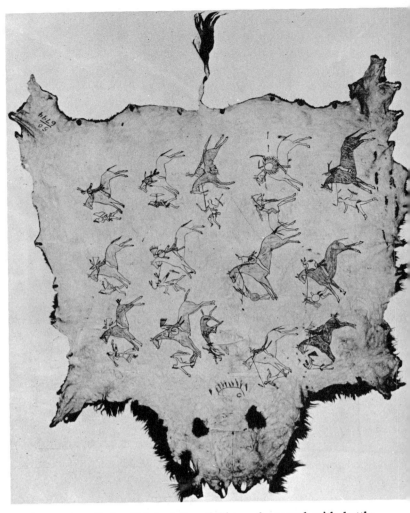

Buffalo robe of the Oglala tribe of Sioux decorated with battle scenes. *Courtesy of American Museum of Natural History.*

Calendar robe painted by Anko, a Kiowa, covering events of thirty-seven months from 1889 to 1892. Plains art was developing in two directions, towards a lively realism, and from that to symbols with fixed meanings that might in time have become a form of writing. The Kiowas kept a number of calendars, most of them recording the outstanding events of each year for a series of years, the longest covering the years from 1826 to 1901. The Sioux kept similar "winter counts," a remarkable extract from one of which is shown on page 167. *Smithsonian Institution.*

endurance, sure-footed, and trained to come up alongside a buffalo and stay in just the right position for a lance thrust or a close-in shot with bow or gun.

When the first of the game was being butchered, the liver was sliced and eagerly eaten raw, for it was packed with vitamins, and after their winter diet the people were suffering vitamin starvation. White men who wintered with the Indians, or in the same manner, found themselves craving a delicacy that otherwise would have revolted them.

Then the village was full of food. Among some tribes the meat was divided for all. Among others, the successful hunters considered it a part of their manhood to give to the unsuccessful and old and needy. The Indians feasted on unlimited meat. This was a time when the women were busy tanning and working hides and drying meat, but the

The full flower of beadwork costumes—Lazy White Bull of the Miniconjou Sioux ("Bull" in Plains Indian names refers to the male buffalo). Note the chest-piece of polished bones strung together, an ornament that also was of some use as armor.

Courtesy of American Museum of Natural History.

155

men had both leisure and plenty of energy for fun and games.

The greatest game of all was war. When describing Plains culture, it is almost impossible to find any element that can absolutely be stated to be purely Plains. The farmers to the east of them lived just as they did when they came out to hunt, used horses the same way after they got them, shared a great number of the customs and probably were the source of most of them. Much of the war-game pattern may have come from such relatively advanced tribes as the Omahas. Nevertheless, as it was in historic times, it was a horse game, and as such, whatever its origin, it belongs above all to the purely horseback, hunting tribes.

It was all done in a spirit of fun, with the principal

Arapaho beaded pouches with porcupine quill on the fringes.
Courtesy of American Museum of Natural History.

Curly Bear, a Blackfoot chief, photographed in 1916. His costume includes a war bonnet, gauntlets with a floral design in beads, a necklace of beads and bear's claws, and a medallion honoring the inauguration of Woodrow Wilson.
Smithsonian Institution.

Fringed buckskin shirt, Blackfoot, with porcupine quill embroidery and hair trimming. Porcupine quill was usually dyed red and yellow. Its shiny surface gives a brilliant effect.
Courtesy of American Museum of Natural History.

"Cheyenne Children's Games," by the modern Cheyenne artist, Dick West. The picture mostly shows boys' play; the two girls at the lower left with their dolls, one in a cradleboard, are acting as audience to the dance the three boys in front of them are staging. Some of the boys' play is pure fun, some is practice for war and hunting. An accepted game for Plains boys was to try to steal meat off the drying racks and carry it off for a feast—good practice for stealing a tethered horse out of an enemy camp later on. *Philbrook Art Center.*

Crow Indians an engraving from a sketch by Bodmer made in   1833. Three of the men wear ornamented buffalo robes.
Smithsonian Institution.

objective to gain glory, or to revenge a similar attack. The commonest practice was for a single man, or a party of men, to sneak up on another tribe's camp and see how many horses they could run off. What was especially honorable was to get right into the village circle and steal the favorite horse of some important warrior, which was kept tethered near his tent. Stealing horses was not economic; the tribes owned more of the animals than they had any use for. As with the Indians to the east, it was more honorable to run risks than to kill. Some men carried poles adorned with feathers, coup sticks, as their only weapon, with which they would try to touch as many armed enemies as possible. Some touched the enemy with their bare hands. Not killing the man, but being the first to run up and touch the corpse carried the greatest honor.

When certain young Sioux came back from France after World War I, they asked the old men to initiate them into

Sioux shield. The design was probably revealed in a vision, and is as important as the tough buffalo hide in protecting its owner. *Courtesy of American Museum of Natural History.*

Crow horse trappings, about 1900. The man carries a combination bow and lance that was used by the northern Plains Indians. *Courtesy of American Museum of Natural History.*

Cheyenne necklace, captured in 1876. The owner, High Wolf, a considerable warrior, adorned it with the left-hand middle fingers of enemies he had slain. *Smithsonian Institution.*

"Sioux Teacher," by Oscar Howe. The man describes to the boys the exploits painted on his tepee. Plains Indians had no modesty about depicting or telling about their achievements, but they had to be absolutely accurate or they would be disgraced.

Philbrook Art Center.

One of a series of autobiographical drawings by Sitting Bull, the great leader of the united Sioux against the whites. The buffalo in the upper right-hand corner gives his name. The black object hanging from his hand shows that he has killed and scalped one Crow, whose body lies on the ground. Now he proves his worth by counting a coup on another, hitting him with his bow, although the Crow is armed with a gun and narrowly misses him.

Smithsonian Institution.

Model of a tepee cover, tribe not known. One half is painted with pictures bearing on hunting—buffalo, elk, antelope, and bear. The other shows two war incidents. The mounted man with a war bonnet is striking his enemy with the muzzle of his gun, thereby counting a coup.

Courtesy of American Museum of Natural History.

the soldier societies. It turned out that, while these young men had killed a fair number of Germans, it had all been done by shooting. None of them had been in a bayonet fight, none had actually touched an enemy. Shooting people with rifles might be a useful thing to do under certain circumstances, but as a qualification for rank among warriors, it did not count. They were refused initiation.

It was a deadly game. Nobody aimed to get killed, but plenty were killed. To keep the game honest, the tribe that was being raided, if it detected the raiders before they got away, did its level best to kill them. So, too, when two war parties met, the man who rushed in with a coup stick was likely to be met with arrows, or preferably, lances.

There was also true warfare on occasion, usually because one tribe wanted to move into another tribe's territory. In the mountain country west of the Plains there were many tribes that wanted to get into the act, such as the Nez Percé, Shoshone, Ute, and the Jicarilla Apache tribe already discussed in the last chapter. Such groups kept pushing into the buffalo country and had to be pushed back. They were horseback people, they lived in tepees, they took over varying degrees of the Plains culture, so that on the west as well as on the east you cannot easily draw a line and say that the area of the Plains culture ends just here. It blends into the next areas.

The Jicarillas were described in the last chapter as a bridge between the Southwest and the Plains. They farmed, their mythology is Southwestern, their ceremonial a mixture of Southwestern, Basin, and original northern Atha-

pascan, but here is a story they told me that shows how Plains they were, too.

One time when the whole tribe was camped together, two brothers, warriors of ability, were angry with a famous warrior and powerful leader named Luna. (This happened not so very long ago; Luna died of old age in the 1920's.) Luna was known to have very powerful war medicine, which he wore in a small bag hung from his neck. Personal medicine of that kind is a Plains trait, not a Southwestern one.

The brothers challenged him to combat by drumming and singing a song that mocked him. Luna accepted the challenge by drumming and singing back at them. The duel was arranged in a narrow, shallow valley, where everyone could line up along the sides and watch.

Luna started from one end, cradling his rifle over his arm. The brothers started at the other end. They came together slowly, until they could almost touch each other, then Luna said so that everyone could hear, "Well, why don't you start fighting? Here I am."

One of the brothers answered, "You are wearing something that is too much for us." This meant the war medicine.

Luna slipped the thong over his head, lifted the bag, and threw it to one side. "All right," he said, lifting his rifle, "here I am."

That the great man was so sure of himself as to be willing to throw away his sacred power was too much for the brothers. They lowered their weapons and called off the fight.

This incident could have occurred nowhere else within the Southwest.

In the north, in Canada and just inside the border of the United States, some of the Chippewas and the Algonkian Crees, whose original culture was developed in cold, northern forests, also moved towards the Plains and partially adopted Plains ways. They provided some fine fighting for the Sioux, whom earlier the Chippewas had harried out of the woodlands.

War achievement led to honors and rank. Many of the men that whites called "chiefs" were simply warriors who had proven their mettle, were honored accordingly, and were sought out to lead war parties. They had no governmental authority. The list of honorable deeds varied from tribe to tribe. Generally it included leading a successful war party, which meant one that stole horses or killed enemies or made coups, and on which no one from the home tribe was killed. Making a coup, snatching a bow or gun from an enemy, stealing a picketed horse, were important. ("Coup," pronounced "coo," is simply the French word for "blow." A coup could be made by touching an enemy with a bare hand or a stick, or killing him with a hand weapon. If someone *shot* an enemy, not the shooter, but the first man to run up and touch the body got the high honor.) Although they took scalps, few tribes gave special honors to a scalp taker.

A successful Crow captain of war parties trimmed his shirt and moccasins with hair; one who had struck coups attached wolf tails to the heels of his moccasins, the warrior who had snatched a gun or bow decorated his shirt with ermine skins. The Blackfeet used decorations of white weasel skins to indicate honors. The Sioux, more than any others, developed a "feather heraldry," by which eagle feathers worn in the hair or in a headdress told of the wearer's achievements. From this developed the "war bonnet" that has become so familiar, a sort of hat surrounded by a crown of eagle feathers which slope backwards and fan out slightly, with or without a tail of feathers hanging down the back. In early illustrations we see that tail fairly often, attached to a headdress of skin with a pair of horns attached to it. Entirely feathered war bonnets are seldom shown.

The basic elements of the High Plains horse-and-buffalo culture had been established long before 1700, mostly in the country farther east. In its full form, which provides the original for the picture that comes first to all our minds when someone says "Indians," it did not begin to develop until the middle 1700's. It was in its full flower less than a century later. Very rarely have we an opportunity to see how the introduction of a new element or two can cause a cultural revolution. In this case the principal element was the horse, aided by the trade articles such as metal and woven goods, which were traded from tribe to tribe well ahead of the advancing white men.

Rain-in-the-Face, famous chief of the Hunkpapa Sioux. His name really meant something like "His Face is Like a Storm." Often the white officials learned names and terms from interpreters who spoke little English; also, names that were short in the native language became long in translation, so the white men shortened them. Another famous example is Young Man Afraid of His Horses, whose name really said that he had stampeded the enemy's horses. *Smithsonian Institution.*

War Eagle, a Yankton Sioux, in full regalia. These horned headgear were worn just as much as the all-feather kind, if not more. The leggings are made of woven material with beadwork strips sewed on. The shirt may be an heirloom, as it is buckskin decorated with masses of porcupine quill. *Smithsonian Institution.*

As we might expect when people move into a territory from many different directions—in this case from the east, the north, and the west—they differed in many matters. They all adopted a similar material culture. That is, their clothing, tents, tools, diet, and so forth became very much alike. Material culture is the easiest thing to imitate. You see a large tepee handsomely painted, and if you have the necessary skins and poles, you make one like it, and paint yours. But unless you have spent some time talking with the owner of the first tepee, you do not know what symbolic or sacred meaning his decorations may have; instead, you use meanings and designs of your own. Nonmaterial culture spreads more slowly. The war-and-honor pattern already described is an example of nonmaterial culture, consisting mainly of a number of ideas, that did reach to almost all.

The Comanches, who established themselves fully in the Plains, remained a comparatively simple people, very loosely organized, their rituals and myths reflecting the thinner culture of the occupants of the mountain country from which they came. They became allies of one of the most highly evolved and puzzling tribes, the Kiowas. As already noted, the Kiowa language is related to the Pueblos' Tanoan. So far as scientists can trace them, the Kiowas were always in or near the Plains, always purely hunters, and made neither pottery nor basketry. Yet they give the impression of being a people with a rich tradition behind them, which shows in their social order, their myths, and their ceremonies as well as their high artistic sense. Their myths suggest an ancient Southwestern origin. There is a historical puzzle here as yet unsolved. It is less surprising that the Cheyennes should have a

Much of the time, chiefs did not wear all their feathers. This is Red Cloud, head chief of the Oglala Sioux, on a visit to Washington in 1884. On the whole, a survey of early photographs of Plains chiefs shows many more wearing a single feather than wearing all their regalia. *Smithsonian Institution.*

Sitting Bull, the great Sioux leader, a Hunkpapa under whom the Sioux tribes united in their resistance to the white invaders. Although he was at one time a member of the Kit-Fox Society and had a fine war record, he was a medicine man and organizer more than a war captain. *Smithsonian Institution.*

relatively rich nonmaterial culture, since we know that not long ago they were farmers, and can see how they probably relate to old, high cultures.

The Kiowas were notable for the distances to which they raided. In the 1860's, starting in Oklahoma, they sent at least one war party westward past Santa Fe to the Navaho territory on the farther edge of New Mexico. They reached deep into old Mexico. They tell of a raid that some authorities interpret as having crossed the whole republic and ended in British Honduras. This seems impossible, but it is certain that they got far enough to see monkeys and parrots.

As usual in North America, war and peace alternated, often in rapid succession. In time of peace there was trade. These tribes were wide ranging; friendly as well as hostile dealings might occur between any of them. All told, on the Plains and just surrounding them, there were six different linguistic families and over twenty-two separate languages. As a means of communication, they developed the international "sign language," a system of gestures by which intricate conversations could be carried on. To some degree this spread to tribes beyond the buffalo area; today it is all but extinct and English has taken its place.

There were tribes with clans descended through the mother, others with clans descended through the father, some without clans. Among some, a husband moved to his wife's camp, among others, the other way round. Most of them had a somewhat romantic pattern of courtship, including playing tunes on simple flutes. Elopements occurred, but the preferred way of marriage was by courtship followed by the formal purchase of the bride from her family. The purchase price was paid in horses. This does not mean that the bride was "sold." The number of horses paid for her was a testimony both to the husband's love for her and the high esteem in which her family held her. The same thing, incidentally, was true among the Navahos, where it was an honor to a woman throughout her life that a large number of horses had been given for her.

Organization was loose and democratic. At special times, as during a hunt, the police imposed rigid discipline; at other times public opinion was the main force. Chiefs were respected, they were advisers, but they did not give orders. If two men started a fight, chiefs might come between them carrying sacred pipes and urge them to stop, but no force was used. Among the Cheyennes, who had a complex system of law, murder was taken very gravely. It damaged the whole tribe. It profaned the Sacred Arrows, their holiest possession and the center of their sacred power. The murderer came before the council of chiefs, and might be exiled for as long as ten years.

Among the Crow, murder was a private matter between the killer's clan and the victim's. The police came into the picture, not to make an arrest or to try to punish, but to try to persuade the killer and his people to make an adequate payment to the bereaved, so as to avoid the starting of a harmful feud.

The power of public opinion was great. The Blackfoot had a system of mockery that could make life intolerable for a man, and drive him out alone on a quest for death or war honors with which to redeem himself. In some tribes, it was a particular relative's duty to rebuke a man

The war bonnet in full flower—White Whirlwind, an Oglala Sioux. *Courtesy of American Museum of Natural History.*

who had behaved badly. The rebuke was given publicly, and the shame felt was an intense punishment.

Behavior between relatives was exactly defined in most tribes. There were those with whom one was expected to joke and rough-house—who might be the same ones whose duty included the rebuke—and those with whom one dealt always in terms of great respect. Some tribes maintained a beautiful relationship between brothers and sisters. Brothers felt great responsibility for sisters; sisters, in turn, did their brothers many favors such as making especially fine moccasins for them. When they grew up, an extreme form of the respect relationship was required, under which they could barely speak to each other. This did not mean coldness; it showed the lofty and strong nature of their feeling for each other. Mutual service and help continued through life, and from all accounts, the affection also continued very strong.

The Plains "societies," also found among the farming tribes west of the Mississippi, are curious. Some tribes had both men's and women's societies, others only men's. They might be purely religious, like the Crow Tobacco Society, which planted the sacred tobacco and held rituals connected with the plant for the good of the whole camp, or primarily military with religious elements, like the Dog Societies of the Mandans and a number of other northern tribes. In writing about the West we often run into references to "Dog Soldiers" or similar terms, by which the Dog and sometimes the Kit-Fox Societies are meant. These often performed the police functions already described and were also pledged to extreme heroism in war.

In their fullest development, the men's societies had a unique age grading. Young warriors, desiring to confirm their standing, would come to the members of a society of slightly older men and try to buy their insignia, songs, rituals, and privileges. After much bargaining the deal would be made. The older group would then buy out the next older club, and so on up, until the oldest, having sold out, retired from the honors and activities of society membership.

Intangibles such as these were far more valuable than usable possessions. Anyone who amounted to anything practiced open-handed generosity in a conspicuous manner. Chiefs often reduced themselves close to poverty helping the poor. What we think of as property was lightly held. But powerful songs, sacred bundles, the knowledge of how to conduct a particular rite, were valuable. Even when someone's own father or mother possessed the knowledge and the articles that went with it, they had to be paid horses, robes, and other goods before they would turn them over.

Religion, much like that of the Western farmers, was strongly shamanistic but with some large rituals and many minor ones requiring priestly training. Visions were important not only for the Indians along the Mississippi but, as has been told, for the Iroquois and others. The Plains Indians and their nearer eastern neighbors developed the vision pattern dramatically. Magical-religious power, the gift of healing, which made a true "medicine man," the authority for making a sacred bundle, came from visions. A vision might be the reason for starting or for calling off a war party. Women, also, could have visions, although they were primarily a man's business.

More than this, a man really could hardly function without a vision. At various ages, usually in the late teens, young men went to seek their visions, riding out alone, fasting, often cutting off a joint of a finger or otherwise mutilating themselves as a sacrifice and to win the pity of the spirits. They had heard many descriptions of visions, been reared on the myths about the sacred beings and how they behaved. Hunger, loneliness, pain, and intense expectation led most of them, in the end, to have a dream experience that fitted the general pattern and told the seeker that from then on his friend, his adoptive father, was a spirit elk, a buffalo, a whirlwind, or whatever it might be.

"Dog Soldier Dance," by Dick West, the Cheyenne artist. In the foreground sit the drummers and singers, and on either side of them a pair of women with rattles dance a quiet step. The Dog Society members put on a lively dance of warlike character. The dancer on the extreme right has the same headgear as the Mandan chief shown on page 103. *Philbrook Art Center.*

From this patron he received, or believed he had received, a few prayers. His vision showed him what objects to put together as a charm that would protect him and bring him a good life. These charms we call "medicine," just as we are inclined to call all Indian priests "medicine men." Those are white men's terms, and as usual, show the thorough ignorance of those who bestowed them. A very strong vision, or series of visions, might show that a man was intended to take up some part of religious practice. Visions could teach him new rites and prayers. A man who was unable to obtain any vision at all, could buy the use of the vision and "medicine" of someone who had been especially blessed. The successful dreamer would teach him his songs or prayers and permit him to copy his charms.

Analysis of these dreams and visions makes an interesting psychological study, which we cannot go into here. One example, however, must be included. Earlier in this book the custom of *berdache* was described, under which male homosexuals dressed and lived as women. The Omaha, the farming Plains-edge tribe among whom so much that is "Plains" may have originated, believed that young men became *berdaches* as the result of their first vision during puberty. The Moon would come to the youth, in one hand holding a warrior's bow and arrows, in the other a woman's pack strap. As the visionary reached out

Calumet and beaded pouch for carrying it. These pipes were important in Plains ceremonial.

Courtesy of American Museum of Natural History.

Blackfoot medicine man. His necklace, the decorations on his fur hat, and the manner of painting his face all relate to his magical power.

Courtesy of American Museum of Natural History.

"Religious Ceremony," painted by Catlin in a Sioux camp in 1832. It appears to be a greatly simplified form of the Sun Dance, performed by a single votary. *Smithsonian Institution.*

Funeral scaffold of a Sioux chief, after a sketch by Bodmer, 1834. The dead were placed on scaffolds, where they dried out, rather than being buried, a practice that may have originated in Asia. When nothing but bones were left, these were reverently gathered up and placed in rock crevices. Athapascan Indians would have been terrified to have the remains of the dead so near them, but to the Sioux it was more like continuing to have the company of the departed. *Smithsonian Institution.*

Extract from the "winter count" of High Hawk, a Sioux, showing the chief event of the year 1540. In this count, High Hawk reached far back into the legendary and mythical past. This shows the founding of much of Sioux religion and ceremonial, when the divine being, White Buffalo Woman, came to the Sioux and taught them. She stands inside a ritual lodge, the *tipi-okihe*. According to Black Elk, the great Oglala priest, from her revelations stem seven major rituals and also the use of the calumet as a sacred pipe. A horse is drawn on one side, because White Buffalo Woman prophesied the coming of horses. It is interesting that, although High Hawk knew nothing of our dating, the year of this sacred event is the year in which Coronado crossed the Plains. *Courtesy of American Museum of Natural History.*

"And They Moved Without Him," by the modern artist Black Bear Bosin. The man who died has been put on a scaffold, to which are tied the heads and tails of his favorite horses. The band, moving on, is disappearing into the snow, while a woman beside her horse pauses a moment to weep.

Philbrook Art Center.

to take the weapons, the Moon might quickly cross his hands, and the visionary take the woman's emblem. Then there was nothing for him but to turn pseudo-woman.

As we know now, dreams, of which the Indian visions were a form, sometimes show, not what we secretly want, but what we dread. At least one case is known in which a young man had the *berdache* vision, and as a result committed suicide.

As a result of the vision pattern, almost everyone had a sort of cult or sub-religion of his own, inside the general religion. The rituals relating to a man's own "medicine" or to his sacred bundle were held in his own lodge. Many society rituals were also semi-private, and originated in visions.

In addition, there were public rituals that affected the whole tribe and also provided it with entertainment. War and scalp dances, ceremonies to bring the buffalo like the Mandan ones illustrated in Chapter V, involved many people directly and were observed by all. One of the most important, followed in some form by almost all the Plains tribes, is called the Sun Dance by us—as usual, a poor name, since it involved little if any sun worship. Among some tribes it was a yearly fixture; others, like the Crow, held it only rarely. Usually it was sponsored by someone who had made a vow to do so in return for supernatural help. It was a means of having powerful visions and of bringing good to the whole tribe.

Its central feature was dancing in an enclosed area,

Two stages of the Sun Dance, painted by Short Bull, an Oglala Sioux chief. *Courtesy of American Museum of Natural History.*

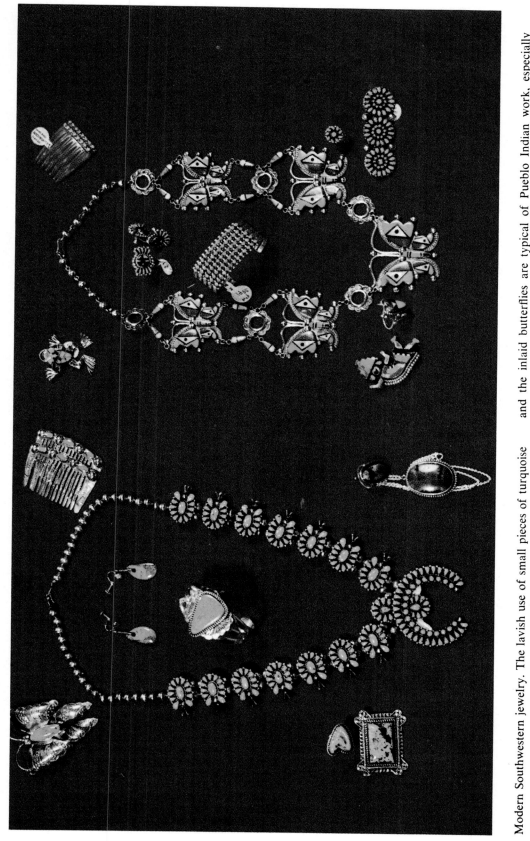

Modern Southwestern jewelry. The lavish use of small pieces of turquoise and the inlaid butterflies are typical of Pueblo Indian work, especially of Zuñi. *Dexter Press, Inc.*

Present-day Seminole women and child in Florida. Their costume is a development over the centuries from one derived from the early Spanish. *Dexter Press, Inc.*

Plains Indian in ceremonial costume.
Peabody Museum of Natural History, Yale University.

Buffalo Dancers of Jemez Pueblo, New Mexico, two buffalo impersonators and "Buffalo Maiden." The fact that these dancers are artily posed on a rock, along with the dance leader on the left, instead of photographed in the Pueblo plaza, shows that this is a team hired to put on an exhibition. Some tribes nowadays perform the smaller, unmasked dances commercially. When they do, they carefully leave out certain elements, which removes the sacred character from the dance. *Dexter Press, Inc.*

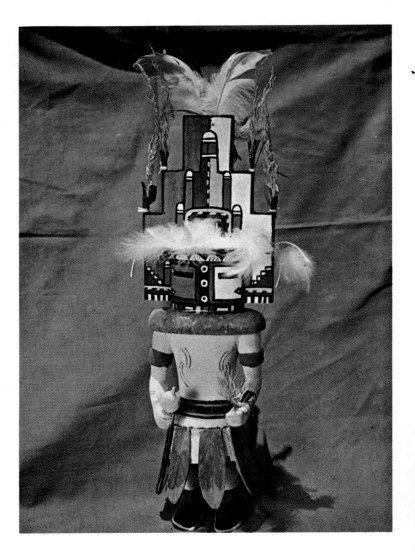

Doll representing the kachina that usually appears in the "Kachina Homegoing," when the kachinas dance for the last time in the year. The mask, as usual, is exaggerated in size. It is exceptional in that phallic symbols are painted on the flat board, called "tablita," that rises above the mask proper. *Reproductions on these two pages from Hopi Kachina Dolls by Harold S. Colton. © University of New Mexico Press. Courtesy of Dr. Colton and the University of New Mexico Press.*

Doll of the He-e-e Kachina, representing a mythical character who rallied the Hopis successfully against an enemy attack. In some villages He-e-e is said to be a woman, in others, a man who had put on woman's clothes as a joke when the enemy arrived.

172

Hopi doll representing Owl Kachina. Great care has been taken to show the knitted cotton leggings worn by the real dancers who impersonate Owl.

Three Hopi kachina dolls, showing variety of types of masks. As in most masks, there is no attempt to portray a face, although there are eyes and mouth, but to symbolize on the "face" the attributes of the particular kachina.

The skin-painting above is the work of an Apache chief named Naiche, second in command to the great Geronimo. Done in vegetable dye on doeskin, using a soft buffalo bone for a brush, it pictures the sacred girls' puberty ceremony. While the rest of the tribe watch from in front of their tepees, which face east towards the rising sun, the dance is performed around the purifying fire. Each pair wrapped in a blanket comprises a young girl and an old woman who will act as her guardian. Fertility is symbolized by leafy trees, corn, and wheat; barrenness by leafless trees. The small figures, called Earth Spirits, at the left of the fire, and the posturing Mountain Spirits with candelabra-like headdresses complete the group. *Courtesy of Oklahoma Historical Society and American Heritage.*

White Mountain Apache on horseback. *Dexter Press, Inc.*

Nez Perce schoolchildren staging circle dance. The boys' costumes include old and modern Indian items and dyed winter underwear. *Dexter Press, Inc.*

George Catlin in 1832 first painted the Bull Dance of the Mandans, a celebration of the buffalo's coming which took place in a clearing between the earth-covered lodges. The disrupting figure at left is the evil spirit, soon to be neutralized by a magic medicine pipe and driven from the village by women.

Courtesy of Smithsonian Institution and American Heritage.

Sioux, they made a sacrifice and demonstrated their courage by a form of self-torture. Two parallel slits were cut in their skin, and under the strip between a stick was run, from which a string led to the central pole or to a buffalo skull or similar object. The idea was to keep jerking against the string until the strip of skin tore out. Other tribes, such as the Kiowa, who had a highly developed Sun Dance, did not practice such torture.

This ceremony became the principal one of the Utes, a mountain people under strong Plains influence. They added to it certain features of their own original culture, such as lines of men and women dancing opposite each other.

Allegedly because of the self-torture features, the Sun Dance was forbidden by the U.S. Bureau of Indian Affairs about 1910. In those days, in flagrant violation of the Constitution, the Bureau lent itself readily to efforts to suppress Indian religions. The Sun Dance was forbidden regardless of whether the tribe practiced the torture or not. The Indian right to religious freedom was finally recognized in 1934, after which some of the tribes revived it in modified form.

Plains Indian religion was a curious mixture consisting largely of primitive thinking and a good deal of poetry. It was capable of evolving to much higher levels. Many of the more learned priests developed a lofty philosophy. Black Elk, the famous Oglala Sioux priest, who died only recently, taught doctrines of such interest, with so much poetic and high religious content, that his teachings were made the subject of two books by two different white men, one a poet, the other a student of comparative religions.

It was great good luck that among the first white men to go among the Plains Indians and their close neighbors and relatives to the east were George Catlin, the gifted American artist, and the naturalist Prince Maximilian of Wied, with the artist Karl Bodmer in his party. Going out in the early 1830's, they recorded a good deal of the culture at its full peak and while direct contact with white men was still rare. As stated, it had developed in less than a hundred years, and the remarkable thing is that this, which we think of as the real thing in the Indian way of life, is entirely the result of the coming to the New World of the white men.

The culture went almost as fast as it developed. Still in the 1830's, the great smallpox epidemic swept the northern Plains and all but wiped out the Mandans and Hidatsas. Our routes from the east to the growing settlements of the Pacific coast ran through the Plains territory. The tribes knew no reason why foreigners should trespass on their land, kill game, and build forts without permission. They raided the intruders to teach them manners, and the intruders struck back with armies.

There were minor wars and then treaties. Gold was found in the sacred Black Hills of the Sioux, so their treaty went out the window and war flamed. In the east, a great demand developed for buffalo robes. In those days, most people in winter went about in sleighs or in unheated wagons, and buffalo robes were ideal to keep out the cold. The buffalo hunters appeared, professional killers who slaughtered the herds from a distance with .50 caliber rifles, solely for the skins. The wholesale, wildly wasteful

Two Cheyenne Indians who had pledged a Sun Dance about 1900. Pledgers, who made the dance possible, might not necessarily take part in the self-torture. They are painted for their special part in the ritual. Note the skirt-like garments on the lower part of their bodies; similar clothing shows in Short Bull's painting.
Courtesy of American Museum of Natural History.

around or facing a pole made of the trunk of a tree that had been "killed" and felled with great ceremony. The dancing was grave and extremely simple, which was true of much Plains Indian ritual dancing, the dancers hardly moving from where they started. As a rule, the "sun" dancers went without food or water through the whole time of the performance, which was often until they fell in a trance and had a vision. In some tribes, such as the

"Sioux Sun Dance," another painting by Oscar Howe. This simple but impressive painting really captures the Indian view of this great ceremony, in which what was shocking to missionaries was beautiful and holy to the eyes of the Indians. Two men continue tugging at the lines that connect them to the sacred tree, to which are attached a variety of symbolic objects. A third, who has just broken free and completed his discipline, scatters the feathers in his hands as he sinks to the ground. *Philbrook Art Center*.

Model of an Arapaho Sun Dance, showing the typical Sun Dance enclosure. *Courtesy of American Museum of Natural History*.

Crow, the Sioux chief who gave the battle cry that opened the Battle of the Little Big Horn, in which Custer and his command were wiped out. *Smithsonian Institution.*

An early U. S. outpost in the Plains country—Fort Laramie, Wyoming. Forts like these served as trading centers, and it was some time before the Indians discovered that they were Trojan horses. *University of Oklahoma. Photo by Walters Art Gallery.*

destruction of the animals profoundly shocked and angered the Indians.

They fought, and soon learned the kind of enemy they confronted, armed with powerful weapons, great in numbers, cold-blooded in killing. There were sporting types such as the notorious General Custer, who won a great victory by leading a charge into a Cheyenne village that had made peace and killing large numbers of Indians of all ages. Custer, a braggart, a poor soldier, a lecher, but excessively brave, finally led his troops against a large, peaceful camp of Sioux, Cheyennes, and Arapahos at the Little Big Horn and subjected his men to what was called the Custer Massacre.

That victory was one of the last great flares of Indian power. One by one the tribes were broken. A great many were concentrated in Oklahoma, which we still thought was territory we would not want. Some, like the various Sioux tribes and the Crows, received reservations in parts of their own country. The buffalo were wiped out in a few years of the white man's commercial hunting, leaving the Indians starving until Uncle Sam issued them rations enough to keep them on the edge of life. Cattle ranchers took over the once free Plains. (Later, many of them in turn felt much as the Indians did when farmers pre-empted the public domain and fenced them in.)

The fighting tribes did not give in readily. There were uprisings, raids of hunger and desperation. Briefly, they had known a wonderful life and had started a new culture that might have evolved greatly had it been given a little time. They tried to hold to that new life, struggling against hopeless odds until everything ended in the massacre at Wounded Knee.

After Wounded Knee, 1890. Sitting Bull, the great leader and organizer, had been coldly murdered by the authorities. Frightened, hungry, ragged, desperate groups of Sioux fled the reservations. One large group was gathered up and surrendered, to be slaughtered, men, women and children, by soldiers' rifles, artillery, and bayonets, their tents destroyed, their bodies plundered. This picture is drawn from a photograph; the photographer placed his camera where dead women and children would not show—or the copyist corrected his error. It is typical of white men's thinking of the time that when General Custer and his cavalry were wiped out because they attacked superior numbers, it was called "The Custer Massacre," but when these Sioux with their women and children were murdered, it was called "The Battle of Wounded Knee." *Smithsonian Institution.*

VIII. Behind the Shining Mountains

The first frontiersmen, the trappers, crossing the Plains, saw them rising snow-capped to face the morning sun and called them the Shining Mountains. Later, duller men gave them the dull name of the Rockies. They are the northern part of the backbone of America, and, together with the true deserts that edge the Southwest, they mark off the land that did not receive the higher cultures, the beginnings of the long march toward civilization, or the special, picturesque, rich culture of the Plains.

That country is now the western parts of Colorado, Wyoming and Montana, Idaho, Utah, Nevada, the northwestern corner of Arizona, California, and all of Washington and Oregon except for a narrow strip along their coasts. The line was nowhere sharp. The northwestern Arizona tribes planted corn. The Utes, well within the high mountain country, were at least half Plains. Farther north, the Shoshones and their close relatives stretch across Wyoming, northern Utah and southern Idaho. Those on the east made trips to hunt buffalo, had grass enough for grazing a fair number of horses, lived in goodly tepees, were trying hard to be Plains Indians and doing pretty well at it. Those at the western end were poverty-stricken desert dwellers.

Usually, anthropologists separate the small zone covering central California west of the Sierra Nevada and the narrower, fairly fertile strip of southern California near the coast from this great area. They may also cut the main part in two, distinguishing the higher country near the Canadian border from the portion to the south. Throughout all of this territory were peoples speaking many languages. There were considerable differences in mode of life. All, however, with a few exceptions at the very border of the Southwest, did no farming, almost all shared the same basic elements, untrammeled by any touch of Mexico. Of all it is true that, while the variety that existed makes a fascinating and almost endless study for specialists, they are dull matter for the ordinary person.

The lower country between the Rocky Mountains and the Sierra Nevada, from the general line of the southern boundaries of Colorado and Utah up into Wyoming and Idaho, is called the Great Basin. Twenty thousand years ago, when the early men were drifting down into the continent, this Basin contained sixty-eight goodly lakes. A thousand years ago there was enough water left to enable farming and other Pueblo practices to spread far into it. Now that is ended. It is formidable, frightening country to see except where modern irrigation has subjugated it. It contains stretches of true desert, not only arid country but the real article, including the famous Death Valley.

The people who lived in this desert and near-desert mostly spoke languages of the Uto-Aztecan family, fairly closely related to Ute, Comanche, and Hopi. They were busy keeping alive. There was no room, in their endless struggle, for fancy cultural items; they stuck to what was useful, and they lived where many white men have died.

It is interesting to consider the variety of the Uto-Aztecan peoples, from the civilized Aztecs and Toltecs of Mexico, through the industrious Hopis of Arizona, to the impoverished Paiutes of western Utah and Nevada. Not so long ago, Hitler, an ill-educated, profoundly ignorant man, beat the drum over the idea of an "Aryan race," and led much of Germany astray on it. He confused race and language—"Aryan" being the name of a language family —and having done so, confused language and culture. Had he had a little knowledge, and a little conscience, the well-known case of the Uto-Aztecans would have prevented his deadly idiocy.

The Paiutes and their relatives in the western deserts could maintain only a "gathering" culture; that is, a culture devoted to the gathering of everything edible. Most Indians know every plant in their territory that can be eaten, even though usually they don't bother with them. In many parts of the dry, Southwestern country there is a tiny potato— at least, it tastes like a potato—attached to some insignificant leaves aboveground. A Navaho, sitting and talking, may idly dig one up and chew on it; the true desert people hunted them painstakingly. They dug for all kinds of roots, for which reason, early white men called them "Diggers." They harvested the seeds of wild grasses— which was how the planting of wheat, corn, and other grains began, but in this environment the practice could lead to no farming.

They also hunted, for such hunting as there was. A group of men would spend days, if necessary, running down a deer, a very large game animal not often seen. Where there were antelope, the scattered groups would assemble once a year for a great drive, when the swift beasts were driven into a brush corral and killed. Then for a short time everyone feasted on red meat, and with so many camped in one place, there could be something like ceremonies, or at least dancing that was fun, and social life.

They hunted prairie dogs, pocket gophers, and rabbits, and were not above mice. Rabbits and birds were often caught by driving them into great nets, some of which were eight by thirty feet. They also hunted grasshoppers. They

Paiutes of the Kaibab Plateau, north of the Grand Canyon in Arizona, photographed in 1872 by Hillers, who was on the famous Powell expedition which first explored the full length of the Grand Canyon. The standing gentleman has been posed as a cigar-store Indian. The fringed, buckskin shirts show Plains influence. The Kaibab Plateau is better hunting country than most of the Great Basin, and deer are fairly plentiful there. The man kneeling at the right is kindling fire by spinning a stick in a strip of cedar bark, held by the other kneeling man.

Smithsonian Institution.

dug trenches, into which they drove the insects, which they roasted. The eating of such foods was used by white men as a reason for despising the "Diggers," hence an excuse for maltreating them. They could not mistreat them on the grounds that they were bloodthirsty savages, because they were not. They were too busy keeping alive to indulge in such luxuries as fighting. When they had to fight, they fought well, using spears twelve feet long and effective bows. They sometimes took scalps.

A sizable family could use up the food within several miles of its camp in a short time. Then it had to move on. The people had to live scattered out. Their dwellings were very simple wickeyups, the minimum necessary shelters of brush. So narrow was the margin of life that, in the most desert sections, very old people who could not longer move with the camp were left to die. An enclosure would be built, if possible by a spring, the ancient would be furnished with a blanket and a little food, and left. Sick infants were sometimes abandoned, also. This was not cruelty or heartlessness; it was dire necessity.

Under such circumstances, nonmaterial culture was extremely simple. In all the area now being described, not only in the Great Basin, true tribes are hard to find except at the edges, or after the deadly pressure of the white men forced people in desperation to unite. What we find mostly are bodies of people speaking alike, holding the same beliefs, who recognize a common relationship. Under favorable circumstances, these could gather once a year or so,

as for the antelope hunt, otherwise each family went by itself. You had, then, recognized wise men, sometimes called "talkers," to whose advice the tribe listened, but you had nothing like chiefs.

There were no clans. There was almost no organization at all. Similarly, religion was pared down to the simplest shamanism. Men inspired by dreams took up healing by means of magic, or were supposed to have the power to ensure a successful deer hunt, or a good supply of grasshoppers. Their position was fairly definite, but their rewards were small and a medicine man who lost a number of patients might be killed.

Power came through dreams or visions, but there was no fancy business here of the vision quest. If you had a significant dream in the night, there it was; if not, you went without.

Their mythology was equally simple, mostly tales about magical animals who had a hand in shaping the world, without any real account of an origin of the world or mankind. The tales are usually dull to our taste, inclined to be humorous, and often coarse. They are what tired people might tell at the end of a long, hard day, in the short time between eating and falling asleep.

There was a popular ceremony in which both men and women danced in a circle round a tree, singing songs about animals. The practice of men and women dancing together seems to be part of the Basin pattern, which spread later both to the Southwest and Plains, sometimes as a sociable element in a ceremonial, sometimes simply as fun. From the Basin also may come the fear of the dead which requires the burning of a dead man's house, forbiddance of using his name, and other observances largely intended to prevent the ghost from coming along to live with its relatives and friends. This fear exists in strong form among the Navahos and some of the Apaches, and is one item of evidence that some of them must have passed through the Basin area on their way to the Southwest.

The Southwest is a land with an abundance of usable clay and stone, which is reflected in the housing. A cotton-raising country, its people went in for woven garments. The Plains was above all a land of skins and hides. Habitations were made of hides, clothing of skins, ingenious uses of both run all through the culture. The Basin was a land of sticks, dry-country trees, and grasses. The people dressed in garments of grass or shredded bark, and also did a crude weaving of strips of rabbit skin worked through a warp of strings to make a warm robe. They practiced basketry extensively. The Paiutes in the south made extraordinarily fine basketry. It may have been from them that the Apaches learned their art. Navaho baskets are hard to distinguish from Paiute ones, and mainly the Navahos traded for their baskets, as they do today, even those used in their ceremonies.

In their life of catching small game, nets were important. Basketry was used for many things. Women wore basket hats. They cooked in baskets, by the process called "stone boiling." Stones are heated red hot and then dropped into a basket full of water, bringing it to a boil. This method is common wherever Indians must cook without fireproof pots. The Plains Indians did the same thing, only their containers were the carefully cleaned stomachs of buffaloes. Some of the Basin basketry and network look very like the ancient Basketmaker products. Very probably they inherited some of the early Basketmaker culture as it was before those people learned to farm, and, because their environment would not let them change, have preserved it to this day.

Human beings can become used to almost any kind of life, and even find beauty in it. The Eskimo produces poetry about his frozen homeland; plainsmen all over the world, on steppe, pampa, or plain, learn to love the fine gradations of light and shifting cloud shadow, the movement of grass in the wind, the sheer space, while mountain people despise the flat country and cling to their sky-reaching glories. The desert Basin people found goodness in their hard life, but it remains that they stayed where they were because they were few, weak, and poor. Through the summers they endured killing heat; in much of their country, their winters were a misery of wolf-fang cold.

Other Indians looked on them with pity and condescension. As late as the early nineteenth century there were Paiutes in the western part of what is now the Navaho Reservation, the driest part of the Navaho country. The

Hopis had contact with them there, and their name became a synonym for ignorance. If a Hopi starts talking about some sacred matter before an uninitiated child or a non-Hopi, someone will remark, "There is a Paiute here," as a way of warning the speaker.

The people described are the extreme; where opportunity offered, the Basin people bettered themselves. In northwestern Arizona, the Havasupais, who settled long ago in a strikingly beautiful, well-watered canyon leading into the Grand Canyon, do as much farming as their situation will permit. It is hard to say whether the Havasupais should be classed as Basin or Southwestern. There is the same difficulty about the Walapais, holding out in the highish, dry country further west. Both of these groups are Yuman by speech.

An extension of the Basin people, both Yuman and Uto-Aztecan, reaches across the hot country of southern California to the sea. To varying degrees their culture contains elements of the culture of the Yumas, described in Chapter VI. To the east, the rim of the Basin is the Rocky Mountains, not country for farming, but good for hunting. Here such tribes as the Utes were strong even before the time of

A piece of the canyon of the Havasupais, one of the most beautiful and isolated places in America. This picture shows the area occupied by the old Agency; the stone buildings are government work. On the right is a Havasupai house, with flat roof and thatched walls, rather like the Papago type.

Courtesy of American Museum of Natural History.

The Utes of the Colorado mountains became at least halfway Plains people. This is Ouray, a chief of the southern Utes who won a great reputation with the white men because of his acquiescence in selling out to them, which made him a "good" Indian.
Mercaldo Archives.

Storage basket of the Yavapais, almost finished (note the awl stuck into the rim at the left). The Yavapais are a northern Arizona tribe, closely related to the Havasupais.
Smithsonian Institution.

the horse, if the traditions of other tribes can be believed. After the coming of the horse, they became at least halfway a Plains people, although the perpendicular country they inhabited included nothing even faintly like plains. In historic times, they were feared even by such fighters as the Navahos.

As you go north, the Basin country rises steadily, to become the high Plateau country of Idaho, Oregon, Washington, and western Montana. Here the hunting was better, and the western tribes had access to rivers up which came the salmon from the Pacific. A form of lily, the camas, the root of which is excellent eating, grew plentifully in many places. Here we find two new language families, Salishan and Shahaptian. In this section tribes were somewhat more organized. In the summer, people scattered in search of food, but there were winter gatherings that might bring most of a tribe together.

These, too, were a people of basketry, scanty items of clothing made of bark fibers, rabbitskin robes, and brush shelters. The shelters were larger, often built on a gabled frame, and in the winter they built earth lodges. They also covered gabled frameworks with well-woven mats.

The strength that comes from visions was of vital importance. Women were born with certain powers—perhaps this belief was held because women were important as food-gatherers. Women could also have visions. Young men went to great lengths to obtain visions, tearing themselves with thorns, bathing in icy waters, starving. Through

the vision men received actual guardian spirits, who might return in later life to demonstrate that this man had been blessed. When a vision was due, usually in midwinter, the man gave a public feast lasting for many days, in the course of which he would fall unconscious, revive, sing an inspired song which a medicine man would interpret, then dance and sing around a bonfire. Others who had been similarly blessed would perform, in their turns, the dances and songs that had been revealed to them. Every man, it seems, was something of a shaman, although only the medicine men performed rites for others.

On the whole, these, too, were peaceful people. Most of their fighting was defensive in early times. Taken broadly, their culture looks like Basin culture as it would develop in better surroundings.

The coming of the horse, which reached the Umatilla of Oregon in 1739, made great changes. The tribes, until then foot travelers who also used some bark and dugout canoes, became more mobile. Some pushed toward the Plains, only to be pushed back, time and again, by the Blackfoot. Many were able to get in frequent buffalo hunting. The Nez Perces became on the whole a Plains people, like the Shoshones to the south of them. The way of life of such tribes as the groups now called Flatheads was changed. Those that could not reach the buffalo country were in the line of a new liveliness of trade of such goods as shells from the sea, and the horses themselves, against meat and skins. Plains war ideas spread among the eastern-

Rabbit Skin Leggings, one of four Nez Perce Indians who journeyed to Saint Louis with fur traders in 1831. Two of the Indians died in Saint Louis. George Catlin painted the portraits of the survivors. *Smithsonian Institution.*

Nez Perce woman, of fairly recent times. Her dress shows the strong Plains influence, but she still wears the basketry hat of the ancient Plateau-Basin tradition.

Courtesy of American Museum of Natural History.

No Horns on His Head, one of the two Nez Perces whom Catlin painted when they were returning to their home in the Northwest after visiting Saint Louis in 1831–32. Soon after this picture was painted, No Horns on His Head died. Catlin writes that they "were in beautiful Sioux dresses, which had been presented to them in a talk with the Sioux, who treated them very kindly, while passing through Sioux country." *Smithsonian Institution.*

Jason, a Nez Perce man, photographed in 1868.
Smithsonian Institution.

Chinookan woman and child, painted by Paul Kane about 1850. The shape of her head is due to intentional distortion done in infancy; the child's head is bound so as to cause the same effect. It is curious that this custom existed among the Mayas of southern Mexico and Central America. The woman's costume, a simple fur robe, is typical of the original style. *Royal Ontario Museum.*

Nez Perce couple before their tepee, and dog with travois. The Nez Perces lived in northeastern Oregon and adjacent parts of Idaho. *Museum of the American Indian.*

Shoshone camp in Wyoming, with Washakie's tent in the foreground. Washakie was an important chief of one of the bands of Shoshones that had come under strong Plains influence. Compare the crude decoration of his tepee with the elaborate and technically fine decorations of Plains tepees in Chapter VII.
Smithsonian Institution.

Appaloosa mares (top) and stallion (bottom) on the former Nez Perce range. *F. Haines and University of Oklahoma Press.*

most. The use of tepees spread well to the west, as did buckskin clothing, while canoeing fell off.

In the middle part of California, on the coast, and continuing on into Oregon, can be found a linguistic hodgepodge. Here are small groups speaking languages of almost every family. This seems to have been an area in which conditions were good, the climate mild, with the sea on one side and high mountains on the other, in which fragments of people passing through remained, to be joined by others who for one reason or another came over the mountains to seek refuge.

The northern part of this strip, from about the fortieth meridian on, was occupied by people of the Northwest Coast culture, taken up in the next chapter. South of there is what anthropologists mean when they say "California." The peoples of that portion show in varying degrees the influence of Basin culture, which is probably the original ingredient, Northwest Coast, and both the Yuman and Pueblo branches of Southwestern. The whole situation creates a wonderful playground for scientists and a great confusion for ordinary people.

These Indians had pretty decent hunting and good fishing. They developed ingenious modes of getting the varied game offered them. For instance, a hunter would let a number of wild gourds or other round objects of the right size float downstream past where ducks were feeding until the birds ceased to pay attention to them. Then he would float down with his head in one, and as he went by, grab a duck by the feet and pull it under water. This would not frighten the other ducks; the trick could be worked on the same flock a number of times in succession.

In the area are many oaks, the acorns of which can be made into a nourishing flour. This was a staple food. It took some ingenuity to work out this food, as acorns in their natural state are intolerably bitter with tannic acid. Altogether, six processes of grinding, leaching with water, drying, roasting, and so on were required before the flour could be used for gruel.

Among these groups we find about the finest of all the basket-weavers in America. The work is extraordinary, both for fineness of technique and excellence of design, often unbelievably delicate. Some baskets, into which brilliant, small feathers have been worked, have almost the effect of jewels.

Like the northern Atlantic coast Indians, these had a form of shell money, in this case flat beads of the dentalia shell. The beads they traded westward—necklaces of

Nez Perce Indian, painted by A. J. Miller. This man wears a ring through the septum of his nose, but the tribe got its name, Nez Perces, which is the French for "Pierced Noses," from French fur trappers who saw some of the people wearing dentalium shells in their noses.
Walters Art Gallery and University of Oklahoma Press.

Girl sketched in 1851 by the Salmon River in northern California. Her simple costume and tattooing are typical of the area.
Smithsonian Institution.

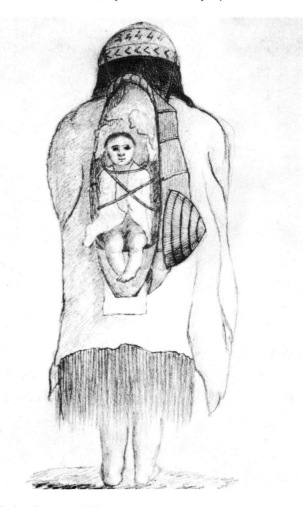

A sketch by George Gibbs of a northern California woman and child, seen at the junction of the Klamath and Trinity Rivers. She wears a basket hat and a simple robe over a grass skirt.
Smithsonian Institution.

Painting by Arthur A. Jansson, "Daily Life of the California Indians," tribe and location not specified, but probably toward the south. The woman at the right is grinding acorns into meal, the one at the left is cracking them, and at the extreme left a man with a helper is boring a shell to make a bead, using a stick similar to that used for making fire.

Courtesy of American Museum of Natural History.

such beads are highly prized by Arizona and New Mexico Indians even today—and used among themselves, where their value was fairly well fixed. The amount of shell paid for a wife might determine her and her children's future standing, and shell money featured in many other transactions.

During the summers, these Indians kept much on the move, gathering food. Seldom can people find enough wild food in one place to enable them to stay put. The pickings were good enough, however, to enable them to stay in sizable groups, and to take up a village life in the winter. Tribes were pretty clearly defined, most had clans with descent counted through the father, and many of them were divided into moieties or halves, which did various services for each other.

The men often went naked, or wore a breechclout of skin, or wrapped skin around their waists; women wore aprons in front and behind, of shredded bark or strings. They went barefoot most of the time, but also wore sandals made of fiber or crudely shaped skin moccasins. The men

Woman with baby in carrying board, and young chief, of the Yurok tribe of northern California. The sword-like object in the chief's right hand may be one of the obsidian blades that were painstakingly chipped for ceremonial use. Such blades were of no practical use, since a piece of obsidian or volcanic glass that size would shatter at the first blow. This drawing was made from a sketch drawn by Gibbs in October, 1851.

Smithsonian Institution.

189

Basket ornamented with shell beads and bright feathers, Wappo tribe. *Courtesy of American Museum of Natural History.*

Model of a Hupa woman, of the northern part of California, leaching the tannic acid out of acorn meal. The Hupa tribe actually belongs within the Northwest coast culture described in the next chapter, but being at the extreme southern edge of it, their way of life is transitional in part between that of the Northwest coast and of the main part of California. The costume and the method of preparing acorn meal are typical of California.

Courtesy of American Museum of Natural History.

Pomo woman weaving a large "mush bowl" basket. The Pomos of California are among the finest basketmakers in the world.

Courtesy of American Museum of Natural History.

Engraving of California Indian women originally published in Schoolcraft's *History of the Indian Tribes*, 1857.
Courtesy of American Museum of Natural History.

portance. The California tribes made a major ceremony of boys' and girls' initiation. They, too, felt that visions were essential to men, and they ensured that boys would have a vision during initiation by giving them a potent drug, a brew made from the root of the Jimson weed or *Datura stramonium.*

They were not exactly warlike, but quarrelsome. Each little tribe guarded its pocket of territory jealously, and acted immediately against trespassers. One tribe, the Maidu, even kept sentries posted along its boundaries. Often, when there was serious trouble, two tribes would line up, then each would pick a champion to fight it out for the tribe. After the fight, there was long consulting and haggling, ending with payments of shells, which settled the matter. Some scalps were taken, and when they were, it was not just a small piece off the top of the head, but everything, including the ears.

About half the tribes cremated their dead, like the Yumas, and had similar follow-up ceremonies. Often the moiety to which the deceased did not belong handled the funeral arrangements, so that the bereaved moiety was not contaminated. The house and valuable articles might be burned, including specially woven, extremely fine baskets, after which the taboo on mentioning the dead person's name was lifted. That taboo, it should be pointed out, is far more troublesome for primitive tribes who name people after objects than it would be for us. If the deceased's name is "White Deer," or "Oak Leaf," for instance, a couple of words in constant use must be dropped until in some way you can get around the taboo.

By and large, the North American Indians encouraged generosity, often of a somewhat showy kind. Such tribes

decorated their heads with arrangements of bright, small feathers. They made rabbitskin robes, and also feather blankets. Great quantities of feathers were tied to strings, which were then woven.

In the southern part, houses were cone-shaped, a framework of poles solidly thatched with grass, often tied on roots and all. Some had smoke holes, some did not, but almost all had two small doorways opposite each other. In the north, the houses were more solidly built, and many were partly underground.

Their religion and ceremonies, as might be expected, fell in between the scanty practices of the ever-wandering desert people and the elaborate fixed rituals possible to farmers. They had ceremonies for such purposes as ensuring the coming of the salmon, some of them had masked dancers, and some had dancers completely disguised with feathers who seem to relate to the kachinas of the Pueblos. A number of tribes made a crude kind of ground painting, suggestive of the Southwestern "sand paintings," by pouring dry colors on a circle of smoothed earth.

Where rituals are few, a good deal of attention is likely to be paid to the strange things that happen when a girl becomes a woman, and similar attention may be extended to a boy's turning into a man. A very poor people, like those in the desert, cannot give too much time to such matters, while for peoples such as the Pueblos, with their great, elaborate rituals, these individual matters lose im-

Large, conical basket made by the Pomos.
Courtesy of American Museum of Natural History.

191

Models of Hupa man and woman in aboriginal costume. The man holds a flat, broad bow. These bows are powerful, and in recent years non-Indian archers in California have modified the English bow form somewhat under the influence of this type, producing an excellent hunting bow. These Indians could get yew, the same wood as used in England for bows.

Courtesy of American Museum of Natural History.

as the Hopis, who knew the famine that a drouth year can cause, might keep a year's supply of corn laid by, but even among them there was a great deal of giving and sharing. Perhaps because of the strong development of shell money, many of the California tribes preached the opposite, a rather mean thrift. Amassing quantities of shell became an end in itself.

The Spanish occupied Southern California as they did New Mexico. In California they established strong missions. The priests gathered in the roving Indians, with no little use of force. The idea was to settle them in villages, teach them useful arts, including farming, and make them into an exploitable, Christian labor force. A good many of the wanderers found this new way of life confining, and the clothes they were made to wear stifled them. Some died of it. The others became accustomed to the new mode of life. They did not become self-sufficient, but dependent upon the priests; essentially, they were not farmers but farm laborers.

When Mexico became independent, funds for support of the missions were cut off and most of them closed down. Then the "Mission Indians" were lost. They neither knew how to survive as they had in the old days, nor how to take care of themselves in the new manner. They suffered

Washakie's great-granddaughter poses as Sacajawea, the Shoshone woman who accompanied and guided the Lewis and Clark expedition to explore the Northwest. The mere fact that a woman and baby accompanied them was a tremendous help, since that immediately showed the new tribes they met that they were not a war party. *U. S. Dept. of Interior.*

made remarkable efforts to continue as groups, maintaining their identity and ancestral values.

At first the white men wanted only to pass through the Basin and Plateau areas, so that they troubled the Indians relatively little. Later, they began to take up the land. Not many of the tribes were well enough organized to offer serious resistance. The finding of gold and silver in Nevada brought great trouble to the Indians there. Throughout, the increasing white population destroyed the narrow margin of food. Many of the desert people became hangers-on around white settlements; some never received title to any land until the 1930's. The stronger tribes of the Plateau country fared somewhat better.

One group, a part of the loosely organized tribe called Nez Perce of Idaho and Oregon, did put up a resistance that is famous. One of their leaders was a remarkable Indian named Chief Joseph. They faced an all too familiar situation. They had accepted a reservation peaceably. Then they agreed to cede part of it. Part was not enough; the white men wanted Chief Joseph's homeland. Some of his young men resisted, and started fighting. With other

The eastern, Plains-like Shoshones befriended the white men, who for long wished only to pass through their territory. Washakie, shown here, was one of their strongest chiefs. Fort Washakie in Wyoming is named for him. He is credited with one of the shortest and most effective formal speeches in history. An Indian Bureau official was sent out to persuade the Shoshones to take up farming. After he had made his speech, the ordinary men and lesser chiefs had their say pro and con. Then Washakie rose to summarize. Summoning up what little English he knew, he said, "God damn a potato!" *Smithsonian Institution.*

greatly. To add to their sorrows, came the discovery of gold in 1849 and then the gold rush that filled California with white men. The little groups were thrust aside, and now, too, the tribes farther north were overwhelmed.

A series of treaties was negotiated, by which the Indians gave up most of the country in exchange for small reservations. Pressure from what had become the new state of California prevented the treaties from being ratified, although the Indians had moved out of the land they had surrendered therein. There was nothing for the unfortunate little tribes to do but drift about, scrabbling for a living as best they could. Finally pieces of land were set aside for them, usually the poorest there was. The result was a curious mess, with 116 reservations in the state, ranging in size from over 25,000 acres to 2 acres. Few of the shattered tribes could keep their culture, although some have

Chief Joseph of the Nez Perces, one of the ablest statesmen the North American Indians ever produced. After his surrender, General Miles, his antagonist, constantly befriended him out of admiration and personal liking. *Mercaldo Archives.*

Nez Perce bands, they fought magnificently, but they were hopelessly outnumbered, so they decided to move to Canada, where, as all Indians knew, treaties were not broken. They conducted a fighting retreat, with their women and children accompanying them, that is considered one of the great retreats of military history.

Cold, weary, near starvation, they were caught and surrounded almost within sight of the Canadian border. Chief Joseph was offered honorable terms, and he surrendered. The terms were promptly forgotten, and he and his band were shipped to Oklahoma, where many of them died in the low altitude and the heat.

Looking Glass, one of the great war leaders of the Nez Perces, photographed in 1871. He was killed during the famous retreat with Chief Joseph, in 1877. His leggings are made of a Hudson's Bay Company four-point blanket, his buckskin shirt shows Plains influence, while his headdress is evidence of contact with white men. His horse has been painted in stripes. *Smithsonian Institution.*

IX. The Eagle, the Raven, and the Whale

At the extreme northwestern corner of the United States, beginning on the coast of the north end of California and continuing along a narrow, coastal strip to British Columbia and on up along the tongue of Alaska that projects southward from the main part of that great territory, a remarkable native culture developed with very little outside help. The discoveries and inventions that made possible the advancement of the Southeast and Southwest, shaped the Iroquois, changed the character of the Algonkians, created the Midwestern farmers, and even affected the mounted nomads of the Plains, could not reach here.

The culture is called "Northwest Coast." The people belong to a number of language families, in which they resemble the little language islands all along California. Starting in Alaska, the most important are the Tlingit; south of them are the Haida in British Columbia. Both of these groups (they are not tribes) speak languages related to Athapascan, but so changed that they must have separated from the main mass of the Athapascans long ago. South of them are the Tsimshian, speaking one of a number of languages that many authorities think may form a single family, for which they propose the name "Penutian." Then come the Kwakiutl and Nootka, whose languages are related to each other and also, more distantly, to Salishan tongues. Tribes of Salish speech, unquestionably immigrants from the Plateau area, are the Bella Coola of British Columbia and Coast Salish of Washington. The Chinook were along the Columbia River which divides Washington from Oregon, another group suggested as belonging to the doubtful Penutian family. North and south of them was an assortment of small groups, some of which were straight Athapascan, and in California three side by side, belonging to three quite separate families—the Karok, of unknown relationship, the Athapascan Hupas, and Algonkian Yuroks. So much diversity in a small space must mean that the long, very narrow coastal strip was occupied little by little, by many groups of different origins.

In the name of the culture, the word "Coast" is important, for it was based on access to the sea and the mouths of rivers. When we look for influences, we find archeological evidence of an early, Eskimo-like culture in the area, and various ways of doing among the historic Indians that seem to be elaborations of Eskimo ways. In the Eskimo indications we find also traces of an ancient, primitive Siberian Iron Age culture, and there was even a limited amount of actual iron, mostly worked into knives, probably of Siberian origin.

There are those influences. There are items, as we should expect, from the Plateau people, others that point to the northern Athapascans who lived in Canada behind the high, rugged coastal mountains. Here, however, is something different; instead of a primitive people affected by contact with a far more advanced one, we have a group that took over primitive elements and themselves proceeded to advance. The chief influence is Eskimo, and Eskimo techniques for fishing and for hunting the mammals of the sea—such as seals and whales—are beautifully developed, but the Eskimos, by and large, are not an advanced people.

There is another unique element here. Up to now we have seen what we expect, that cultural progress followed upon farming. Farmers have a food supply that gives them spare time, and farmers do not wander about. Spare time sitting around in one place is what leads to inventions. The Plains Indians had a magnificent food supply, although not through the whole of the year, but their life was mobile. They encumbered themselves with nothing that would hamper mobility.

The Northwest Coast had no agriculture at all, except for a little tobacco planting in a few places. It had a moderate supply of berries, and some access to the starchy camas roots. It had poor to good hunting of deer, bear, mountain sheep, and elk, and some very good hunting of migratory birds. What it had in abundance was the food of the sea. The salmon, in five varieties, ran up the rivers in great quantities every year; there were runs of herring, smelt, and olachen—also known as "candlefish," since it is so oily that you can pull a wick through a dry olachen and burn it like a candle. In addition, there are halibut, cod, flounder, and quantities of shellfish. Add to these the sea mammals—hair seal (not the fur kind), porpoises, sea lions, and whales. There was all the food in the world along the coast.

When the deep-sea fish ran up the rivers in great masses to spawn were the times when food could be caught most easily and in the greatest quantities. Once the people had learned to preserve all they could catch, a rhythm developed of periods of great activity and periods of taking it easy. Having half a ton or so of dried salmon stored up made a family as unlikely to move about as having an equal store of corn. The great lack in the diet was starch, except for the tribes that could dig camas. This lack, plus the need to keep warm in a damp, cool climate, may explain the Indians' great fondness for grease and oil. Many of them took enthusiastically to planting potatoes as soon as they had them. In southern Oregon and northern California the Indians used acorn meal, as did the California cultures.

A prized delicacy for feasts was made by whipping a mixture of soapberry, olachen oil, and cold water into a froth. Ice cream has largely replaced this dish. A "salmon cheese" was made by storing salmon in boxes until it was runny, and more than runny. Many white men love strong cheeses, but almost without exception we prefer cheeses that do not wave at us.

Cooking was by stone-boiling in watertight baskets and boxes, by baking or steaming in pits with hot stones, and by broiling. The Northwest Coast people had leisure to elaborate their cookery, among other things. Around 1900 a housewife of a Kwakiutl tribe gave an anthropologist 150 recipes without coming to the end of her mental cookbook.

The climate of the Northwest Coast ranges from chilly to mild. The Japanese Current makes winters fairly easy even in the north; it also brings an enormous amount of

rain. Right behind the coast in the northerly part rise the rugged mountains, difficult to get through. In Oregon they become lower and gentler, allowing more access to the land behind. In addition to the big rivers that come through to the sea, the great amount of water dropped on the high country produces many small ones. The northern part is a land of off-shore islands and narrow, deep, fjord-like inlets. All in all, although in modern times the United States part of it, at least, has proven good country for certain kinds of wheat and for apples, it is not a land in which to raise corn; but the layout for fishing is splendid.

Hunting land animals was something of a luxury in the north, as well as a hardy sport. It increased in the south, until, when we come to the Hupa and neighboring tribes in California, marginal members of the Northwest Coast group, we find hunting deer a major activity. The tribes up against the steep mountains, however, did successfully hunt mountain goats, a quarry that a modern hunter thinks it rare luck to get within the telescopic sights of a high-powered rifle.

The northern hunters of the Northwest Coast not only killed these animals, but their preferred weapon for doing so was a spear. The method of hunting was for one or a few men to work along, letting their presence be detected enough to make the goats move along in the direction

Impression of Northwest Coast life by the artist A. A. Jansson. In the background, across the inlet, can be seen the village. A chief's canoe is on the water. The dancer in the bow, costumed as Eagle, shows that the chief is on a ceremonial visit. In the foreground two men are spearing salmon, one is cutting cedar bark to strip it from a tree, another is cutting through a log with fire, controlled by water leaking from a box and poured from a dipper. The men would probably not be wearing the kilts shown, but either nothing or a breech-clout in mild weather.

Courtesy of American Museum of Natural History.

Model of the secret shrine of a Nootka whaler. Most dangerous of all hunting, whaling called for the most elaborate rituals.
Courtesy of American Museum of Natural History.

the hunters wanted, but without really frightening them. Slowly the quarry would be worked downhill and into a narrow, steep gorge or other suitable place, where they could be penned. Other hunters, waiting ready, then closed in and made the kill.

This procedure required enormous skill in stalking and climbing, and an exact knowledge of the terrain. To the Indian mind, it required also supernatural help. The knowledge, the right to acquire the skill, the right to use the places where the mountain goats could be trapped, and the rituals, were all possessions. They were the property of chiefs, jealously guarded and inherited according to the system of inheritance of the group. This pattern of property is common in the culture.

It was the prerogative of chiefs, also, to hunt whales. Whaling was almost entirely confined to the Nootka tribes of British Columbia and Washington, who were fine coastwise seamen and skilled boat-builders. They could turn out a seaworthy vessel well over fifty feet long.

The ritual for whaling was elaborate and exacting, the equipment expensive. The chief himself was the harpooner.

The line from the harpoon had to be laid on board so that it ran out without a hitch, as in our own early whaling, but the arrangement was made more difficult by the fact that four buoys of inflated sealskin were tied to the line at intervals. The harpoon was too heavy to throw. The whaleboat sneaked up alongside the whale's left side from the rear, getting close enough for the harpooner, standing with his right foot on the gunwhale, to drive the harpoon home. Immediately the crew paddled for all it was worth to break away to port before the whale crushed them. A second whaleboat, commanded by a relative of the chief, might be along, and have the honor of putting in the second harpoon, when the victim began to tire from dragging the line and floats and from loss of blood.

By and by, if the whale did not destroy the whalers first, it would be worn out. Then a lance with a chisel-like blade was used to cut the tendons of the whale's flukes, leaving it helpless. After that, the killing lance was driven to its heart. If the ritual had been exactly performed, during the chase the whale would have come close to the beach; if there had been some error, it would have gone out to sea.

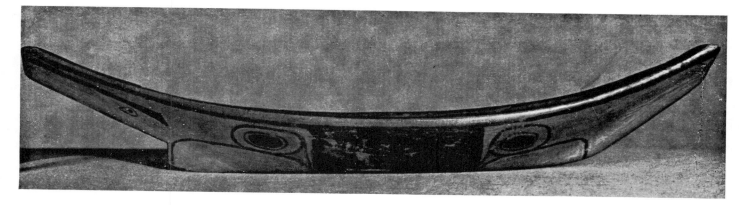

Native-made, painted cedar model of a Haida chief's sea-going canoe. This shows very well the beautiful lines of these boats, the sharp bow leading to the forefoot and the easy curve of the stern.

Northwest Coast bow-lines are believed by some authorities to have influenced the builders of the original clipper ships.
Washington State Museum.

In the latter case, the crew might have a couple of days and nights of steady paddling, towing the beast, before they landed it.

Hunting, or leading the hunt for, other sea-mammals were also chiefly prerogatives. The method of hunting mountain goat is astonishing, the whaling spectacular; all the fishing was ingenious and competent. They used hooks and lines (the hooks made of bone), spears, harpoons, traps, and a variety of nets. They had dip-nets, worked by a single man, and seines handled by a crew. One mode of catching herring, when they were running, is unusual. Two men would go out in a canoe. One paddled, the other handled a paddle-like board with teeth along one side of the blade. While his partner made the canoe go, he moved this much as a paddle is moved, the teeth to the rear, at each stroke hitting and spiking one or more herring, which he flipped into the boat.

The Northwest Coast people were not seafarers as, for instance, the Polynesians were. They did not use sails until after contact with white men, and although some of them made coastwise voyages of a hundred miles or more, they hated to get out of sight of land. Still, they were supremely at home in their canoes. If a canoeman came across an animal such as a deer, elk, or bear swimming, he would catch up with it and beat it over the head with his paddle until he had reduced it to a condition in which, also with his paddle, he could shove its head under and drown it. Then he would haul it on board.

We have described cultures of meat and hide, of crops with stone and clay, others in which bark was of vital importance. The Northwest Coast culture is founded on fish and wood. All along the coast wood was plentiful, above all the great evergreens—spruce, fir, yew, and redwood in the south, and best of all, the easily workable cedar. The canoes were hollowed out of wood, houses built solidly of wood, utensile of all kinds were made of wood. Cedar bark was worked up into yarn and woven for clothing. Mats were made of bark and of reed. A baby's cradle would be lined with bark, pounded and worked into a padding soft as cotton. There were few tricks of woodworking they did not know, from mortising to shaping in a steam box. In their woodwork, they were helped by having a few iron tools, but mostly, in a land where workable stone was scarce, they used chisels, adzes, and knives with blades of sharp, strong shell.

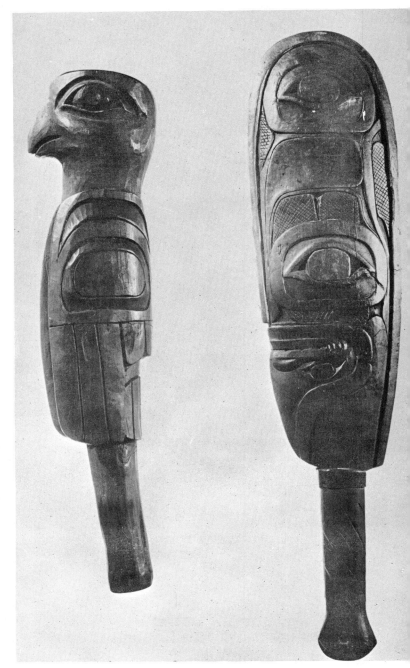

Haida carved clubs for killing halibut after they are caught. *Courtesy of American Museum of Natural History.*

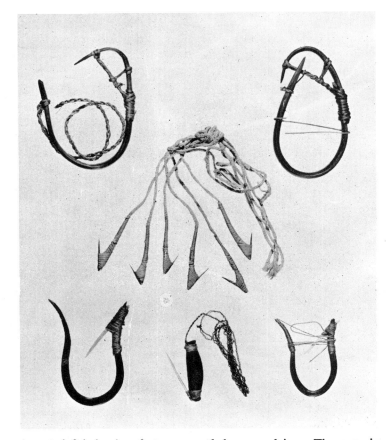

Assorted fish hooks of stone, wood, bone, and iron. The ones in the middle row, with iron points, are for trout. At the bottom, left, is a small halibut hook. The lines and wrappings are made of cedar bark. *Courtesy of American Museum of Natural History.*

Two daggers. The left one, the tribal origin of which is unknown, is carved out of whalebone. The right, from the Tlingits, is of copper. The hilt has a bird design, inlaid with shell and a red bead for the eye. *Southwest Museum, Los Angeles, Cal.*

Stone chisel or stabbing knife, tribe unknown, collected by Captain James Cook in 1778. *Copyright photograph, British Museum.*

Modern Indians of northern Washington and their neighbors from British Columbia lined up for their annual canoe race.
U. S. Dept. of Interior.

Group of Tlingit baskets. The one on the lower left is decorated with fairly realistic killer whales; the designs on the others are purely geometric.
Courtesy of American Museum of Natural History.

Coastal village and people "midway of British Columbia"—probably Kwakiutl—taken in the 1880's. The picture shows the house construction, everyday canoes, and totem poles. The arrangement of the planks vertically, instead of horizontally, came in when the Indians could get nails.
Courtesy of American Museum of Natural History.

Top view of Haida basket hat. The design represents Eagle, split in the typical manner and painted around each side of the crown.
Washington State Museum.

In addition to iron, they had some copper, acquired by trade with Indians in the Canadian subarctic, where free copper can be found. As in other parts of the New World where this metal could be obtained, it was regarded as precious; here it was beaten into sheets of various sizes, called "coppers," which were highly valued. It was also worked into knife blades. Copper is a soft metal for such use, but by hammering it when it is cold, it can be given enough temper to make it serviceable.

Among the articles they made of wood were masks, chests, boxes, bowls, spoons, cradles, rattles, and of course, their houses, their canoes, and the famous so-called "totem" poles. They made waterproof boxes, in which they boiled food by dropping hot stones into the water. With their skill at working wood, they naturally evolved an art of carving, which they then carried over to horn. They carved wood, painted it, steamed and bent it, fitted it, and inlaid it with shell, mica, and copper. They also did a little stone carving, and in the nineteenth century, after our tools became common among them, developed a fine technique of slate carving. Their extraordinary art, however, cannot be understood until after we have had a look at their religious ideas and their social organization.

Their basketry was fine, almost as fine as the best California. They knew the tricks of weaving by twining weft strands through warp strands hanging free from a "half loom," that is, an upper bar with no lower bar. Essentially, this technique is more closely related to basketry than to weaving with a shuttle. It was practiced in crude form by the Basin people and others in the making of rabbitskin robes. Along the Northwest Coast it was developed to a high pitch, producing blankets and other

Model of part of a Kwakiutl village. Two houses, with vertical board walls, are painted. The settlement is placed on the edge of the steep bank above the shore, with platforms built out from the bank and steps hewed out of single logs leading to where the canoes are beached below.
Courtesy of American Museum of Natural History.

Salish interior scene by the mid-nineteenth-century artist Paul Kane. Kane's work was romantic; his paintings, worked up from sketches after he got home, often inaccurate. It is difficult to explain just what sort of dwelling those people are occupying. The whole loom, however, is well shown. By it sits one of the dogs from which the Salish sheared wool. At the back is a woman spinning yarn. To the left, a baby hangs in a Plateau-like cradleboard. Its head is wrapped to flatten the forepart. *Royal Ontario Museum.*

Model of Kwakiutl domestic activities. At the left a woman is twining a cedar-bark robe on a half loom. At the right a seated woman is breaking up cedar bark on the edge of a paddle. The standing woman behind her is drying salmon. The bark-worker's head has been artificially deformed by applied pressure in baby-hood. In the hanging plain cradle is a baby swaddled in cedar bark, with a pad tied over its forehead to alter the shape of its head in the same manner. At the back of the model, one man is painting a box, another picks up a hot stone between sticks to drop into a box of water.

Courtesy of American Museum of Natural History.

garments with elaborated designs in the native colors of yellow, blue, and black plus the background color of the material. The principal type of yarn was made from cedar bark, but mountain goat wool was used, while the Salish raised a special breed of small, woolly dogs, which they sheared as we do sheep. Usually these wools were combined with bark, as by using a wool weft through a bark warp.

The Northwest Coast people lived in a cool, damp climate. They had available good materials for clothing, if to shredded bark we add the various woven materials (all rather scratchy), moderate to good supplies of buckskin, elkskin, and bearskin, sea and river otter and beaver fur, and even some caribou from inside the mountain ranges. Immediately northwards from them were the Eskimos, who made fine, beautifully tailored garments of considerable elaboration. Northwest Coast dressing, however, seems to have been in order to display rank or ceremonial authority plus the minimum necessary to keep out cold and wet. If anything, display counted for more than comfort. While they knew how to make moccasins, they often went barefoot even in snow, and apparently did not mind it.

Early Chilkat (Tlingit) blanket with painted design. The principal figure is Raven shown in profile, with two faces as fillers for the space of his body and two others in the decorative units below. *Inverarity, Art of the Northwest Coast Indians.*

Chilkat mountain goat's wool blanket of a more usual type, black, yellow, green, and white, with highly formalized design. The design represents a diving whale, as may be told by comparison with other designs, but is so conventionalized as to be virtually unrecognizable. Chilkat women, unlike the Navaho, copied designs painted for them by the men. *Washington State Museum.*

In warm weather men went naked unless they had reason to wear insignia of whatever rank they might have. Women wore bark skirts. In cold and wet weather, robes or capes, often of shredded cedar bark, and a basket hat gave protection. The Salish, who had the most advanced weaving techniques, including the use of a "whole" loom, also made robes of downy feathers strung on threads. The Chilkat branch of the Tlingits, famous for their weaving, frequently went through the mountains into the Athapascan country in the interior. From the Athapascans they copied a one-piece trousers-and-moccasins outfit, on the order of a fisherman's waders or small child's pajama trousers, and fringed buckskin shirts with porcupine quill embroidery. Buckskin, we might note, is not a good material in a very wet climate, as it soaks up water like chamois and becomes equally slippery and nasty when really wet.

The tribes from the Nootka in Washington northwards were definitely warlike; those to the south perhaps might be described as quarrelsome and not afraid of a fight. After trade with the white men began, tribes that had suffered from the piratical conduct of many of the seafarers who came to deal with them, did not hesitate, in retaliation, to attack the next ship that came along. In 1799 the Russians established a fort in Tlingit territory near Sitka; three years later, the Tlingits wiped it out. As late as 1852, the Chilkats sent an expedition three hundred miles inland to destroy a fortified Hudson's Bay Company post, because until that post was established they had had a monopoly of trade with the Indians of the area. They behaved remarkably humanely, turning the people

Bella Coola group in ceremonial costume, drummer seated at left, engraving after a photograph taken before 1878. The group is unusual for the number of feathers worn directly in the hair. Four of the men wear Chilkat-type robes, the others simpler, cedar-bark ones, except for the man standing at the right, whose robe might be of woven fur or feathers. *Smithsonian Institution.*

they captured loose with a strong warning to stay out of the region.

The Lewiltok branch of the Nootka dominated part of the passage between Vancouver Island and the mainland. They levied tribute even on strong war parties going through. This caused them to be attacked frequently, but they stood off the attacks and went right on.

Nootka men in everyday summer costume, on the beach by their canoe. Photo taken in 1873. Several men have short beards.

Northwest Coast Indians had more face hair than most Indians, and were often markedly light-skinned. *Smithsonian Institution.*

Chinookan Indian, painted by A. J. Miller, an early visitor to the far west. The Chinooks, living along the Columbia River, became famous as middlemen and traders between the coastal tribes just west of them and the Indians in or near the buffalo country.
Walters Art Gallery and University of Oklahoma Press.

From the Nootkas north we find true war, so rare in North America, waged to wipe out or drive out another tribe. We do not find the pattern of self-advancement through brave killing or running risks, the war honors system that begins in the Southeast and carries through, with so many changes, to the western end of Plains influence. The reason for the warfare was that here was one of the few places in North America where there was something like a crowding of population. The land between the steep, bleak mountains and the sea was narrow, in places so narrow as to make it hard to find good sites for villages. The fishing was good all over, but there were places better than others. There were many reasons why a group that was increasing might desire to eliminate a neighbor, even if it was of the same language and customs.

South of the Nootka the fighting was mostly in feuds, vengeance by relatives of a slain man. Vengeance brought counter-vengeance. Feuds were ended by payment of indemnities for the men killed. Deaths on each side did not cancel each other out, but each man was the subject of long haggling, according to the dead man's rank. Among the groups in California, the worth of a slain man was the amount of shell money paid as his mother's bridal price.

Feuds of this kind occurred in the north also. Among these more warlike people, it was sometimes impossible to come to an agreement on the price to pay for the killing of a man of importance. For the good of the group, a chief or noble related to the killer, of approximately the same rank as the victim, might offer himself. He put on his finest regalia with his highest insignia, and came from his house to the enemy dancing a stately dance that was part of his inheritance. If the other side had good manners, it would wait until he had come close to the warriors before killing him.

There was also plain raiding, one of the main purposes of which was to capture slaves. As the general economy stood, there was not much need for slaves, but having a few around the house showed that a chief was either a successful war leader, or rich enough to buy an expensive article. Also, in the potlatch exhibitions described later, a fine way to show off one's wealth and one's prodigality was to have a slave killed, using for the purpose the correct weapon, commonly called a "slave killer."

Captives taken from neighboring villages were usually ransomed without delay. Slaves that were kept were taken from farther away. After the Yankees entered into the Northwest Coast trade, they often bought slaves in California and carried them north to trade with the Alaskan tribes.

When an important chief died, many tribes felt called upon to stage a raid, so that the chief might be accompanied by others, or, as some said, so that others might be mourning, too. On such a raid, the party would kill the first eligible victim that came to hand and might even choose a member of their own group, if they met him alone in his canoe.

Weapons included bows, a variety of clubs, spears, and an efficient knife for infighting, with a long, heavy blade and a second, short blade fastened to the upper end of the handle. Some of the big war canoes were built with a high shield at the bow, pierced for archery, making them into a useful type of landing craft for beach operations. The Indians also used armor. Helmets were made of wood, usually carved into horrifying faces. Slats strung together were wrapped around the body, or cuirasses of heavy hide were worn.

Social organization and religion were closely interwoven. Each village was an independent unit, and might make war upon other villages of the same speech and customs or might be loosely allied with some of them. Villages were grouped around a core of relatives. In the north, there were clans, with descent traced through the mother. In the south, many groups counted descent as we do, through both father and mother, with emphasis on the father's line. Inheritance, which was of vital importance here, went the same way. Where the clan system obtained, the village was organized around a clan. Some had moieties, usually Eagle and Raven or Raven and Wolf. Common clan names were Eagle, Raven, Wolf, and Blackfish, the last name referring to both the killer whale and black whale.

In the north the important thing was that within the group, however organized, there were lines of descent, or lineages, of different rank. The highest of these traced their descent back in a straight line to a supernatural animal, such as Raven, Eagle, or Bear, or to a human who had had a special experience with a supernatural being and from it received special powers and rights. In this we can see an original element of the familiar shaman concept, but it has been formalized into something quite different. The individual's ancestry, and certain other experiences subsequent to the original one, including unusual achievements, gave him the right to certain insignia, or "crests," such as are carved on the so-called totem poles. From the accumulation of these things, and also by certain methods of purchase, came also such possessions—as the Indians thought of them—as the right to dance certain dances, sing certain songs, perform certain rituals, the ownership of salmon-catching areas, the right to hunt whales, and so forth. In the south, the hereditary principle weakened, and purchase became more important.

Out of the variety of crests, rights, and prerogatives developed a detailed system of grading—from chiefs, who had a great deal, down through the nobility to the common people, the poorest of whom had no honors or special rights at all. Below them were the slaves.

What the individual, commoner or noble or chief, owned, was not purely his own. It was also property of the group as a while, giving them all status as compared with other groups, working to their benefit. Thus when a chief was called upon to give a great feast to the chiefs and nobles of another group, everybody gladly pitched in to help and contribute, and in due course the chief paid everybody back.

In the religion, there was a clear base of shamanism, greatly elaborated. The usual magical tricks by which shamans proved their power were elaborated into real theatrical devices. Many major ceremonies were put on by firelight inside the great houses, a situation that made deceptions easy, since such details as fine strings that made masks open and become something else, or by which objects were made to fly through the air, could not be seen. Supernatural figures came flying down through the smoke hole. Magicians were put into wooden boxes, the boxes burned, and the magician reappeared unharmed. Speaking tubes made of kelp enabled performers to make voices sound from strange parts of the building.

An important factor in bringing about the shift from shamanism—dependence on the religious magic of inspired individuals—to formal religion, is the existence of some cycle in time of vivid importance to the people, usually connected with their basic food supply. This we have already seen among the farming peoples. In the Southwest in early July, everyone is waiting for the rain

Tlingit wooden helmet, decorated with tufts of hair. The horrible face carved on it was probably intended to frighten the enemy.

Helmets of this kind were worn with a collar of wood underneath, to take up the force of a blow and protect the neck.
Museum of Anthropology; University of California.

Haida slate carving illustrating the legend of the origin of the Bear Clan. According to the story, a woman was captured and taken as wife by the king of bears, by whom she had a child, half human and half bear. She was finally rescued by a group of hunters. The carving shows the great pain she suffered when she nursed an infant with bear's teeth. The projecting lower lip is standard in representations of women; it derives from an enlargement of the lip caused by inserting a labret, or ornament of shell or other decorative substance. *Smithsonian Institution.*

Another slate carving of the ancestress of the Bear Clan When we compare this with the first example, we see that on the Northwest Coast, unlike in most of North America, men had reached the quality of true artists as distinct from gifted craftsmen. In the Southwest, for instance, a subject of this kind would always be shown in the same manner, as in the carving of Hopi kachina dolls. Here, as in our sacred art, the individual artist expresses his conception. In this version, the interest is less in the pain of the mother and more in her character as a person of royal status. She wears a headdress with Bear's ears, appropriately, and has other Bear attributes, such as hair on her cheeks. The child is shown as a bear cub, rather than as a human with bear's teeth. The general effect is one of dignity and loftiness rather than action.

Courtesy of American Museum of Natural History.

Tsimshian potlatch mask of cedar, representing Man-Burned-in-the-Fire, for which there was a special dance. The teeth are bone, the scars of the burns are human skin tacked on.
Provincial Museum, Victoria, B. C.

Kwakiutl wooden rattle trimmed with fur. The main body of the rattle represents a crane. The crane's tail becomes a mountain goat's head, and the goat's horns form the legs of the spirit shaman, who is split into two halves, riding the crane's back.
Washington State Museum.

Kwakiutl wooden mask portraying a mythical character called Tlaolacha, also used in potlatch dances.
Provincial Museum, Victoria, B. C.

Tlingit mask representing Hawk. The sharply hooked beak is all that identifies the bird, since this is not "a hawk," but a special Hawk spirit of a semi-human, semi-divine nature.
Inverarity, The Art of the Northwest Coast Indians.

An unusual Tsimshian mask. It is painted white, with red lips, nostrils, and a red line on the nose. Originally it had a mustache and goatee of animal hair tacked onto it. It represents a white man, and is almost surely a portrait of a particular individual.
Provincial Museum, Victoria, B. C.

Tlingit wooden headdress, painted black and decorated with human hair. It represents Whale, as shown by the symbols of the high fin and round eye. Northwest Coast headdresses appear to be derived from masks, and have much the appearance of masks worn on top of the head instead of over the face.

Washington State Museum.

Kwakiutl chief's headdress, carved, painted, and inlaid with aba- lone shell. The design includes Whale at the top, Raven, and a human head, and relates to a myth of the lineage.

Wolfgang Paalen Collection, Vancouver, B. C.

Collection of rattles. In most parts of the United States, rattles were made by putting small stones or similar articles inside a globe made of dried skin, wood, or a gourd. Here they were often made simply of shells or bird's beaks strung so as to rattle against each other when shaken.

Courtesy of American Museum of Natural History.

Tsimshian mask representing the moon.
Courtesy of American Museum of Natural History.

Kwakiutl wooden mask, larger than life size, representing a clan ancestor who came to earth in the form of an eagle. He turned himself into a human being, but could not change his beak into a nose. *Courtesy of American Museum of Natural History.*

Kwakiutl masked dancers photographed in front of a chief's house about 1910. The effect of these when performing indoors, by fire-light, can be imagined.
Courtesy of American Museum of Natural History.

Kwakiutl chief, holding a copper, photographed shortly before 1895. He wears a trade blanket decorated with shell buttons and pieces of native worked shell. *Smithsonian Institution.*

with intense anxiety. To leave the bringing of it to a few specialists would be emotionally impossible; everyone wants to help.

The cycles here were the yearly return of the various spawning fish, especially the salmon. Salmon hatch high up in the rivers. As small, un-salmonlike fish called parr they swim down the rivers and disappear into the sea. No one knows where they go. After a number of years, when they are full-grown, these creatures return to the exact place in which they were spawned to spawn in their turn, and literally kill themselves to do so.

The Indians saw the salmon running up the rivers each year. They saw how those that they themselves did not kill finally died in the high waters. They did not associate the parr with the salmon. They came to the conclusion that these fish were immortal. The fish swam into the rivers voluntarily to feed mankind (and bears), died, and were reborn in the ocean. Here was something that called for major ritual in order to keep it going, as well as for great care in returning all salmon skeletons intact to the water. The ritual involved everybody, but tended to attach itself to the chiefs who owned the fishing grounds.

The same beliefs, naturally, were held for the herring, smelt, and olachen. Then they were extended to deer and other animals. With them came more rituals.

The position of a chief was a curious blend of ritual prerogatives which were also duties, inherited rank, and wealth, which in themselves enabled him to acquire more wealth. As part of his position, he sought to exhibit his

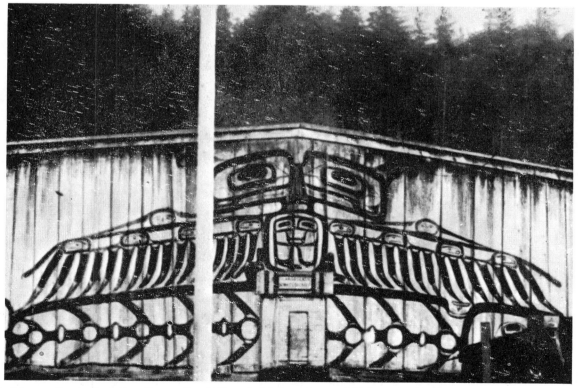

Painted Kwakiutl house front, depicting the myth of Thunderbird carrying off a whale. This is a good example of how subjects were formalized to make balanced decorations. Thunderbird's head, shown full face, is developed into a design that harmonizes with the matching wings. The whale is shown in "X-ray" view, so that its backbone and ribs fill the space with a decorative pattern. *Inverarity, The Art of the Northwest Coast Indians.*

Tlingit food-storage box, carved and painted. The sides are made from a single piece of cedar, steamed and bent into shape. The technique of splitting the object represented is well illustrated here, as in the face at the bottom, each half of which makes a profile, the whole a full face. The principal element in the design is a sea spirit. *Washington State Museum.*

After section of a Haida ceremonial canoe in the American Museum of Natural History. The figures are models, but most of the objects are the real thing. The party in the canoe is shown as en route to a potlatch. The chief, in full regalia, stands in the stern. In front of him is a bear dancer, and further forward a professionally unkempt shaman is drumming.
Courtesy of American Museum of Natural History.

crests, the evidences of his rank, in every possible manner. This, combined with the general reverence for such animals as the killer whale, raven, eagle, bear, beaver, and wolf (or rather, for certain divine members of these species), and for such mythical creatures as the thunderbird, shaped an art.

Over and over these animals and experiences connected with them were represented, both as pure and applied art. Some of the work was simple and realistic, much of it was stylized into formal decorative schemes. There was a tendency to cover all the space on the object decorated, resulting in the use of fillers, such as faces carved on animals' chests, conventionalized eyes placed to mark all joints, or insertion of minor figures without special meaning. The work, then, ranged from pure, representational art to about equally pure design. A common trick was to show the animal as if split in half, one half in profile to the left, the other to the right. Sometimes the head was split, and shown as two profiles, sometimes it was handled full face. The body might be quite unrecognizable, the creature identifiable only by the peculiar beak of an eagle, the killer whale's big teeth and sharklike fin, or the beaver's chisellike front teeth and crosshatching to represent his scaly tail. It sounds rather odd, but out of these conventions came by far the finest North American Indian art of historic times.

When we think of the Northwest Coast, we think first of totem poles. The name is a poor one, since what are carved on them are not, technically speaking, totems, but crests and insignia; but the name is established beyond change. Totem poles were erected in memory of departed chiefs by their heirs, as part of the procedure by which they validated their inheritance. The new chief thus hon-

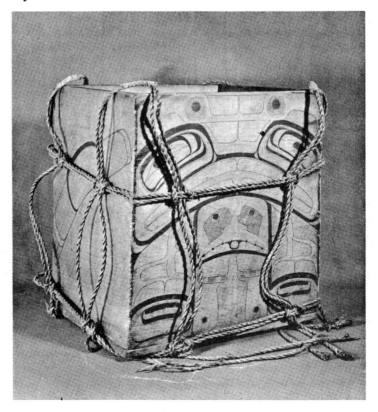

Haida painted storage box, with native-made ropes for tying. *Washington State Museum.*

Haida jointed wooden puppet. This particular one, representing a mythical, man-eating creature called Olala, was used as a headdress in dances of the Olala secret society. The top of the dancer's head went into the hole under the ribs. Figures similar to this were also made to fly "magically" through the air during shamanistic performances. *Smithsonian Institution.*

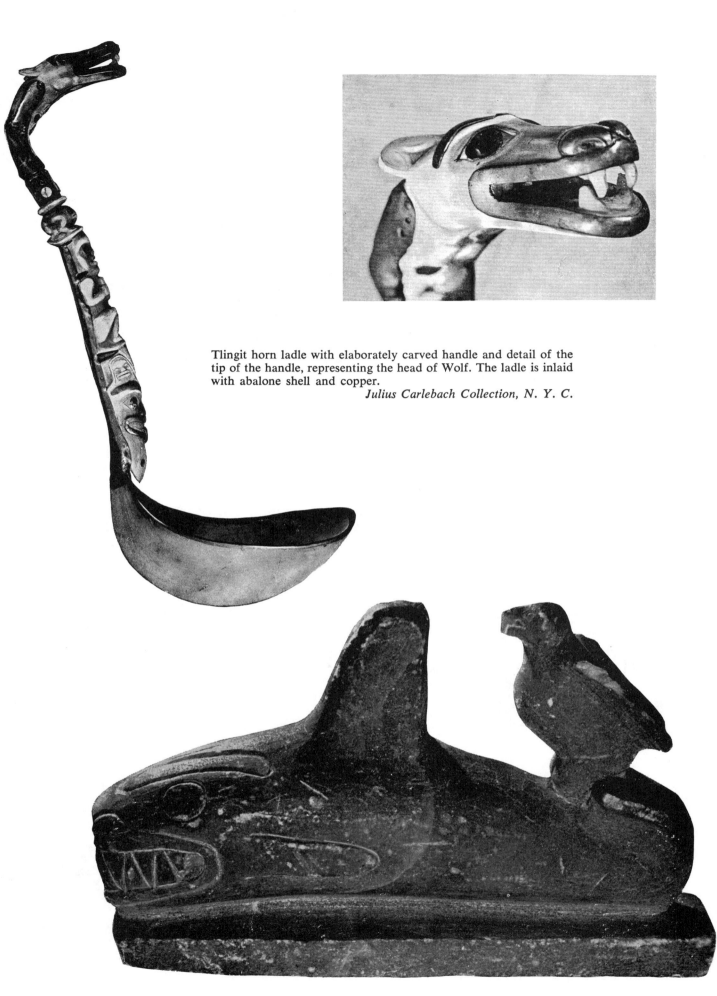

Tlingit horn ladle with elaborately carved handle and detail of the tip of the handle, representing the head of Wolf. The ladle is inlaid with abalone shell and copper.

Julius Carlebach Collection, N. Y. C.

Kwakiutl sandstone carving of Eagle on the back of Whale.   *Anthropological Museum, Univ. of British Columbia, Vancouver, B. C.*

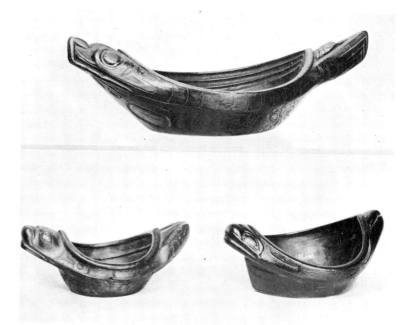

Haida and Tlingit food dishes.
Courtesy of American Museum of Natural History.

As the mask run earlier shows, white people intrigued the native artists. This is a Haida carving on slate of a white woman. The artist, with some humor, brings out the primness of the subject.
Southwest Museum.

Seated bear carved out of cedar and painted black and red. Tribe unknown. *Museum of Anthropology, Univ. of California.*

ored his predecessor, and at the same time published his own importance. They were put up by the graves of chiefs, or actually were their graves, the body being placed inside. They were erected to display some special privilege of the owner. Some groups put up poles attached to the fronts of their houses, with the door cut through them.

Recent as well as ancient events and triumphs could be recorded on them. A pole honoring one Haida chief carried several figures of Russian priests. The chief had been very proud of his successful resistance to attempts of the priests to convert him and his people. The figures represented that triumph and also were a method of publicly ridiculing missionaries.

Most Americans have at least heard of the function called potlach, although popular ideas about it are even vaguer than about totem poles. Potlatches could be described as social ceremonials. They were assemblages at which a chief, with the help of his group, fed a great number of guests, gave away property and destroyed property, in order to validate his own rank and privileges, or to confer certain crests, names, or rights on others, or both. When a chief had died, his successor might give a potlatch or a series of potlatches in his memory. At these the honors and powers he had inherited would be recited, crests would be displayed, ancestral contacts with divine animals might be dramatically enacted. The guests served as witnesses that the new chief's claims were correct; the food and gifts they received were their payment; the lavishness of the whole thing testified to the chief's high position and the position of his lineage group.

A potlatch might be given to announce an heir presumptive, or, where inheritance was in the mother's line, to hand over certain crests and prerogatives to a son-in-law. The son-in-law would hold them as custodian for his children, to whom in due course he would pass them with a potlatch. Among some tribes, if a chief had suffered some humiliating accident, such as falling down in public, he might give a potlatch to restore his prestige. Among the southern tribes, where the hereditary principle was weaker, potlatches were the means by which men bought, in a sense, the rank to which they wanted to succeed.

It was at potlatches that the coppers already mentioned became most important. As has been said above, these crude sheets of metal were considered very valuable. Among the northern tribes, it was essential that one or two be destroyed, by breaking them up and throwing them in the fire or by throwing them in the sea, at the first potlatch given by a dead chief's successor. Farther south, coppers increased in a value every time they were given away at a potlatch or as a dowry, so that some of them became worth thousands of dollars.

There has been a lot of disagreement among anthropologists about the extent of the "competitive potlatches" given with the hope of shaming and eliminating a rival. It seems likely that these did occur in early times occasionally, when there was a question as to which of two chiefs

Costumes worn at a Tlingit potlatch about 1900 or slightly earlier. Here we have a mixture of native and trade articles. The man at the left wears an overgarment of cloth or canvas on which native designs have been skillfully painted. A number of the men wear nose rings. *Smithsonian Institution.*

Painted Tlingit wood carving of a woman being carried off by a sea monster. Her expression of terror is touchingly shown.
Wolfgang Paalen Collection, Vancouver Island, B. C.

Haida dishes, carved from slate and inlaid with shell or bone. The upper right-hand one, of modern workmanship, includes the American eagle. Slate carving became common after the acquisition of our tools. At first the products were rather dull imitations of typical American sailors' "scrimshaw" whittling. Later, the craftsmen moved over to native designs, producing much handsomer objects, and achieving refinement of technique such as is shown here *Courtesy of American Museum of Natural History.*

Model of the mortuary pole of a Haida chief, He Whose Voice is Obeyed, at Skidegate. The chief's crests were Bear, shown near the bottom of the pole, and Moon, shown at the top. The man in the moon holds a piece of saladberry bush in one hand and a bucket in the other. Planks on top in the form of a grave box shows that this post was raised in memory of a deceased chief.

Courtesy of American Museum of Natural History.

Totem poles at Kitwanga, British Columbia. The houses behind are of relatively modern construction.

Canadian National Railways.

218

Model of Haida house, showing totem pole attached to the front with the door cut through it, and carved and painted corner posts. The cylinders on top of the hats on the highest, human heads show the rank of the chief of the house.

Courtesy of American Museum of Natural History.

219

ranked first. This situation could arise when two groups, formerly independent, united. In the mid-nineteenth century, a number of Kwakiutl groups moved in around a Hudson's Bay post at Fort Rupert, and a number of Tsimshians similarly settled near a post at Fort Simpson. Both of these gatherings formed rough confederacies. The ranking of chiefs and nobles within each group was clear enough, but how they rated in regard to the chiefs of other groups had never been worked out.

The result was a terrific competition. One chief would give a potlatch at, rather than for, a rival, at which he would give away or destroy what he hoped was more wealth than the other could possibly amass. Blankets, both trade blankets and the far more valuable Chilkat ones, were burned, coppers destroyed or pieces hacked off them, a slave or two killed.

The second chief would call on his people, and they would make a tremendous effort to outdo the original pot-

Kwakiutl house posts, carved in the totem-pole manner. The one at the left has an arm developed as a crotch to carry a beam. House posts had supernatural abilities, such as being able to give warning of danger.
Courtesy of American Museum of Natural History.

latcher. Goods might be borrowed from outsiders, to be returned at a fixed rate of interest within a year—in itself no slight burden. Eventually one rival or the other would have to give up, and it would be established that he and his group were of lesser rank. At its height, when the Indians were prospering mightily from the fur trade and their stock of material possessions was such as existed nowhere else in North America, the competitive potlatch system became a vicious thing, an endless procedure of amassing wealth for the purpose of ruining others. Even so, the groups sometimes managed to soften the business. Two chiefs might feel called upon to assert themselves yet neither of them would desire to be ruined or to come near to beggaring himself and his group to win. They would get together privately and agree to give a potlatch and counter-potlatch at which the gifts and the things destroyed would come out exactly even. This gave the mass of the people an exciting show and resulted in no great damage.

The three California tribes counted as part of the culture were marginal. Their potlatch was simplified, and did not include the giving away or destruction of wealth. Instead, thriftily, it was merely displayed. Their most important items were the white skins of albino deer, decorated with bands of brilliant, small feathers, and the shell money mentioned in the last chapter. Men of wealth hired dancers, who progressively, as the ceremony went on, displayed more and more of these possessions and other articles, such as obsidian blades of great size, manufactured only for show. Whoever displayed the most got the most glory, and when the performance was over, the owners carefully retrieved all their goods.

The first well-established contact with the Northwest Coast Indians was made by Bering, the Dane for whom the Bering Straits are named, exploring for Russia. He sent a boat ashore, which never returned. Instead, a number of war canoes came out against Bering's ship, and he sailed away. In 1778 the great explorer, Captain James Cook, visited the Nootkas, who gave him some sea otter skins. When members of the expedition reached China, Cook having died in the Hawaiian Islands, they discovered that the Chinese would pay tremendous prices for the furs. This was the beginning of the Northwest Coast trade, which the Americans, especially, developed as a highly profitable triangular affair, taking cheap goods to the Northwest Coast to buy sea otter fur, trading these at a high premium with the Chinese for tea, which was cheap in China, and selling that in Boston at another high premium. The trade resulted in the virtual extinction of the sea otters, but while it lasted, everyone profited.

The Indians became choosy about their trade goods. An enterprising Connecticut Yankee named Collins made a business of manufacturing, at Hartford, the kinds of knives, axes, and other blades the Indians preferred. From this he branched out into providing similar goods for natives in other parts of the world, with the result that to this day Collins and Co. dominates the machete market of the world, and in parts of Latin America that tool is no longer called *machete* but *un collín.*

The sea otter trade was replaced by trade in other furs, largely carried on through posts of the Hudson's Bay Com-

Engraving, published in 1895, from a photograph of a Kwakiutl chief delivering a speech at a potlatch. In front of him is a pile of blankets to be given away. The members of the audience have been carefully seated according to their rank, and gifts will be distributed in the same order. *Smithsonian Institution.*

Copies of totem poles being made by Indians as part of a CCC project in the 1930's. As would be expected, wooden poles do not last too long in a wet climate. *U. S. Dept. of Interior.*

The North California substitute for a potlatch—Hupa Indians performing the White Deerskin Dance, which is in part the ending of a long ritual for "renewing the world" and assuring abundance, but more a means of displaying wealth, especially the white skins and large obsidian blades such as those carried by the two men in front. *Courtesy of American Museum of Natural History.*

pany and other firms, in the early nineteenth century. The coastal Indians dealt in furs of their own taking and in those that they traded from Indians farther inland. They became rich in goods of all kinds, and through the middle of the nineteenth century they flourished.

Actual migration and settlement by white men came relatively late. Disease, liquor, and crowding had their usual effects. Slowly the culture faded, although as yet it is by no means dead. Commercial salmon fisheries and canneries pre-empted many of the fishing grounds, and for a time, until brought under governmental control, threatened the destruction of the salmon. Today the surviving tribes are getting along unevenly. Still men of the sea, they work for the fisheries and canneries when they can. Some groups, with federal aid, have set up cooperatives with the hope of getting into the industry on their own.

The tribes in Alaska were greatly handicapped by the fact that non-Indians and the commercial interests suc-

White deerskin, originally property of a Karok Indian, decorated with strands of brightly colored feathers, for use in the White Deerskin Dance. Among the tribes at the north tip of California who shared in part the Northwest Coast culture, such skins had much the value of Chilkat blankets farther north.
Museum of the American Indian.

cessfully prevented them from receiving reservations. They had title to little more than the sites of their villages, and such fishing grounds as they still controlled were always in danger of being seized by powerful white firms. Cut off from their subsidiary sources of livelihood, such as hunting, all too many tried to live from salmon catch to salmon catch, spending much of the year in enforced, demoralizing idleness and struggling endlessly with accumulated debt. In 1972 the tribes shared in the Alaska Native Claims Settlement Act, which recognized that the Eskimos, Aleuts, and Indians were the true owners of Alaska. The native peoples were permitted to select and retain a total of forty million acres as their own and to receive $962,-500,000 over eleven years as payment for the rest of the state that they relinquished to the whites. The money would go to twelve regional corporations of natives, set up to invest and use the funds in projects, like educational and economic enterprises, that would benefit all the native populations. It was a complicated act, representing compromises among the federal government, the state of Alaska, and the 60,000 or so native peoples of Alaska, and only time can tell if it will work out well for the different Eskimo and Indian villages. One advantage it had, however, was to secure for the natives a firm title to considerable land around their villages, which whites, otherwise, might eventually have seized.

In Oregon and Washington, fragments of many tribes, shattered by contact with white men in the mass, have gathered on a few reservations under such circumstances as to destroy their original tribal distinctions, and as a result have lost a great part of their culture. Throughout the area nowadays, those who have dealings with tourists or who otherwise capitalize on their Indian heritage are likely to store away their ancient, meaningful insignia and put on war bonnets, that the white men may see what they intend to see.

X. Ghosts and Drugs

American Indian religions varied from the most primitive shamanism—little more than the exercise of magic, usually beneficial, by self-elected practitioners—to organized, priestly systems based on high philosophies. Whatever the type, one thing is constant: religion permeated daily life. There was no such thing as setting aside a portion of every seventh day for relations with God or the gods.

For such people, when they saw the very framework of their lives collapsing, there was an inevitable turning to religion. In worship might be found the cure, or failure in worship might explain the creeping disaster that was destroying them, that was robbing life of all that made it worth living.

When primitive peoples are overwhelmed by a totally alien, higher culture, they have three choices. One is nativism—to reject the higher culture altogether and make a special effort to preserve all old ways in purity. In our modern age this seldom if ever works. The millions of men of the Machine Age press too remorselessly; also they offer too much that is useful and attractive. To take an extreme example, refusing to use metal tools would verge on insanity. For a generation or more, one tribe in the Southwest forbade its members to use a cultivator in their fields, insisting that its members stay "pure" by cultivating with hoes, which themselves were white men's products. Too many men came to realize how much horse-drawn cultivators could help them; in the end the ban was relaxed.

In another tribe, the "old heads" who govern it are still refusing to allow piped water or electricity in their village. It will not be long before they are forced to yield, for all their young people know the convenience of these things, and in time the elders must yield or the younger generations will revolt and reject them entirely.

The second choice is complete acceptance of the higher culture, entirely abandoning the old one. This, also, seldom works. There are exceptions, but as a rule the native who has cut himself off from all of his own tradition is an incomplete and uneasy man. There is too much learned in infancy, the warmth of certain types of family relationship, the satisfaction of certain ways, a mode of thinking of one's self, a set of values, that nothing can satisfactorily replace. Given a proud tradition, a sense of the goodness of belonging to a certain race and having the history a given tribe

has, a profound desire to continue to be members of that tribe and to keep it in being—which we find almost everywhere among our Indians—and you can begin to understand how some tribes remain still Indian after two hundred years or more of contact with the white men, and after having been moved hundreds of miles from their original homes.

The third choice, and the most hopeful one, is making a new adaptation, taking what is good of the higher culture, keeping what is good and can, as a practical matter, survive of the older. In great degree this is what most Indians are trying to do. They have a hard time of it, not only because the white men habitually push them around, but even more because most white men hold the curious conviction that no people can become progressive unless it becomes *exactly* like themselves.

This explains why so many missionaries think that a man cannot become a good Christian unless he dresses as the missionary does, lives in the same kind of house, eats the same food—despite the fact that, as Indians sometimes point out, Our Lord wore His hair long and wrapped Himself in something very like a blanket. The same line of thinking led well-meaning schoolteachers on the Navajo reservation to propagandize their pupils urgently against eating the "disgusting" parts of sheep, until a study by the Association on American Indian Affairs showed that only by eating the whole animal could the Indians achieve a balanced diet, and that those who followed the teachers' advice were more susceptible to tuberculosis than those who did not.

In terms of religion, the three choices could be somewhat inaccurately identified with religious developments intended not only to bring back the old days, as the Ghost Dance Cult, but conversion to Christianity, and the modern, in-between, Peyote Cult or Native American Church. The identification is not accurate. Such tribes as the Iroquois or the Zuñis of New Mexico show that an Indian can be "pagan" and progressive at the same time. Indians who hold strongly to tribe and tradition make excellent Christians, bringing to Christianity a sense of the constant presence of religion in daily life and a habit of participation in religious activities that we should do well to copy.

Nativistic or reactionary religious revivals and new sects

appeared early after the white men grew strong on the continent. We have no report of any special religious development back of King Philip's desperate, futile counterattack in New England. Perhaps there was none, or perhaps the Puritans did not bother to record it. In the 1760's, the Ottawa chief, Pontiac, nearly drove the British out of the Illinois-Ohio region. Back of Pontiac's success and the confederacy he formed were the preachings of a Delaware prophet, whose name is unknown. The prophet did not preach war, but a complete return to old ways, so that the good old days would return. Pontiac made the logical extension of this idea, that if the white men were cleared out, the good old days would come even faster.

Tecumseh's war against the Americans, described in Chapter V, was based on another revivalistic movement for return to the old, pure ways, led by his brother, Laulewasika. The records on this man are ample. He had been an alcoholic, who reformed after he had a shaman-type vision, and proceeded to become a prophet. Like the forgotten Delaware, he did not preach war. He taught a return to purity, and in his doctrine the bringing back of old times, ample elbow room, and ample hunting were constant major elements; but he did not teach a simple return to the old-time religion. Rather, he offered a new variant in which Christian influences are apparent, and with such revolutionary novelties as ordering the destruction of sacred bundles.

The movement spread strongly among Indians who ranged from uneasy to desperate. Tecumseh, the doer, the war leader, seized upon it as the source of the necessary emotional element for his war.

The influence of Christianity shows in many of the cults, sects, and religions that sprang up among the Indians. The concept of a single, active, high God has been hit upon only a few times in human history. When that concept was brought to the Indians, there were plenty of competent religious thinkers who, although they rejected the new religion, were strongly influenced by this fundamental element of it. It resulted in giving a new coherence to old systems, and to the development of new variants.

After the Revolution, the Iroquois were a defeated people, their power gone, their empire cut down to reservations. They, too, felt hopelessness, frustration, and the sad sense of the dying away of the old, rich life. Among them in 1799 arose a prophet, Handsome Lake. He, too, was an alcoholic who reformed after a vision. He preached that the old Iroquois had had a good life, but that it was incomplete because they knew God incompletely. His new dispensation made the old religion complete. He combined established, old ceremonies with new ones. Originally he taught an extreme reaction against white ways, but later he modified his stand, even to the extent of agreeing to the use of ploughs. This was a more important change than it seems at first look, because ploughing is a man's activity. The introduction of plough farming ended the women's monopoly and affected their whole position. Handsome Lake's ministry did not result in any fighting. It helped the Iroquois to survive and to fight the plague of drunkenness, and it gave their religion a form that could survive strongly to the present day.

Far more famous than any of these early religious revivals is the Ghost Dance Cult. Its history is curious. It is directly the result of Christian mission influence, and it started, of all places, among the Paviotso, a branch of the Paiutes, in Nevada. There, about 1888, an Indian with a history of mission contacts, Jack Wilson or Wovoka, began having visions. The visions produced a doctrine that was in part derived from an older relative of similar background, Tavibo, probably an uncle, who had had some visions and taken a try at being a prophet in 1870. The new religion combined Christian ethical ideas and the general idea of a messiah to come, with rituals intended to make the white men disappear and bring back the vanished game and the dead Indians. Wovoka specifically preached peace and forbade fighting anyone.

Word of this teaching reached the Plains tribes when things were desperate. The buffalo were gone, and everyone was hungry to the verge of starvation. All the tribes had been defeated and put on reservations. Life was wretched, and they did not know what way to turn. Delegations went to talk to the prophet. What they brought back was not what he taught, or else his doctrines were quickly changed after the delegates got home. War against the whites was an essential part of the Plains Ghost Dance doctrine. Dancing in a circle, Basin style, would bring back the dead buffalo and their own dead tribesmen, but it was their own power, magically fortified, that would clear their land of the great enemy. Through the rituals and by the use of various symbols that developed around it, they could make themselves bullet-proof, or endow a shirt with the property of turning bullets.

Wovoka, the originator of the Ghost Dance Cult, photographed with the adjutant general of Wyoming.

Smithsonian Institution.

Oglala Sioux Ghost Dance, from a painting by Frederic Remington. *Courtesy of American Museum of Natural History.*

Composite painting of Arapaho Ghost Dance from photos taken by James Mooney, a great early ethnologist. The Basin-type "round dance," with women participating, was new to the Plains. It survives among many tribes today as a purely social dance.
Smithsonian Institution.

Some of the Sioux, the Arapahos, Cheyennes, and Kiowas accepted the doctrine most completely. It led to a strange ferment, endless dancing, and the announcement of many visions in which people saw the buffalo, talked with the returning dead, prophesied the new millenium. There were sporadic acts of hostility. The white men became badly frightened. The situation led to the killing of Sitting Bull in his own home, by Sioux police hired by the government, an affair that has been the subject of controversy ever since. Finally it led to the "battle" of Wounded Knee, which was started by white soldiers' nervousness and ended with the death of 31 soldiers and 128 Sioux. After that the cult died away. It is almost forgotten now, except that among the Nevada Indians some still perform dances in a form Wovoka established.

None of these religions lasted except the Handsome Lake dispensation, and that never spread beyond the Iroquois. What is powerful today is the most curious of all—the Peyote Cult. Peyote (pronounced pay-YO-tee) is a small, spineless cactus of which only a very small piece, the "button," shows above ground. This button may be chewed or steeped to make a tea. It contains a number of alkaloids, which produce trances in which the taker has extraordinary visions, usually of an extremely happy nature, accompanied by colors of astonishing beauty. Definitely not habit-forming, the plant does not come under the Federal Narcotics Act, although some states prohibit it.

Arapaho Ghost Dance shirt. Decoration of these shirts was usually confined to painting. This is the type that was supposed to be bullet-proof. *Museum of the American Indian.*

From a photograph of a moment in the Arapaho Ghost Dance ritual, by Mooney. *Smithsonian Institution.*

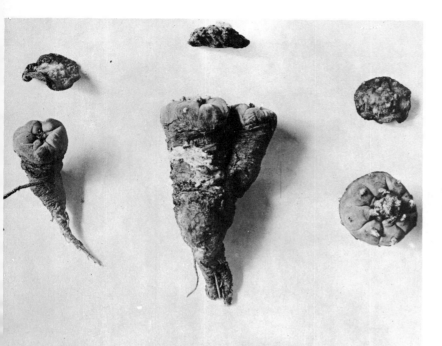

The peyote plant (*Lophophora williamsii* Lemaire) and "buttons" cut from it. *Smithsonian Institution.*

Drawing by Skybuck, a Kickapoo, of a peyote ceremony. The artist has shown the tepee as cut away to expose the ceremony within. The Kickapoos were a wigwam people transplanted to Oklahoma; the use of a tepee in the peyote cult is probably the result of having learned it from neighboring Plains tribes. Many of the essential ritual elements can be seen—the fire and altar shaped like a crescent moon, rattles, a small drum, a feather fan in one man's hand, the staff in another's.

Museum of the American Indian.

It had long been used by a number of Mexican tribes, in connection with important ceremonies occurring once a year. From them, it seems to have spread to the Tonkawas and Karankawas of Texas in the nineteenth century. It reached the Kiowas about 1870, but did not become important with any Plains tribe until the middle of the 1880's.

With the plant traveled a cult, which, as it became known in recent times, had been vastly changed from the original Mexican. Use of peyote was no longer annual; a peyote ceremony could be held at any time. The visions it caused naturally tied in neatly with the vision complex of the Plains Indians and their neighbors. Today these visions are regarded as methods of experiencing God. The peyote ceremonies begin at nightfall and continue through the night, ending with a feast in the morning. Participants describe their feelings at that time as peacefulness, happiness, and a sense of being blessed.

The rituals and the beliefs range from almost purely Indian to at least semi-Christian. At the center, always, is the plant itself, which is regarded as sacred and the consumption of which is in part a form of communion.

As peyote does not grow much north of the Mexican border, in many places it is hard to get and often scarce.

When there is, say, only a single button for a sizeable congregation, it may simply be displayed on the primitive altar, without anyone eating it. The actual eating is accompanied by solemn ritual. A peyote session is anything but an orgy. The variation in belief is exemplified by the idea held in one tribe that the staff used by the leader of the ritual is "the staff of life," while another tribe holds that the staff is Christ's.

The use of peyote has spread throughout the many tribes now gathered in Oklahoma, northwards across the Cana-

"The Burning of the Cedar," a phase of the peyote ritual painted by the modern Potawatomi artist Woody Crumbo. Compared to Skybuck's simple realism, this handsome painting is distinctly romanticized. It shows the drummer, one singer with rattle, and the officiant who is scattering fragrant powder on the fire.

Philbrook Art Center.

Peyote ritual in a Kiowa tepee, photographed in the late 1880's. The crescent altar enclosing the fire is plainly shown.
Smithsonian Institution.

Comanche peyotist of the 1880's, with rattle, staff, and feather fan. *Smithsonian Institution.*

Latter-day peyotists of the Iowa tribe, now in Oklahoma. The man in front holds the peyote rattle and feather fan.
Museum of the American Indian.

dian border among both Plains and Woodlands-Western Farmer tribes, reached into Oregon, and in recent years has made great progress among the Navahos. Those who take up the cult abandon their old religions and are usually immune to conversion to Christianity. They enter into a new, intertribal religion, the sharing of which gives them a sense of belonging to something larger, less helpless, than their own small group.

Because of its relation to the old religions and Christianity, the cult in some places aroused violent controversy. It was made more violent and more confused by the fear many people felt toward "taking a drug," although many careful experiments have proven that this is no drug. Opponents made statements ranging from one that peyote causes bad teeth to allegations of fantastic orgies and the utter ruination of those who use the plant. Peyotists state, apparently with considerable truth, that members of their cult do not drink and usually are quiet, steady citizens. Many hold that the plant will cure sicknesses, which is dangerous (although impartial witnesses testify to certain cures). The element of escapism in the religion is not surprising when we consider the Indians' present situation, so commonly marked by frustration, the sense of past glories and satisfactions forever lost in exchange for a harsh present and a dubious future, all too often including extreme poverty and the constant pain of being subjected to racial discrimination.

In order to meet the attacks upon the cult, especially

Members of the Bannock and Shoshone tribes, Fort Hall, Idaho, at a peyote ceremony in 1939. Although the Indians of this reservation live in houses, a tepee is put up for a peyote session. The fire and crescent altar are as usual, but other paraphernalia seem to be absent—perhaps simply put aside so as not to let it be photographed. *U. S. Dept. of Interior.*

The morning feast following the ceremony shown in the last picture. At the moment, the participants appear to be listening to a blessing recited by the man at the end of the spread. The Indians of the Fort Hall reservation have long been poor for reasons beyond their control; it is not surprising that they did not produce handsome Indian costumes for this occasion.

U. S. Dept. of Interior.

drives to forbid by law the possession or use of the plant, many of the peyotists organized themselves into the Native American Church, a formal, nonprofit corporation. The very fact that this "Indianistic" movement can do so modern a thing is an interesting example of the third choice mentioned earlier in this chapter—making a new adaptation out of parts of the old and parts of the new.

Today this new Indian church is still spreading, gaining adherents in many tribes.

XI. The Non-Vanishing Americans

Anything like a complete description of the Indians of the United States as they are today would require all of a book the size of this one. It is as true of them now as it was before the white man came, that there is hardly any general statement that can be made about the Indians as a whole that does not call for a long list of exceptions.

One big fact stands out. The Indians are not vanishing; they are increasing—in fact, at a rate faster than that of the rest of the population. It is probable that the Indian population dropped as low as 220,000 around the turn of the century. Today there are approximately 500,000 Native Americans living on or near reservations, or who are otherwise recognized and provided services by the federal government. This includes about 60,000 Indians, Eskimos, and Aleuts in Alaska. Moreover, there are another 350,000 or so Indians who are living off reservations in cities or rural areas, or on reservations that have no relationship with the federal government.

These last include certain tribes, like the Penobscots and Passamaquoddies in Maine and other cohesive groups in the eastern states, that are presently being considered for recognition by the federal government and for eligibility for federal services. Among such groups are peoples like the Chickahominys of Virginia, the Wampanoags of Massachusetts (including the Gay Head band on Martha's Vineyard), and the thousands of Lumbees of North Carolina. Some of them are formally recognized by the states in which they live, have land set aside specially for their use, and may receive some services from their states. Others, like groups in Connecticut, receive only token acknowledgement of their existence by their states. On the whole, these groups are scattered and for many years seemed lost and forgotten among the surrounding non-Indian population. Many are poor and a long time ago lost virtually all their old customs and traditions. In recent years, however, most of them have gained a new pride in their Indian backgrounds and have revitalized some of their old traditions.

When you look for the strongest, most readily identifiable Indian groups that retain their tribal organizations and many of their old values and customs, you are most likely to look to the peoples who have the status of Indians under federal law, from the 9,000 or so Iroquois in New York State to the large tribes of the plains and Southwest. The greatest centers of Indian population are in Arizona, with almost 120,000; Oklahoma, with 84,000; New Mexico with 82,000; Alaska, with some 60,000; California, with 49,000; and, surprisingly, North Carolina, with about

45,000. The native peoples in Arizona, New Mexico, and most of the western states are native to those states; most of those in Oklahoma were moved there under the old policy of concentrating as many tribes as possible in an "Indian Territory" that, it was believed, white men would never want. That was before we knew the worth of the black gold called petroleum, or how to find it.

In the north, in the two Dakotas and adjacent states, there are some 35,000 Sioux. The scattered groups of Indians in California add up, as we have stated, to almost 50,000, and Indians in considerable numbers are to be found in Oregon, Washington, Nevada, Idaho, Montana, Wyoming, Wisconsin, and Minnesota. Elsewhere they are few, a few hundred here, a thousand or so there.

In previous chapters there have been brief descriptions of the later history of the various groups. The story always seems to be monotonously and sadly the same. There are three main types of tribal history. Some tribes, especially in the East, were wiped out. Many were forcibly moved out of the white man's way, sometimes many times over, until finally they landed in some unlikely spot where they have been allowed to remain. Others, especially the stronger Western and Southwestern tribes, have been allowed to keep some part of their original homeland.

Until the 1870's we dealt with the tribes as little nations having a limited sovereignty subordinate to our sovereignty, making regular treaties with them each time we wanted a new arrangement. Finally, in 1871, Congress stopped the treaty-making, and since then we have dealt with the Indians as people under our jurisdiction, though we did not recognize most of them as citizens and denied them citizens' freedoms and rights.

Whether we had treaties with them or only made agreements and promises, it is the unhappy truth that there is no tribe with which we have not at some time broken our word.

When gold was found in the country of the progressive Cherokees, who were moving so rapidly toward full civilization, we drove them out. Since at that time the non-Indian population of the South was increasing rapidly and wanted all of the rich land it could get, while we were at it, we drove out all of the Five Civilized Tribes that we could catch.

We did not get them all. As was told earlier, some Cherokees held out, and now occupy a reservation in North Carolina. So did a number of Seminoles, after a campaign of extinction that cost us fifteen hundred

Sioux girls arriving at "Carlisle Barracks," 1879. Note the expressions of eager anticipation on the girls' faces and the friendly and affectionate way in which the teacher on the left looks at them.

U. S. Dept. of Interior.

casualties in Army and Navy forces and millions of dollars. Finally these invincible people were given title to tracts of land in Florida, where they still are. Feeling that they had never surrendered to the United States and had never made peace with us, the Seminoles—together with a group that separated from them and is now an independent tribe in Florida known as the Miccosukees—long resisted all services offered them by the Bureau of Indian Affairs, including education. In 1957, a treaty was finally signed between the Seminoles and the United States, ending the longest war in history, and in 1962 the Miccosukee tribe (which still retains its native religion, though most of the Seminoles are Christians) was officially recognized. Federal services came to both tribes, and recently the Miccosukees, under contractual arrangement with the Bureau of Indian Affairs, took over the control and management of all its own affairs, one of the first of all tribes in the United States to do so.

Many Choctaws managed to hold out, mainly in Mississippi. Today there are about 3,200 of them, living on a federally recognized reservation in that state. Their lot has not been an easy one. Within Mississippi they were subject to Jim Crow segregation laws and, as their lands dwindled away through the years, they were largely neglected and forgotten. About 1916 a series of epidemics brought them to the attention of the Senate, which conducted an investigation. This was followed, at last, by a government land-purchasing program for them, which built up their lands again, and by federal recognition and services. Today, the tribe, with some government help, is continuing to try to pull itself up by its own bootstraps, so to speak. Its people are very proud of their tribal background and history and are playing an increasing role in regional and national Indian affairs.

The story changes as we move westward. When gold was found in the sacred Black Hills of the Sioux in South Dakota in the 1870's, the government tried to make our citizens respect the Sioux boundaries guaranteed to them by the Treaty of 1868. They could not stem the gold rush, and when the government gave up and offered, instead, to buy the land from the Sioux, the Indians refused to sell. It was not only that it was their homeland; it was the seat of their religious beliefs. Nevertheless, the government drove them from it, sending armies under Custer and other generals to force the Sioux onto smaller reservations away from the Black Hills. The Indians fought back, wiping out Custer, but finally were overcome by the army's superior forces. The Sioux were not driven entirely from their own country, but they were penned on reservations, and in recent years they have reminded the government with increasing insistence that the Black Hills and other lands "guaranteed" to them forever in 1868 were stolen from them. It was one of the causes of the Indians' dramatic armed "occupation" of the area around Wounded Knee, South Dakota, in 1973. The Indians demanded that the government discuss that broken treaty. To end the Wounded Knee episode, the government agreed to talk about the treaty which had been made and broken a century ago. Talks did take place, but the government negotiators said they did not know what to do. The stolen land was now so thoroughly occupied and used by white ranchers, farmers, towns, industries, and cities that they did not see how it could be restored to the Sioux. Thus, as with many broken treaties, a kind of impasse continues: the Indians remember the theft of what was theirs, holding it up to the white man's conscience, and the white man and his government try uncomfortably to avoid the subject.

To some extent, Indian lands and resources are better safeguarded for the tribes than they have been in the past. Among the general public there is considerable respect for the Indians' rights in their lands—a respect strengthened by the Indians' growing ability to protect themselves both through their appeal to public opinion and through their recourse to the courts. Our federal courts have always been the most faithful defenders of the Indians' rights, and the tribes have learned how to take the initiative in going to them. But despite the better situation, almost all tribes must stay constantly on the defensive, carefully guarding what is theirs, and warding off unending attempts to whittle away at their reservations and resources. It makes for a situation in which the tribes can never enjoy real security or peace. Even today, Paiutes in Nevada and many other tribes in arid parts of the West are battling for water that was actually stolen from them or is now being threatened. In Arizona and Montana, Hopis, Navahos, Crows, and Northern Cheyennes are fighting against the exploitation, pollution, and even destruction of their lands by coal strip mines and big power plants. And in New Mexico and elsewhere, various tribes are resisting white men's conglomerates that wish to build large new cities and recreation projects for whites on the reservations.

The complexities of the relations between tribes and white industrial interests that wish to use reservation resources can be seen in events that have occurred on the Navaho reservation. About 1920 a rich oil structure was found on the Navahos' lands. There were oil people who wanted to take this land away from the Indians, but there was no question of getting away with any such thing. Instead, following the procedure established by law, leases were negotiated which required the consent of both the Navaho tribe, represented by its tribal council, and the Secretary of the Interior, who is the superior of the Commissioner of Indian Affairs. The Navahos at that time were not equipped to judge an oil lease, but they had good advice, and a special advantage in that one of the sons of their council chairman had recently received his LL.B. degree. They received profitable terms.

From then until now, there has been a continuous series of discoveries of oil, gas, helium, uranium, vanadium, and coal within the Navahos' boundaries. The number of educated Navahos has greatly increased; its tribal council has become an impressive, modern governing body. It has many tribal economic and development organizations, led and staffed by technically educated Navahos, and not one attorney, but a staff of them. Well aware of its rights, it grants no leases or permits to prospect without being convinced that it is getting the best possible terms. Despite all this, however, it is still too often true that white men's deceit has been used to do the "convincing," and this has led to trouble within the tribe. The Secretary of the Inte-

Seminole spearing fish. He stands in a pirogue, the traditional dugout canoe of the South. *U. S. Dept. of Interior.*

Seminole C.C.C. worker, Florida, working on a cattle guard.
U. S. Dept. of Interior.

rior, approving what was often arranged by the Bureau of Indian Affairs, has on occasion used his power and influence to get the Navahos to do what eventually turned out to be not in their own best interests, or something that a large part of the tribe would have opposed. In the 1960's, for instance, the Department of the Interior induced the tribal council to approve giving away some of its valuable and very scarce water rights to the builders of a power plant. The council did not understand what it was doing until it was too late. Again, in leasing coal for strip mines, the council came under heavy criticism from many of the Navaho people, some of whom opposed the strip mines and other developments on the reservations, and others who felt that the Navahos had not gotten good enough terms for the various deals. In all cases, there was ample reason to feel that the federal government had favored the white corporations and their developments, and had not fully informed or protected the tribe.

The modern Indian picture contains all sorts of economic tales. A very few tribes, such as the Osages and the Jicarilla Apaches, have at times received a considerable income from oil and similar leases. With the sudden acquisition of money, following poverty and deprivation, came a new white man's stereotype about Indians: they were oil millionaires! Oil-rich Indians, however, are very few, nor are most of these as rich as popular belief makes out. An Osage with as much as $1,000 a year in oil money is above average.

Cherokee ball player in North Carolina being scratched before the game, according to the old ritual. On his chest can be seen the marks of earlier scratchings. *Smithsonian Institution.*

Mississippi Choctaw drummer. The drum is of the European type, beaten with two sticks. On his chest are three metal gorgets, probably heirlooms. He is drumming for the dance that precedes the traditional Choctaw ball-game. *Museum of the American Indian.*

As has already been told, the Iroquois were strong enough to receive reservations in their own country in New York, where about nine thousand of them remain to this day. Mostly mixed in blood, they are still proudly Iroquois. Several generations ago, a steel bridge was built across the St. Lawrence River, one end of it being on the reservation occupied by the Mohawks. Indians got jobs as common laborers. Much interested in what was going on, they showed remarkable ability in climbing all over the structure, an apparently inborn sure-footedness, and lack of fear of heights. Presently some of them were promoted to jobs on the actual steel; in the end there were Mohawk riveters.

Interest in this type of work spread among the tribes of the League. Today, structural steel work, and especially work on the "high iron" of skyscrapers and great bridges, is an Iroquois specialty. Iroquois, both Christians and the followers of Handsome Lake's revision of the ancient faith, have worked on most of the important steel structures in the country, clear across to the Golden Gate Bridge. Because New York City provides a great deal of such work and the Brooklyn Navy Yard was a source of steady employment, there is an Iroquois colony in Brooklyn. The Christians attend a church with a minister who preaches in Seneca, the traditionalist "longhouse" followers hold simple ceremonies in their apartments, and all go home at intervals to maintain contact with their tribes.

I got into an argument one time with a Seneca and an Oneida, both of whom were steel workers, and a North Carolina Cherokee who was a physical instructor. All three had played on Jim Thorpe's famous Carlisle football team, and all three looked it. They were three of the handsomest men and finest physical specimens I have ever seen. I do not remember what the argument was about now, except that it dealt with Indian affairs and that my disagreement with them came from the belief that they—who had better than a high-school education, spoke perfect English, and were thoroughly experienced in making their own way in the white man's world—wanted to apply principles that would work for them to Indians who had no such advantages. What sticks in my mind is the sense of how deeply Indian they were for all their sophistication; their concern for all Indians regardless of their own ability to go it alone; and the fantastic difference between those three, for all their Indianness and, say, a Navaho singer with his long hair done up in a queue, turquoise in his ears, and no knowledge of English whatsoever.

Mentioning Thorpe, the great Sac and Fox athlete, and Carlisle calls for a little enlargement. Carlisle Indian

Seminole girl educated at the Cherokee boarding school in North Carolina, in full tribal regalia, using the sewing machine at the Indian day school on her home reservation for the appliqué work that is a Seminole specialty. *U. S. Dept. of Interior.*

School was founded in Pennsylvania for a purpose of inspired and brutal benevolence. Indians of high-school age were taken—often almost literally kidnapped—from the Western reservations and sent there, to remain for four, six, or more years. The idea was to break them completely away from their families and their tribes, forbid any speaking of their native languages or any manifestation of their native culture, and put them through a course of sprouts that would make them over into white men. For the summer vacations, they were placed in the homes of farmers or

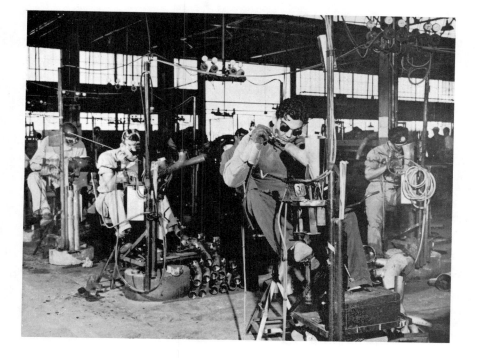

Skilled war workers at the Ryan Company plant near Phoenix. The man farthest back is white, the other three are Indians, tribes not identified. *U. S. Dept. of Interior.*

Navaho Marines in the South Pacific. Some 3,600 Navahos served in the armed forces in World War II. Humiliation over the number of men who were rejected because they were illiterate and non-English-speaking was one factor in the awakening of the tribe to the importance of education. *U. S. Dept. of Interior.*

Navaho communications team in the South Pacific in World War II. The Marines recruited a select group of Navahos and gave them special training. By sending over the air in Navaho, they could deliver and receive messages in a code that the enemy was unable to break, without any of the loss of time involved in the usual processes of encoding and decoding. *U. S. Dept. of Interior.*

Another Indian winner of the Congressional Medal of Honor, Lt. Ernest Childers of the Oklahoma Creeks. *U. S. Dept. of Interior.*

Lt. Jack C. Montgomery, Oklahoma Cherokee, receiving the Congressional Medal of Honor from President Roosevelt while his family looks on. *U. S. Dept. of Interior.*

An older Blackfoot lady in best costume, in her tepee at the annual Sun Dance gathering, Montana, 1951. A grandchild hangs in an improvised but secure hammock on the left. *U. S. Dept. of Interior*.

Fort Hall Indian baby being carried in an old-style, well-decorated cradleboard. *U. S. Dept. of Interior*.

Navaho children in the boarding school at Tuba City (which is no city) on the reservation. Boarding children as young as this is another example of the frantic efforts to provide schooling in a land of vast distances and almost no roads.

U. S. Dept. of Interior.
Photo by Milton Snow.

Indian women employed in the office of the Bureau of Indian Affairs in Washington. For this publicity picture they borrowed Indian clothes; not one of them is wearing the dress of her own tribe.

U. S. Dept. of Interior.

Old Choctaw spinner, Oklahoma, with her spinning wheel. Like others of the five tribes, the Choctaws learned the use of the wheel in colonial times. Today, among those who live in the barren hill country, spinning can add two or more dollars a month to incomes running around $48 a year plus a small amount of crops.

U. S. Dept. of Interior.

A bunch of San Carlos Apache cattle. These white-faced short-horns have come a long way from the "pink and green" collection of odd creatures with which the tribe started. A couple of animals towards the rear show traces of the early, longhorn strain.

U. S. Dept. of Interior.

small-town people, mostly Quakers or Pennsylvania Dutch, who worked them hard and treated them well. There is no question that they learned a lot, but de-Indianizing them did not work. The Carlisle graduates who were the most valuable were those who returned to their tribes and, after a rather painful process of restoring contacts with their own people and the old ways, became leaders among them.

Carlisle went in heavily for athletics and produced magnificent football teams, the greatest during the time that Jim Thorpe was there. They regularly whipped the big Eastern university teams. They were so ingenious that the rulebook had constantly to be revised to meet their bright ideas. For instance—there was nothing in the book that said you could not deflate the football. They equipped their backs with leather stomach pads the same color as a football, then ran a fake in the course of which the quarterback stuck a needle in the ball and flattened it. The backs spread out and ran separately, all acting as if they had the ball, or as if no one had it. When that was stopped, they produced a runner with an extraordinarily hollow back. The quarterback swiftly stuffed the ball inside that man's jersey, a fake was run around right end, the man with the hidden ball strolled in a lost way around left end, then ran in the clear. Of their remarkable contributions to the art of football, perhaps the most durable is the shoestring play, which is still occasionally worked. That is the play in which, when the teams line up, one player on the offensive team—usually an end—remains on the sideline, apparently tieing a shoelace and unaware that he is missing the boat. The signal for the play is usually called the play before, so that as soon as the teams are in position and before the defense has had time to notice the missing man, the ball is snapped. Immediately the shoestring tier races down the field to receive a long forward pass. If not spotted by the defense before it starts, this play is usually good for a touchdown.

The school was closed and its plant taken over by the Army in World War I, and it was never reopened.

In this chapter there have been references to federally recognized Indians, and throughout the book there have been references to reservations. It is time to explain the somewhat complicated question of what a reservation is and what the status of an Indian is.

Reservations originally were areas of land reserved for Indians, to which they were supposed to be confined. The idea of confinement has long been forgotten. A reservation today is a tract of land, large or small, good or worthless, reserved for the exclusive use of a specific group of Indians and held in trust for that group by the United States. It is exempt from taxation, and so is income derived from it. No part of it can be sold, given away, taken by foreclosure or other process, rented or leased without the consent of both the owners and the trustee. The trustee in important matters is the Secretary of the Interior, in minor ones the Commissioner of Indian Affairs. The government is also responsible for ensuring that the land is properly used and its resources not wasted. One tribe, owning a valuable stand of timber, talked the trustee into agreeing to a sale of the timber that resulted in great waste and damage and a poor return to the tribe. When the Indians woke up to what they had let themselves in for, they turned around and successfully sued the United States for several million dollars of compensation since the trustee had failed in his duty!

Such land is called "trust land," because it is in trust, and "restricted land," since its owners are restricted to some extent in their use of it, more so in disposing of it. Granted the restrictions, the ownership of such land, tax exempt and producing tax-exempt income, is obviously a desirable thing; any of us might like to enjoy the same right.

A reservation has another important quality. In legal language, it is "Indian country." With certain exceptions, Indian country is exempt from state law, and state courts and police have no authority within it. It is subject to federal law, lawsuits arising within it are tried in federal courts, major crimes are controlled by federal statutes. For the Indians within Indian country, lesser crimes, including some we rate as felonies, and such matters as marriage, divorce, and ordinary business relationships are under the jurisdiction of the tribe. This jurisdiction is the foundation on which tribal self-government, even the continued existence of tribes as tribes, exists. All strong tribes maintain their own police and courts, and jealously guard their right of home rule.

An Indian may leave his reservation any time he likes, without asking anyone's permission (except for a couple of Pueblos in the Southwest, which still enforce their old law requiring permission from their own government before a tribesman can absent himself). He can come back

ADAHOONIŁIGII

THE NAVAHO LANGUAGE MONTHLY

VOL. 2 NO. 3   WINDOW ROCK, ARIZONA   JANUARY 1, 1947

'AHKEAH HONEESNÁ 'ÁKO BÉÉSH BĄĄH DAH NAAZ NILÍGÍÍ YÁ DAH NÁNÍDAAHÍ SILĮĮ'!!

Niłch'its'ósí ńdízídéę bighi' Naabeehó binant'a'í béésh bąąh dah naaznilígíí yá dah nánídaahii dooleeł biniighé Sam 'Ahkeah dóó Chéé Dodge diné naaltsoos bá 'adayiiznil. Sam 'Ahkeah naaltsoos dįįdi miil dóó ba'aan naakidi neeznádiin bá 'aníídee. Chee Dodge t'éiyá naaltsoos naakidi miil dóó ba'aan naakidi neeznádiin bá 'aníídee'.

Sam Ahkeah k'ad naanishtsoh haa deet'ą, 'éí hoł bééhózin. Sam Ahkeah t'éiyá Naat'áanii Néézdéé' naaghá dóó k'ad 'ashdladiin binááhai lá jiní. Fort Lewis Colorado hoolghéedi 'ííłta' dóó Naat'áanii Néezgi dó' 'ííłta' jiní. 'Ólta' yits'áníyáá dóó Colorado bighi' 'akał bistłee'ii ła' yá naalnishgo tseebíí nááhai jiní. 'Áádóó Gad Deelzha hoolghéedi (Mesa Verde) nináánálnishgo tseebííts'áadah nínáánááhai jiní. Bilagáana bitahjí t'éiyá 'aghá naagháá ńt'éé jiní, 'áko ndi t'áadoo bidine'é yóó 'iidíí'ąą da. Bilagáana bitaajigháago t'áadoo le'é bíhojiił'ą'ąą shįį bee Naabeehó dine'é bee bide'ádahoot'éhígíí binjilnisngo díkwíí shįį ńdoohah. Naabeehó dine'é t'óó 'ahayóí haa dadzólí dóó shįį naat'áanii 'ídlįįgi hwééhodoozįł. T'áá bí 'áníigo t'éiyá t'áá 'ii' shéłjaa'ígi bee shidine'é bá ndeeshnish ní jiní.

NAHASDZAAN NAALTSOOS BIKAA' BE'ELYAA

'Anaa' baa na'aldeeh yęędą́ą́ nihe'ena'í danlíinii ha'át'íishįį "rocket" deiłníigo doo deighánígóó nahashkáá' ńdadijahgo 'ádayiilaa lá jiní. 'Éí bee'eldǫǫh bikǫ' yii' hééł 'ańdayiil'įįhgo yee 'ádanihi'niiłdįįd ńt'éé' lá jiní. 'Áko 'éí bits'ą́ą́ bénálkáá' dóó k'ad nááńáłahgo choo'įįgo 'ályaa jiní. K'ad t'éiyá bee 'ak'inda'a'nílí (camera) biih nát'áahgo deigo dadildon jiní. Deigo hastą́diin dóó ba'aan 'ashdladi tsin sitą́ągóó 'ánálgho'go 'áádéé nahasdzáán naaltsoos yik'i niyiiniíł jiní.

NAABEEHO ŁA' TIDIILYAA JINI

Díí kwii be'elyaaígíí t'éiyá 'Ahéhéshįįhdi 'ólta'ági 'áhoot'é. Kwii t'áá 'áłaji shí nahalin. 'Áłchíní doo da'ólta' dago kwii hodootł'izhtahgóó ndaanée łeh. (Ph. courtesy Sherman Inst.)

NAABEEHO LA' DIYOGI YEE HONEESNA

Hoozdo hoolghéedi Arizona State Fair baa na'aldeeh yęędą́ą́ Naabeehó 'asdzání Mabel Burnside Myers gholghéé léí diyogí ch'il bee da'iiltsxóhígíí bee 'ályaago yee honeesná jiní. Mabel Myers t'éiyá Naat'áanii Néezdi 'ólta'ági diyogí 'ál'įįgi bíhoo'aah jiní. Diyogí ts'ídá 'agháadi 'ánoolinígíí dó' yee honeesná jiní.

CHEE DODGE DAATSAAH

Chee Dodge t'áá yéigo daatsaahgo

TSASK'EH BA HOOGHAN DIILTŁA

Hayíiłkąągo Atlanta Georgia hoolghéedi tsásk'eh bá hooghan ńt'éé' diiltła lá jiní. 'Éí Bilagáana t'ááłáhádi neeznádiin dóó ba'aan dįįts'áadah yilt'éego nabistseed dóó neeznádiin yilt'éego t'éiyá t'óó tídadiilyaa lá jiní. T'áá 'íídáą́' ła' hadádahodeezk'ą́ą́ lágo 'inda kǫ'ígíí hadazdees'įį' jiní. Ła' t'áá 'ákóne' dazhdíílid dóó ła' t'éiyá tsésǫ'déé' hadah dahidiijéś'góo dazhneezná jiní. Ła' tł'óół 'ádayiilaago yee hadah dahideeshch'ą́ą́l ńt'éé' níyolgo biniinaa t'óó hadah 'ahizhneezdee jiní. Ła' 'áníigo t'éiyá ch'éénísdzid ńt'éé' diné hadah 'ahinidéehgo yiiłtsą ní jiní. 'Éí shįį be'esdzáán yił naa'aashgo dóó t'óó bééhádzidgo nihee honiigaii lá ní jiní. T'óó nihitsiiji bik'í'deediz dóó "fan" deiłníigo niłch'i 'ádeił'ínígíí haiigiz ní jiní. Diné kǫ' deiniłtsésígíí ła' 'áníigo t'éiyá 'asdzání ła' tsésǫ'déé' ba'áłchíní naaki

Public health nurse immunizing Navaho children. The Indian health service was transferred to the U. S. Public Health Service in 1955.
U. S. Dept. of Interior. Photo by Milton Snow.

The Navaho tribal saw mill, which brings income to the tribe and provides employment for a number of Navahos. Other tribal enterprises intended to improve the condition of the people include motels, trading posts, a supermarket, furniture factory, and a ceramics factory, as well as an arts and crafts marketing organization. *U. S. Dept. of Interior. Photo by Milton Snow.*

Class in a "trailer school" on the Navaho Reservation. The school itself is a Quonset hut; the associated buildings are trailers. More than anything else today the Navahos demand universal education, and the best achievement of the Eisenhower administration was getting the great majority of them into some sort of school. *U. S. Dept. of Interior. Photo by Milton Snow.*

Working conditions away from home—housing and sanitation for Navaho agricultural laborers off the reservation in New Mexico.

Poverty allows no choices. A Navaho *family* with an income of $1,000 a year from all sources is doing well.

U. S. Dept. of Interior.

Paul Jones, elected chairman of the Navaho Tribal Council in 1955. Well-educated, able, and devoted to the welfare of his people, he continued the line of exceptional chairmen that has been the Navahos' good fortune.
U. S. Dept. of Interior. Photo by Milton Snow.

Scott Preston, former Navaho vice-chairman. This picture does not show it, but Mr. Preston wears his hair in the traditional Navaho queue. *U. S. Dept. of Interior. Photo by Milton Snow.*

whenever he chooses. It can clearly be seen that reservations are *not* "concentration camps," despite much hysterical talk and even some hysterical books to the contrary.

Joint Indian-federal jurisdiction over Indian country goes back to the beginnings of our legal history and has been upheld over and again by the Supreme Court. It is an expression of an ancient, limited sovereignty subordinate to the national sovereignty.

Why do the Indians fear the state jurisdiction that the rest of us take for granted? Why are they so anxious to stay exempt from what one writer has called "the tender mercies of state sovereignty"? The answer is no credit to us, although in the states with Indian populations you will find individuals and groups, even special local organizations, sincerely friendly to Indians and working for their welfare and advancement. Good consciences are not localized in any one part of America. Yet it is true today as it has been true throughout our history that those who adjoin "Indian country" are those who discriminate most strongly against Indians.

A number of factors work together to make this true. Very early, as we have already seen, the frontiersmen adopted wholeheartedly the belief in the worthless, evil Indian, the concept that the only good Indian was a dead one. This belief, with the emphasis shifted now from the idea that the Indian is savage to the idea that he is shiftless and useless, continues, always reinforced by the widespread American prejudice against even moderately dark-skinned people. As you move away from where Indians live, you find this belief replaced by a somewhat romantic one, related to the old idea of the "noble red man." You find a sharp drop in race prejudice.

The hostile attitude—that they are shiftless and worthless—toward Indians serves a useful purpose. It makes it difficult or impossible for Indians to compete with non-Indians for jobs. It is used as a justification for trying to separate Indians from their property—above all, today as always, from their land. If today it often cannot be used to separate Indians from their land, it can be used to prevent them from exploiting it, thus enabling white men to get the use of it cheap.

For instance: Parts of several Apache tribes were settled on the San Carlos Reservation in Arizona, where for many years they sickened in idleness and survived on government rations. The reservation embraced a lot of good grazing land. Neighboring cattlemen argued that Apaches never could or would use that range; white men should have it. Under duress, under the eternal threat of troops, the Apaches were led to sign away about a quarter of the reservation.

All the good rangeland on the remainder was leased to a few powerful cattle companies. When, with the guidance and encouragement of a fine superintendent, in the early 1920's, the Apaches started running some small bunches of cattle of hopelessly mixed breed on the most worthless parts, the cattlemen were only amused. Then, by the most intense efforts, the Apache cattlemen began making a little money and buying good bulls, so that their herds were working up to where they were presentable, salable beef cattle. With the superintendent's support, the tribe refused to renew certain leases, needing the range to expand the Indians' own operations. Immediately the pressure became heavy upon senators and congressmen and upon the Indian Bureau, with outraged demands for the superintendent's removal.

The senators from Arizona showed conscience, the Indian Bureau was firm. There was a good deal of backing and filling, but by 1932 there were some 28,000 head of Indian-owned cattle grazing the range and all the leases had been ended. Still, the cattle interests had a string tied to the whole thing, for the Apaches were not allowed to breed their own bulls.

Their herds had started with odd longhorns—some from Mexico—dairy cows, anything they could get their hands on. To get decent "grade" beef cattle required careful breeding with registered bulls and continuous culling of off-colored cows. To produce suitable bulls, you must have a bull-breeding herd of registered cows and registered bulls. Otherwise, you must be constantly buying expensive bulls from other breeders. As the big Apache operation grew prosperous, the Indian cattlemen were required to spend thousands of dollars of their profits yearly buying good sires from non-Indians. Registered heifers they were forbidden to buy.

Under the same superintendent, a man no one could frighten, they solved their problem during the great drought of the 1930's. In this they had the cooperation (some non-Indian cattlemen would say the connivance) of the Commissioner of Indian Affairs. As a relief measure, the government was buying cattle from drought-devastated ranches. Some "drought relief cattle" were issued to Indians, many were butchered and distributed as food for relief purposes. The superintendent spotted a herd of registered heifers that was due to be bought before the creatures starved to death. The heifers were quietly shipped to the San Carlos Reservation. They were in such miserable condition that nobody thought twice about them. On the Apache grass they prospered, and suddenly the cattle interests were presented with something done and finished —the Indians had a registered bull-breeding herd. The fuss finally ended, the situation was taken for granted, and in time the San Carlos cattlemen were *selling registered bulls to white men.*

These Indians were also plagued by a petty war of attrition—fences cut, cattle "strayed," calves mavericked— an endless small harassment and thievery. It was difficult to cope with, since the missing animals were outside Indian country, where state law prevailed. The San Carlos Reservation lies in two counties. The situation improved at last, when the Apaches made it very plain that they would vote solidly for those county officials, especially sheriffs, who gave them equal treatment. It is remarkable how a solid bloc of several hundred votes can reduce a man's race prejudice.

This is only one example, and it happens to be one with a happy ending. Others, many with quite different

Navaho sheep on an exceptionally good piece of range where soil conservation practices have been fully established.

U. S. Dept. of Interior.

endings, can be found wherever the Indians are. In towns near reservations, Indians are often discriminated against. They are abused by the police, get the book thrown at them in local courts, are exploited for their money and contemptuously rejected for other purposes. This is no universal picture, but all too widely true. Some states have shown real conscience toward their Indians; others seem to be waking up, but still others, like South Dakota, Arizona, and Oklahoma, still contain areas with strong anti-Indian feeling. Recently, in Nebraska and South Dakota, white men have murdered Indians and have got away with it.

Here is one example. In a Nebraska town, near one of the Sioux reservations over the border in South Dakota, a white man looking out his window saw a Sioux named Standing Bear, against whom he had a grudge, coming down the street. He seized a baseball bat, ran out, and beat Standing Bear over the head with it until the Indian fell unconscious. Police picked Standing Bear up and threw him in jail, where he died in a few hours. The white man was arrested, pleaded guilty to manslaughter, and got

An Apache wickeyup of several years ago on the Fort Apache Reservation, Arizona. *U. S. Dept. of Interior.*

This picture, taken earlier in this century, shows the old Hopi village of Walpi, Arizona. The odd rock formation on which two boys are sitting is called "the dance rock," as in front of it most dances are held. Immediately to the left of it the poles of a ladder leading down into a kiva can be seen. On rooftops in the background are three clay jars with their bottoms knocked out, serving literally as chimney pots.

Courtesy of American Museum of Natural History.

Two-story house built in San Ildefonso Pueblo by the artist Wo Peen. After Wo Peen's right hand was shot off in a hunting accident, he successfully taught himself to paint with his left. In front stands his wife, a Taos Indian.

U. S. Dept. of Interior.

Life as it was about twenty years ago on the Fort Apache Reservation. To the left can be seen part of their wagon. Wagons replaced pack horses, and pickup trucks replaced wagons. Today these Apaches operate successful tribal enterprises, including a timber industry, a cattle herd, and recreational operations.

U. S. Dept. of Interior.

"Progress" under the allotment system—Sioux home on the Fort Totten Reservation, North Dakota, one of those that was thoroughly broken up by the workings of the Allotment Act.

U. S. Dept. of Interior.

a two years' suspended sentence. This, please note, is only one example; it could be multiplied many times. From the Indians' point of view, the rub is that had this crime been committed in Indian country, the defendant would have come up in federal court and would have got his just deserts, which leads to the even bigger point that had the white man encountered Standing Bear in Indian country he would not have dared kill him.

Hence the Indians with few exceptions hold strongly to their ancient right of home rule and federal protection. Hence, for all their constant dissatisfaction with the Bureau of Indian Affairs, they prefer its jurisdiction to that of the states. Hence their great alarm and sense of betrayal when in 1953 there was enacted, without debate and without hearings, over strong Indian protest, a law authorizing any state to assume civil and criminal legal jurisdiction over Indian tribes any time it wished to do so. The law, intended to hasten the integration of Indians into the rest of American society, and designed as part of a policy to terminate federal relations with the tribes (more on this below), has been used by different states ever since to try to exert various kinds of authority—including the right to tax—over the tribes. Just as consistently, it has been fought by the tribes.

The Indian use of the vote has come up a number of times in this chapter. Let us look now at the actual status of an Indian in the United States. It has changed greatly since the nineteenth century when Indians were in fact wards of the government, often forbidden to leave their reservations without a permit, but on the other hand forcibly carried off to far distant schools, subject to the intervention of the old-time "Indian agents" in their smallest affairs—regardless of whether the intervention was legal or no—their religious practices often forbidden, everything possible done to smash their tribal organizations and to break anyone who showed signs of becoming a real leader.

In 1924, in recognition of the Indians' splendid record

as volunteers in World War I, Congress passed a law extending citizenship to all of them. At the beginning of the Roosevelt administration, most of the laws restricting Indians' individual liberty were repealed and the Indian Bureau junked the outrageously unconstitutional regulation under which it controlled Indian worship. Some remaining restrictive laws were repealed at the beginning of the Eisenhower administration.

Since 1946, a series of important federal and state court cases has conclusively shown that Indians are no longer wards. The government has no more legal authority over an Indian's personal actions and choices than it has over other citizens'. "Legal authority" should be stressed. The trustee of the property of impoverished and all too often grossly uninformed people can find many ways of exerting pressure; for instance, frequently Indians cannot have access to their own funds without the consent of Congress, or the Department of the Interior, or both, and withholding of funds can be used to force agreements. The old paternalistic habits die hard. As recently as 1950 a superintendent issued an order forbidding gambling games on the Blackfoot Reservation after six P.M. His reason for doing this was that the old people were staying up late at traditional games that take the place that bridge, gin rummy and canasta do with many of ours. The Blackfeet appealed to their attorney, and the order was rescinded.

Indians have certain special rights as Indians, other than their jurisdiction over their land and exemption of that land from taxes. Their education, health service, and a number of other services that most of us get from counties or states are federal responsibilities, acknowledged as owed to the Indians for the lands they gave up. Generally, they have been available to Indians only so long as they reside on reservations. When an Indian has moved off a reservation, he has been regarded by the government as being on the same footing with everyone else, although in practice most federal Indian schools and hospitals have received nonreservation Indians. Recently, with the great increase in the number of Indians living in urban areas, it has been questioned whether nonreservation Indians, by right, should not be eligible for every benefit and service available to those on reservations. In other words, an Indian, it is argued, is an Indian, wherever he resides. Various statutes bearing on the subject have been interpreted both ways, and it will be up to Congress eventually to settle the matter. Meanwhile, some of the lines separating Indians from non-Indians have disappeared. For instance, the number of segregated Bureau of Indian Affairs schools for Indians is decreasing, and more and more Indians are attending state public schools, which receive federal subsidy payments for their Indian pupils. For many years these payments were made directly to the state school systems. But their flagrant misuse in some states (the money might be spent for non-Indian students, or on capital improvements for all the students, or the schools might have reported more Indian students than they actually had) has recently brought about changes, and the money is now being paid in most cases to the tribes, which then give it to the schools, making sure that it is used correctly for their own children.

Mrs. Anne Wauneka, daughter of the late Chee Dodge, first chairman of the Navaho Council, herself a delegate to the Council and chairman of its committee on health. Mrs. Wauneka is one of the most forceful and effective members of the Navaho governing team and has done a great deal to improve the tribe's grave health situation. *U. S. Dept. of Interior. Photo by Milton Snow.*

Mrs. Wauneka explaining a health exhibit to tribesmen at the Navaho tribal fair. *U. S. Dept. of Interior. Photo by Milton Snow.*

Tuberculous Navaho girls at the Fort Defiance sanatorium on the reservation. The building was old, in need of renovating (note peeling paint), and hopelessly inadequate. Arrangements were made by which most serious Navaho cases got sanatorium treatment, their cases actively followed up by the tribe's committee on health. The tribe itself has appropriated considerable sums of money to aid in fighting the scourge. *U. S. Dept. of Interior. Photo by Milton Snow.*

Indians do not get pensions from the government. Uncle Sam does not feed them. One of the many frustrations Indians encounter when they go to the cities seeking work is that employers, and also people concerned with relief, if the Indian winds up out of luck, will say, "Why don't you go back to the reservation and let the government take care of you?" The government won't take care of him. Indian rights to relief are the same as anyone else's, less what some states refuse to give. Occasionally, in extreme cases, where some disaster has a whole community starving, the Indian Bureau will manage to finagle some surplus commodities out of the Department of Agriculture and sometimes a little money out of Congress, but these are exceptions.

In the 1880's, wars with the Indians were about ended. Then began the system of attacks upon them by legal means which has never been entirely stopped. By 1880 almost all tribes were on reservations of some sort. Their total holdings amounted to 155,000,000 acres. It was then that well-meaning persons came up with a wonderful idea for civilizing them quickly. The theory was that tribal ownership of the reservations strengthened the existence of the tribes, hence held the individuals back; that the finest thing that can happen to any man is to own his own land with a fence around it; and that if each Indian were given an allotment of land in his own name, all would quickly become hard-working farmers. Since the Indians were a doomed and dying race, if everyone got an adequate allotment of land right away, there would be no need to worry about having more land available for the future. As the allotment system was finally worked out, the typical arrangement was to give 160 acres to each adult, 80 to each minor child.

Allotments would remain in trust, on the same basis as reservations, for twenty-five years. By then, the oldest and most conservative would have died off, the younger people would have civilized themselves, and the "Indian problem" would be ended. After twenty-five years, patents in fee would be issued to the allottees, and to all intents and purposes they would no longer be Indians. Their lands could be sold or mortgaged, or otherwise used as they thought best, and that would be that.

The well-intentioned proponents of this program overlooked a number of points. Most Indians did not think in terms of individual ownership of land, although they might have a strong sense of individual *use* of it; to some of them, parcelling out the earth, the mother of all, was blasphemous. No steps had been taken, nor were any adequate steps planned, to prepare Indians to manage their business affairs; to the contrary, the Indian Bureau's paternalism denied them all experience. A great number of the tribes to be allotted had no tradition or knowledge of farming whatsoever, and further, the greater part of the land involved was unfit to farm and could be profitably used only for grazing, which requires large units with both summer and winter ranges.

A great many people who had no love for Indians at all saw other possibilities in the allotment plan. Setting aside the Southwest, where no one wanted the land and most tribes were obviously far too primitive to have the scheme applied to them, if all Indians got allotments there would be great chunks of reservations left over, which would be declared "surplus," bought from the tribes for a song, and opened for homesteading or purchase. Here was a chance to grab off a lot of Indian property quickly. Then, in twenty-five years would come the fee-patenting. Knowing the realities of the Indians' preparation for outright ownership, many of their neighbors realized happily that anyone who couldn't swindle newly "liberated" owners out of what he wanted must have a hole in his head. So, with a whoop of joy the despoilers joined the well-wishers, and in 1887 the General Allotment Act was passed.

Some tribes resisted allotment vigorously, standing upon their treaties. A few managed to keep some reserve of land in tribal ownership, but very few indeed, outside of the Southwest, where allotment was hardly attempted, could stand against the pressure brought upon them. The reservations were allotted, the surplus lands ceded, and in due course came the issuing of patents in fee.

As noted, successful grazing in the West calls for large units of land. There are many areas where it takes from ten to twenty acres to support a cow year-round. You must have both summer and winter range, or else summer range—the typical, high, open country of the West—plus good land on which you can raise winter feed. Above all, you must have water, and water sources are often far apart. If you have no access to water, your lands are useless. Small operators, family outfits running fifty to a hundred head of stock, cannot afford to buy feed or to drill 1,000-foot wells in hope of striking water. What works for them is an operation such as the San Carlos one—pooled herds on a large area of land held in common, providing a decent living for over 1,500 people.

It was, and is, unnecessary to buy all the range to control it. See to it that the man on whose 160 acres the water is gets his patent in fee, or do the same for those who received the sheltered, winter range. Offer this man and that one $3,000—it is more money than he ever heard of in his life and he can imagine no end to it. If necessary, get him drunk. Talk him into signing a mortgage he cannot pay off, does not understand that he must pay off, and in due course foreclose. Now you have the range. There is nothing for the other owners to do but lease to you, cheap, and most big cattle companies prefer leasing the bulk of their land, if the price is right, to tying up capital by buying.

That is the system. To it must be added another factor. Indians have a high birthrate and die early, and most of them die without making wills. In a surprisingly short period of time a given piece of land will have been divided equally among the heirs of the original allottee, of his children, and of some of his grandchildren. It will have a

dozen or so, in some cases scores, of owners. An heir may receive a check for one cent in payment of his share of a year's lease. In some cases the paper work for a single lease costs more than a year's rental. In desperation, the Indian Bureau officials seek to end the mess by getting the land fee patented and selling it. This is the easy way out; the hard way, that both the Bureau and Congress have shirked for seventy years, is to arrange a system of credit by which the tribes could buy up the land and keep it in Indian use.

Soon, it became painfully obvious that automatically issuing fee patents at the end of twenty-five years would be grotesquely wrong, and the Department of the Interior began extending the trust periods from year to year. Even so, the record of the Allotment Act is painfully clear. There were 155,000,000 acres left to Indians out of what had once been the entire United States. After the Act was passed, better than 5,000,000 acres were added to the Navaho Reservation, making a total of over 160,000,000. By 1933, when the Roosevelt administration put a temporary stop to the ruination of the Indian estate, 47,000,000 acres remained. Nearly 75 percent had been lost to Indian ownership. Under Roosevelt, an attempt was made to enable tribes to buy in land and to recapture "surplus" land that had not been occupied, and for the first time in our history Indian land holdings increased. Today Indian tribes own approximately 55,500,000 acres in the "lower forty-eight states" and 40,000,000 acres in Alaska.

We begin to see the gimmick in the theoretically favorable legal status of Indians. From administration to administration the policy has changed, but until 1929 it had a general direction, which was to de-Indianize by breaking up the tribes, destroying tradition, preventing group action, doing everything possible to make it impossible for the Indians to make themselves heard. Along with this went a grim travesty of education, schools that held

Tribal Court of the Shoshone-Bannocks on the Fort Hall Reservation, Idaho. In this case a woman was convicted of assaulting another. As she was the sole support of her children, she was not put in jail, but sentenced to work out her time washing the agency windows on Saturdays. *U. S. Dept. of Interior.*

Navaho furnishings, inside a log hogan. Poverty and crowding invite disease. *U. S. Dept. of Interior. Photo by Milton Snow.*

sick and hungry children to long hours of manual labor, a system of training that had as its highest aim making girls into domestic servants (an occupation Indians deeply dislike), boys into farmers and day laborers.

Add to this the great susceptibility of Indians to the new diseases we brought among them, and especially the ravages tuberculosis can make among under-nourished, discouraged people in wretched housing and with no concept of sanitation. Add a medical service that was an even grimmer farce than the education. Add the abuses to which Indians are still subjected, already described. Consider that these people, after two hundred years of bitter experience, have every reason to hold that becoming "just like a white man" is a poor thing indeed. You will begin to understand why the Indians did not progress, you will wonder, indeed, how they have survived.

Reform, especially in education and simple respect for human dignity, began under President Hoover and gained pace under President Franklin D. Roosevelt. It is an interesting story of our own times, because, despite setbacks, it brought about great changes—changes that even in the 1970's were continuing to take place with increasing speed. It really began with the Lewis Meriam report in the late 1920's, which pointed out to the government the scandalous conditions of the Indians and recommended many reforms. In 1934, responding to the Meriam survey, Congress passed the Indian Reorganization Act, which provided, among other things, firm authority for tribes not only to set up and run their own local governments but to form corporations for business purposes. It set up a revolving credit fund to help the Indians get themselves on their feet economically, and made it possible, if tribes could find the money, for them to buy in allotments. Also, it directed the restoration of freedom of religion for the Indians, and encouraged the tribes to revive their own cultural traditions.

The Indian Reorganization Act soon came under attack from many whites who feared that the Indians, through their tribal organizations, would be able to protest wrongs done to them and to defend their rights. But the most serious questioning came from many Indians themselves. They liked most of the features of the act, but one of its provisions, though well meant, was opposed by a number of tribes, and as time went on, it was proved that they were right. This was the provision that authorized tribes to set up and run their own local governments. On the surface, it seemed like a forward step. Most tribes had had no self-government since their defeat by the white men and had been governed entirely by Bureau of Indian Affairs agents, soldiers, and missionaries, many of whom had behaved like dictators on the reservations. Now the Indians were to be able to govern themselves. The trouble was that the act imposed on all tribes a uniform type of constitution and government, modeled on the white man's system. Some tribes, lacking any form of self-government, were agreeable to trying the white man's system. But others found it strange, totally alien to their own needs and customs, or disruptive because they still had a traditional government that functioned effectively for their people.

Thus, most of the Hopi towns were still well governed by their traditional religious leaders and saw no need for another government, especially a white man's government that would be in conflict with their religious leaders. Many of the Sioux people, also, still looked to their traditional chiefs, headmen, and holy men as counselors and leaders and found it difficult accepting the white man's idea of how they should be governed. The result was that on many reservations, a majority of the people did not vote for the new constitutions and the new type of government, and, as it turned out, never gave it support. This had bad consequences. In time, on many reservations, the so-called self-government degenerated into tribal councils composed of cliques of Indian politicians who were elected by minorities and ignored or boycotted by majorities. In such a situation, the gaps between the councils and the public majorities widened, so that the governments were not truly representative of the tribe and were neither responsive nor responsible to the people.

The situation was worsened by the fact that the self-government itself was seriously limited. The councils were like the legislatures in British colonies, with little or no control over anything important. The real boss on the reservation was still the Bureau of Indian Affairs agent, who usually told the council what to do and had a veto power over financial affairs and almost everything else that mattered. The people could recognize this, and, as a rule, they had little respect for their political officeholders, considering them more as rubber stamps for the white man and the federal government. The officeholders' position was really a difficult one. Many of them wanted to be responsible to their own people and do what was best for them, but they could see that they really had to be responsible to the Bureau of Indian Affairs. If they bucked the agent, they could get into all sorts of trouble. They could anger him enough to cause him to cut programs and federal funding or even to oust the officeholder from his position. The dilemma could never be solved until the Bureau of Indian Affairs was stripped of all authority and "bossism" over reservation affairs, and full freedom was given to the Indians to really run their own affairs for themselves, like all other people in the country. As we shall see, this became a big issue in the late 1960's, when the Indians began to demand freedom and the right to have governments of their own choosing on the reservations.

Meanwhile, by the end of the 1940's, the Indian Reorganization Act had come into desperate trouble at the hands of white opponents. Not only did Congress not appropriate enough funds to make its various provisions workable, but bureaucrats in the Bureau of Indian Affairs

Flathead Indian, Montana, operating the band-saw sharpener belonging to his family's lumber company. *U. S. Dept. of Interior.*

were definitely hamstringing and sabotaging the carrying out of the act. In reality, despite all the handicaps and opposition, Indian progress in many ways had been great. I remember when a new school was building on the Navaho Reservation in 1930. The only work Navahos got out of it was quarrying and hauling a certain soft limestone. Ten years later, with other construction going on, the bulk of the workmen, straw bosses, and foremen were Navahos, and there were Navahos in the drafting room. Within the next few years there were Navaho graduate engineers as well. All across Indian country, a spirit of initiative, pride,

Modern tribal self-government—voting in the Navaho general election. A special system of ballots on which the pictures of candidates are printed is used, since most Navahos cannot read. *U. S. Dept. of Interior.*

Unemployed Indians' shanties in Pinoleville, California.
U. S. Dept. of Interior.

and self-confidence was taking hold. A new day was being born, pointing not only to economic improvement, but to an atmosphere of renewed Indian dignity on the reservations.

Unfortunately, it was all soon nipped in Washington. Congressmen, seeing only the failures (much of which was their own fault, through lack of funding) and thinking that Indian progress was not taking place fast enough, decided that the only answer was to get rid of "the Indian problem" once and for all by terminating all federal relations with the tribes as fast as possible. In 1953 Congress shocked almost every Indian in the country by passing a "termination" resolution which proclaimed its intent to turn the Indians over to the states in which they resided. Arbitrarily, against the wishes of the tribes, it meant the breaking of all the treaties and the ending of the rights that had been guaranteed by the treaties. It would put the Indians, their lands, and resources, at the mercy of state governments, which would amount to opening them to the aggrandizement of local white interests and state politicians. It would be up to the states to provide services to the Indians, almost all of whom were desperately poor and ill-equipped to compete in the white economy. Few states, it was clear, possessed the funds or resources to care for the Indians, even if they wished to do so. The future of the reservations was plain for all to see. They would cease to exist. In time, there would be no more tribes and no more Indians. They would melt into the white population, and only memories would remain. This, in fact, was Congress's goal. What it envisioned was the forced assimilation of the Indians so there would be no more Indian problems and no further need for Indian appropriations and drains on the taxpayers for federal services to the Indians.

The "termination" policy, pushed with a great degree of insensitivity and ruthlessness by Senator Arthur Watkins of Utah, was carried out without adequate planning or preparation, and over the objection of the Indians, against a number of tribes, including the Menominees of Wisconsin, the Klamaths of Oregon, some Utes in Utah, various Paiute

bands, some western Oregon tribes, and the Alabamas and Texas Coushattas in the South. Particularly in the cases of the Menominees and the Klamaths it was a disaster, bringing hardship and new wrongs to the affected tribes. The Menominees, for instance, found their reservation turned into a county in Wisconsin. Indian resources could not meet the needs of supporting a county, including the usual hospital, police, and other services, and the tax demands on the people soon broke them. They ran through their tribal and individual savings and had to begin opening their lands and forests to white real estate developers and other exploiters. Even that was not enough. Wisconsin became saddled with a huge welfare program which it could not underwrite, and eventually the state had to ask the federal government for help. So, in a short time, large sums of federal welfare funds had to be appropriated by Congress for the Menominees whom the government had thought it had gotten rid of. By the end of the 1960's, the Menominees had had enough of termination. New leaders arose and united most of the people behind a demand that the termination of the Menominees be repealed. Led principally by a brilliant and able young Menominee woman, Ada Deer, the cause received substantial backing in Congress, and by 1973 it seemed certain that the people would again receive federal recognition as a tribe and that steps would be taken to rectify the hurts and damages of the termination period.

The termination policy was paralleled by another government program, which also aimed at hastening the Indians' assimilation. It was called a "relocation" program. Indians on reservations were screened, and those who seemed that they could "make it" in the cities were sent to such places as Chicago, Denver, and Los Angeles, where Bureau of Indian Affairs officials helped them find jobs and homes. Some Indians made the transition successfully and have continued to live among the whites in the urban areas. But the program was considered vicious by most Indians because it was not balanced by help in remedying the distress on reservations, and because in most cases the government lost interest in the "relocated" Indians after they had been in the cities a short time. When Indians lost their jobs or homes, they became stranded persons in strange and alien surroundings. Many of them returned to their reservations, but others suffered greatly and had to be cared for by church and charitable institutions in the cities. The "relocation" program was eventually considered more of a failure than a success, and, during the Johnson administration, was all but abandoned.

Still another program, begun in 1946, was motivated by the hope of ending the "Indian problem." This was the establishment of an Indian Claims Commission, which provided the opportunity for every tribe to present evidence of unfair land dealings in the past so that the government, where fairness demanded, could pay compensation to the tribes for whatever lands they had lost unfairly or ceded for less than they should have received. The idea was that every tribe that still smoldered over the loss of its lands in the past could have its grievance settled, and, with the slate thus wiped clean, the government could then terminate the tribe with a clear conscience. The Indians took advantage of the opportunity and lodged more than 580 claims. By the end of 1972 some $450,000,000 had been paid to settle more than half of nearly 400 claims decided. Approximately 200 additional claims were still to be settled before the commission's expiration date in 1977.

Because of the opposition of the tribes, the distress caused to the Indians, and the obvious immorality of what was being done, the implementation of the termination policy came to an end in the early 1960's. The resolution of 1953 continued on the books, understood as the ultimate intention of Congress, and legislation affecting some tribes contained warnings that they should prepare for termination. But the Kennedy and Johnson administrations dropped all talk of termination, and in 1970 President Nixon announced that, as far as his administration was concerned, termination was dead. Nevertheless, the events of the 1950's had been a terrible shock to the tribes, and they have continued ever since wary and watchful for any sign of a renewed termination threat.

The fear that termination might be slipped over them in some other guise, in fact, contributed to a whole new set of relations between the tribes and the federal government that began to emerge in 1961. In the summer of that year, a conference of hundreds of tribal representatives and individual Indians from all over the country, meeting at Chicago University, took the offensive, and in a "Declaration of Indian Purpose" demanded self-determination for the tribes and their right to participate in the management and control of their own affairs. Congress and the Kennedy and Johnson administrations were slow to respond, but during the 1960's the Indian voice grew stronger and more insistent, and by 1967 President Johnson was forced to acknowledge in a message to Congress that Indians should have those rights.

But, as the Indians well knew from experience, white men's words were one thing, and their actions another. The Johnson administration almost deliberately ignored any substantive changes that would increase the Indians' control of their own lives, but concentrated, instead, on trying to devise and carry out programs that would improve the Indians' lot and raise their standard of living. These efforts had some curious and unforeseen results that served to increase the Indians' political restlessness and their irritation with white men who continued to think up and impose programs on them. In the past, Indians had rarely shared in federal programs designed for the general population. The custom had been that all programs for Indians were designed and carried out especially for them by the Bureau of Indian Affairs, and those programs were all they got. In the early 1960's something of a precedent was set when reservations were included as beneficiaries under the Area Redevelopment Act, which had been designed primarily to aid the depressed Appalachian region. In 1964, when the Economic Opportunity Act was being planned as the keystone of President Johnson's "war on poverty," Indians were not included in the first drafts. Hundreds of Indians and white friends of Indians gathered in Washington in May at a great Capitol Conference on Indian Poverty and, in a masterful public relations job, persuaded Congress and the Administration to include Indians in the final draft of the act.

The result was a momentous breakthrough for the Indians. Under the workings of the various programs of the Office of Economic Opportunity, established by the act,

Oglala Sioux women on the Pine Ridge Reservation, South Dakota, preparing beef for drying as their ancestors once prepared buffalo meat—in much larger quantities.
U. S. Dept. of Interior.

A successful, well educated Shoshone farm family on the Fort Hall Reservation in Idaho. The husband and wife still carry the baby about in a cradleboard. These devices have many advantages for handling infants, and frequently white families who live among Indians adopt them. *U. S. Dept. of Interior.*

the tribes themselves could suggest and devise their own programs. Once they were approved, funds were made available to the Indians, who ran the programs themselves. It was the first time that tribes were actually managing and controlling their own affairs, assuming responsibility for programs that really met the needs of their people as they —and not non-Indian bureaucrats—saw it, and, by and large, they proved that they were fully capable of carrying out functions that previously had been executed for them by federal officials.

The experience was a historic one. Indian attitudes, based on a new self-confidence, changed almost overnight. Individual Indians, tribes, and regional and national Indian organizations like the National Congress of American Indians and the somewhat militant National Indian Youth Council, led by young, mostly college-educated Indians, now increased their demand for self-determination, and the right to participate in the designing of all programs for them and to manage all reservation affairs. The Office of Economic Opportunity example was lost on the Johnson administration, however, and it was left to the Republicans of the Nixon administration to evidence the first meaningful acknowledgment of what the Indians were demanding.

By the end of the 1960's, therefore, two developments could be noted. The economic measures of the Kennedy and Johnson administrations had brought some material benefits to the reservations. New programs and increased funds had made a start at improving housing, sanitation, and health facilities, at expanding manpower development and vocational training, and in getting more Indian students into schools and colleges. At the same time, Indians had become more assertive in their demands and in drawing attention to their grievances.

Their problems were still numerous and overwhelming. Despite the growing affluence of the rest of the country, there was still grinding poverty on the reservations. Most Indian housing was still substandard. Many reservations had no running water, little or no sanitation, scant electricity or other utilities, inadequate medical and dental services, and few roads. Rates of unemployment and underemployment were astronomically high. Average incomes were far below the national level. Life expectancy was lower than that of whites; the death rate was still higher than that of the rest of the population; and the suicide rate of Indians living lives of frustration and desperation was far higher than that of non-Indians. The education of Indians, moreover, was stigmatized as a national scandal by a Senate subcommittee that investigated the subject in 1968. Schools, teachers, curricula, and teaching materials were deficient or inadequate. Indian children were taught without reference to their cultural backgrounds, their tribal histories, or their special needs. Their dropout rate— or, as it was termed, their "pushout" rate—was consequently high.

By the end of the 1960's all these factors, together with others, were having an effect on a new generation of young Indians, many of them reared in urban areas among whites, many of them well educated. Resentful over the continuing neglect and injustices suffered by their people, and finding a new pride in their own Indianness, they began to form various organizations devoted to the Indians' cause. Undoubtedly, many forces influenced them and made possible the new phenomenon they represented. Among them were the Blacks' civil rights struggle and the emergence of "third world" nations among former colonial peoples who had been oppressed like themselves. Moreover, these young Indians represented a generation more mobile than that of their elders; they were able to get around the United States and even the world, seeing peoples with higher standards of living. They were familiar with the use of modern communications and could confront whites with the whites' own methods and technology. Meeting one another on college campuses, at conferences, seminars, and powwows helped to draw them together in something

Dennis Banks, an Ojibwa (Chippewa) Indian who had been making his way successfully in the white man's world working for a large corporation, began to fight for justice for the Indians and became a national leader of the American Indian Movement. He is seen here during the occupation of the Bureau of Indian Affairs building in Washington, but he participated also at Wounded Knee and at other confrontations with whites. *Richard Erdoes.*

more than a dozen states. Federal officials finally ousted the Indians from Alcatraz the next year, but even more dramatic actions were in the offing.

There were causes for what were to take place. In July 1970, President Nixon started the government on a new course, announcing to Congress that his policy would be one of self-determination for the Indians without termination. To back up his words, he sent legislation to Congress designed to enable tribes to achieve self-determination and, at the same time, ordered a shake-up of the Bureau of Indian Affairs so that it would better serve the Indians and meet their demands for the right to run their own affairs. So far, so good. A new commissioner of Indian affairs, Louis Bruce, son of a Mohawk and a Sioux, brought innovative young Indians into policy-making positions in the Bureau of Indian Affairs and began a quiet revolution in federal-Indian relations. Still, so far, so good. Then, as had happened during the Indian Reorganization Act days, internal government opposition and sabotage began.

The crux of the problem this time was fear that if the Indians got the right to run their own affairs, white men would lose the ability to control the Indians' lands and resources, which were becoming increasingly valuable. It so happened that a massive assault had already been launched by American industry against Indian property. Dozens of tribes in the Southwest were fighting for their water rights, which were being taken from them for white developments. The lands of the Hopis, Navahos, Crows, and Northern Cheyennes, as stated earlier, were being leased for coal strip mines and polluting power plants. Other tribes were losing lands on long-term leases to builders of huge cities and resorts for whites on the reservations. In every case, the tribal councils were being advised and guided by the Department of the Interior and the Bureau of Indian Affairs, which encouraged the white ex-

of a Pan-Indian movement composed of individuals of all tribal backgrounds. From this grew quickly an Indian nationalism that became steadily more militant and activist, reflecting also the general spirit of protest and change that characterized the times.

In 1969, a group of Indians of all tribes in the San Francisco Bay area occupied Alcatraz Island, which had been abandoned as a federal prison. The episode, dramatically focusing non-Indians' attention on Indian grievances, inspired similar actions by other Indian groups in

Angry Indians, many of them members of the American Indian Movement, confront a line of helmeted state police, after the killing of an Indian by a white man at Custer, South Dakota, in 1973. The Indians protested the lightness of the charge placed against the white man, and claimed it reflected the region's prejudice and discrimination against Indians. *Ken Norgard.*

Thanksgiving, 1969, was observed with a buffet-style feast by Indians of All Tribes occupying the former federal prison on Alcatraz Island at San Francisco. The Indians claimed the island under an old treaty that had promised the return of unused federal land to the Sioux. They intended converting it to an educational and cultural center for all Indians, but were eventually driven from the island by federal officials. One of their leaders, Richard Oakes, a Mohawk, was soon afterward murdered by a white man in California.
Wide World Photos.

ploitation of the Indians' resources, approved the permits and leases, and, in the process, proved that they were not protecting the tribal resources as they were supposedly bound to do under the law. The truth of the matter was that the Department of the Interior, often encouraged by members of Congress, was accommodating powerful interests in the white man's business world. As long as it could maintain control over the Indians' affairs, it could continue this accommodation. Once the Indians got control, the game was through.

So, increasingly, President Nixon's policy and Commissioner Bruce's programs were undermined and nullified. Congress pigeon-holed the bills that President Nixon had wished passed, and finally all of Commissioner Bruce's authority was taken from him and given to his assistant,

who proceeded to halt or reverse the new programs. The Zuñis in New Mexico and the Miccosukees in Florida had been given the right to run their own affairs by Commissioner Bruce, but it ended there. Other tribes, standing in line for similar treatment, were turned away. A nationwide Indian protest followed, and Bruce's authority was restored to him. But the damage had been done. Indian self-determination had come to a halt, trapped in Watergate-period intrigue and corruption within the Department of the Interior. Collusion between certain government officials and friendly segments of white industry continued to loot the reservations.

These events had aroused the various Indian activists. To them were added other grievances. At Puget Sound, Indians were fighting desperately for their treaty-guar-

The fight to restore their rights and undo the damage caused them by termination saw Menominees struggling on both the state and national levels for many years. Here, Menominee spokesman James White (*right*) lists Indian objections to a white real estate development on their lands during a meeting with the Wisconsin Department of Natural Resources in Madison. *Wide World Photos.*

Activist Indians, armed with makeshift weapons, stand guard at the entrance to the Bureau of Indian Affairs building, which they occupied in Washington, D.C., in October and November, 1972. Members of the Trail of Broken Treaties, they had come to the nation's capital to plead peaceably for justice to all Indians. The group, numbering at times up to 1,000, seized the building in desperation after government spokesmen treated them high-handedly. *Wide World Photos.*

anteed fishing rights. The Indian leader, Hank Adams, was shot and wounded in the struggle. In California the Indian leader of the Alcatraz occupation, Richard Oakes, a Mohawk, was murdered, and his slayer was freed. In South Dakota and Nebraska blatant anti-Indian prejudice had resulted in the humiliation and murder of several Indians. Tribal leaders, who had formed a new, government-supported organization, the National Tribal Leaders Association, were unwilling or unable to protect their people and were called "Uncle Tomahawks" or "apples" (red on the outside, white inside) by the activists.

The explosion came in November 1972. A thousand or more Indians, many of them members of a group called the American Indian Movement, which had been organized in Minneapolis and Saint Paul in 1968 and had spread to many Indian centers, came to Washington in caravans known collectively as "The Trail of Broken Treaties" to present their grievances to President Nixon and the Democratic candidate for President, George McGovern. Unable to see either man, and frustrated on every hand by Department of the Interior officials, they suddenly occupied the Bureau of Indian Affairs Building. Constantly under threat of assault by federal marshals, they held out inside the building for more than a week until White House officials agreed to meet with them and consider their program of twenty points. When they finally left, the importance of their demands and the injustices and suffering which had motivated their actions were lost in the publicizing of some $2,000,000 worth of damage they had done to the building and the fact that they had taken many government records with them.

Little had been accomplished by the sensational confrontation, and little resulted from still another dramatic occupation—this time of the area around Wounded Knee, South Dakota, the site of the tragic massacre of Sioux refugees in 1890. Again, Indians, including many members of the American Indian Movement, led by Russell Means, Dennis Banks, and Carter Camp, were besieged in

February 1973, by heavily armed federal marshals and other whites after the Indians had occupied the buildings at Wounded Knee. The standoff lasted two months and was again ended by a White House promise to meet with the Indian spokesmen. The Indians' demands now included a review of the broken treaty of 1868, made with the Sioux, and a new government for the Indians on the Oglala Sioux Pine Ridge Reservation. Again, the government did nothing.

Such dramatic conflicts, however, drew national attention to the Indians' accelerating demands and showed that a new day was indeed dawning, when such issues as self-determination, the right of tribes to have governments of their own choosing, and the rectification of broken treaties would have to be met with seriousness and honesty.

Flanked by followers, Russell Means, an Oglala Sioux and one of the national leaders of the American Indian Movement, speaks to the press outside the Washington, D.C., headquarters building of the Bureau of Indian Affairs, occupied by Indians in October and November, 1972. *Richard Erdoes.*

Wherever else the increasing Indian assertiveness would lead could only be speculated upon. But one thing was clear. Indian nationalism was growing as a force to be reckoned with. Old ideas that the Indians had no power and did not matter were dead. The past had come back to haunt America, and the Indian minority was at last speaking for itself.

There is an interesting aspect to this. In the past, when few Indians had either the power or the ability to get white men to listen to them, much less to defend their people against the wholesale injustices of white society, various "Indian-interest organizations" of whites were organized to try to assist the tribes, and most of them are still active. Many churches and the National Council of Churches have committees actively concerned with Indians; so have other groups, including the Daughters of the American Revolution and the American Civil Liberties Union. The oldest group devoted entirely to Indian affairs is the Indian Rights Association of Philadelphia, with a fine Quaker tradition. The strongest, with a national membership and both Indian and non-Indian directors and officers, is the Association on American Indian Affairs, which took an active part in the early 1930's in securing passage of the Indian Reorganization Act and ever since has been in the forefront of such groups that are waging fights for and alongside the tribes.

More recently, however, the Indians' own organizations have taken the lead in championing the tribal causes, and

A member of the American Indian Movement, armed with a shotgun, occupies a bunker outside the church at Wounded Knee on the Pine Ridge Sioux reservation in South Dakota in the spring of 1973. Activist Indians, accompanied by their holy men, occupied the area and held it for weeks against encircling federal marshals and white and Indian "vigilantes," calling the world's attention to Indian grievances. *Wide World Photos.*

Bradley Patterson, aide to President Richard Nixon and representative of the federal government, meets with Frank Fools Crow and other spokesmen for the Indians who had occupied the area around Wounded Knee, South Dakota, in 1973. The meeting, at Kyle on the Pine Ridge reservation, witnessed the Indians' presentation of many demands, including a study of all Indian treaties, to the government. The demands were later rejected. *Ken Norgard.*

Typifying the poverty and substandard level of existence that continue to grind the lives of most reservation people are these houses on the Pine Ridge reservation of the Oglala Sioux, descendants of the proud Red Cloud and Crazy Horse, in South Dakota.

Richard Erdoes.

A Hopi Indian ruefully observes a giant Peabody Coal Company steam shovel at work on a coal strip mine at Black Mesa, a Hopi religious shrine on the tribe's reservation in Arizona. Against the wishes of many of the tribe, the Hopi Tribal Council, with the encouragement and urging of the Department of the Interior, leased the Hopi lands for thirty-five years for the exploitation of coal with which to fuel large new power plants supplying energy to white population centers in the Southwest. *Terrence Moore.*

this is the way it should be. It is now pretty much a case of Indians speaking for themselves and being given support and help by the Indian-interest groups. Of great importance is the National Congress of American Indians, whose members include representatives of tribes as well as individual Indians and some non-Indians. There are also such groups as the National Indian Youth Council and the American Indian Movement, already named, and various regional Indian groups, like the United Sioux Tribes and the Northwest Tribal Association. Not to be overlooked, also, is ARROW, Inc., which gives the Indian groups some financial help and also runs practical field programs on its own.

It should also be mentioned that in recent years publications written, edited, and published by Indians have proliferated. They include newspapers like *Akwesasne Notes,* which has been put out by Mohawks and has had a large national circulation; many tribal newspapers; and *The Indian Historian,* a scholarly journal published by the American Indian Historical Society in San Francisco. These publications not only have brought the Indians' various causes to the attention of large non-Indian audiences, but they have served to inform Indians themselves and bring together Indian groups in all parts of the country, fostering a sense of unity.

Behind all these developments, behind all the sensational events, are the Indians themselves. What are they like today? I attempt to answer, reminding you first that no general statement about all Indians is wholly correct. They range from writers like N. Scott Momaday, who won the Pulitzer Prize for his novel *House Made of Dawn,* and Vine Deloria, Jr., who wrote *Custer Died for Your Sins,* to composer Louis Ballard, folk singer Buffy Sainte-Marie, and dozens of internationally famous artists. They include also articulate and patriotic political leaders like Hank Adams, Ada Deer, Leon Cook, and Robert Burnette; scholars like Rupert Costo, head of the American Indian Historical Society; anthropologist Bea Medicine; and Alfonso Ortiz, Princeton professor and president of the Association on American Indian Affairs. They include outstanding tribal leaders like Peter MacDonald of the Navahos, lawyers, doctors, and professional men and women. But they include, even more, the poor and those who have been bent and broken by destitution and sickness. There are the thousands of people in the hills and countryside of the reservations, poorly housed, poorly fed, and scraping along on annual incomes barely large enough to support survival. There are traditional leaders, upholders of Indian cultures and values, like Henry and Leonard Crow Dog of the Dakotas; Thomas Banyacya and David Monongye of the Hopis; Oren Lyons of the Iroquois; and Janet McCloud at Puget Sound. All of them continue to be Indians, holding to the inner quality, the pride, and the integrity of their tribes.

Many Indians are Christians, but many, also, are members of the Native American Church, which combines features of Christianity and native beliefs and is characterized by the use of peyote to establish contact with the supernatural. Others still maintain their old tribal beliefs. The largest of such groups are in the Southwest, although there are others, such as among the Iroquois, as already told. Many tribes continue some of their old dances and other practices because they are fun. In the Sioux country on festive occasions you may find dancing to the latest records going on inside a building, and round dancing to drums and singing outside, with people moving back and forth from one to another. They keep up some of the ceremonies because they are profitable as a tourist attraction, or because they are proud of them as we are of the theater, or because such an occasion as the annual Sun Dance brings all the tribe together and reaffirms tribal unity. The Pueblos of New Mexico are a special case, with their equally devout participation in Catholic and their own old rituals.

Indians today want to progress. They want to progress *as Indians,* with the feeling for the advancement of all their people as well as for the single individual that is one of their great strengths. They see no reason why they cannot be Indians—even more, Apaches or Cheyennes or Iroquois or Sioux—and at the same time be entirely competent in our American world. More than anything else, the sense that this combination of old and new, of progress without loss of identity, has been made impossible underlies the heavy drinking that has plagued so many of them.

I turn again to the Apaches of San Carlos for a sound example of progressive Indianism in action. Those Apaches formed a government and incorporated under the Indian Reorganization Act, thereby receiving certain important rights. Their cattlemen organized into a number of cattle associations. A good many years ago the directors of the associations saw that if they pooled the buying of their supplies, then sold them to themselves at cost plus a handling charge, they could get much better bargains. From this beginning developed the tribal store, an enterprise entirely financed by the Indians' own earnings. As this store expanded into handling more and more ordinary consumer goods, it began to compete with the traders in the reservation and with stores in nearby towns.

I must explain also that at that time, in 1949, Arizona still refused to include Indians in any of its relief programs. The Apaches, therefore, ran a special herd of cattle, the profits from which were used for their relief clients. It occurred to the tribal council that if the clients, mostly old people and orphans, could buy their staples from the tribal store, which had sold only to the cattle associations, their checks would stretch further, so this was authorized. The loss of the relief trade stung the traders into action.

They got the influential Arizona Retail Grocers' Association to protest to one of their senators that the tribal store was socialism, government in business, and should be terminated immediately. Actually, no government funds had ever gone into the store; it was a legitimate enterprise of a chartered corporation. Routinely, the senator sent the letter on to the Commissioner of Indian Affairs, who forwarded it to the superintendent with a request for informa-

Hops are an important commercial crop in the state of Washington, and Indians of the Northwest have long gained seasonal employment from white hop growers. Here, however, are Yakima Indians stringing poles on which the hop vines will climb in a field on their own reservation. *Bureau of Indian Affairs.*

During the 1960's the government emphasized the encouragement of white-owned industries to locate on reservations and provide employment and income to tribes. This 55,000-square-foot rug-making factory was built by Big Horn Carpet Mills, Inc., on the Crow reservation in Montana despite the irritation of some whites in Billings who wanted the new factory in their city. The Crow women are seen here working at a tufting machine.

Bureau of Reclamation.

Many Indians have been trained to become skilled workers in sophisticated modern electronic and space-age plants located on or near their reservations. Here, a young Navajo machinist adjusts a computer that operates a complicated drill press in a Fairchild semiconductor factory at Shiprock, New Mexico.

Bureau of Indian Affairs.

Indian employees of the tribally owned Sioux Tribe Telephone Company work on the lines near Ridgeview, South Dakota.
Bureau of Indian Affairs

An aerial view shows part of the successful Kah-Nee-Ta resort, a multi-million-dollar, tribally owned enterprise of The Confederated Tribes of the Warm Springs Reservation in Oregon. The large complex, composed of hotel-motel and tipi sleeping accommodations, restaurants, swimming pool, and recreation facilities, has become one of the most popular convention and resort centers in the Northwest. *Bureau of Indian Affairs.*

About 20 percent of the $1 million annual income of the White Mountain Apaches in Arizona comes from farming and business enterprises. Here, a helicopter prepares for takeoff to reseed an Apache grazing pasture from the air.
Bureau of Indian Affairs.

A standardized form of Plains dress has spread west as well as east. These are Yakimas, members of a Plateau tribe on the edge of the Northwest Coast area and influenced by that culture. The spread of Plains-type dressing across the Plateau country began early. The old man here wears a pretty fine buckskin outfit; his son's costume (right) is clearly much more modern. Both appear to have artificial braids attached to their headdresses.

U. S. Dept. of Interior.

Indians can be picturesque when they choose. Here two Senecas of New York have arrayed themselves in the now universal war bonnet and some other items imitative of our idea of what the Sioux once looked like. *U. S. Dept. of Interior.*

tion. The superintendent called in the chairman of the Tribal Council, handed the correspondence to him, and told him it was his baby.

The Council notified all traders to attend the next regular meeting at 9:30 A.M. Friday, and the traders came. The secretary of the Council read aloud sections from the tribal constitution and its corporate charter, both of which derived their authority from the Indian Reorganization Act, to the effect that the Council had authority to remove from the reservation persons, other than government officials, not members of the tribe, who acted detrimentally to its interests, and that the Council could issue licenses to nonmembers to conduct businesses on the reservation and could revoke those licenses for activities contrary to the interests of the tribe.

The Council then read and passed a well-worded resolution saying that knowingly misrepresenting the nature of tribal enterprises such as the store was acting detrimentally and against the tribe's interests, and was ground for the revocation of licenses to conduct businesses and for removal of offenders from the reservation.

Then the chairman turned to the traders and said, "You have heard the resolution. Now, by noon we want to see a copy of the telegram you have sent to the Senator."

Well before noon he was handed a copy of the wire, taking back all the false allegations that had been made.

This is the modern Indian tribe in action, and this, again, is why the tribes want to keep their special jurisdiction over Indian country.

By and large, Indians are still very poor. They range from poor to horribly poor. They are, when they wish to be, extremely picturesque, and they are objects of great interest to tourists. For this reason, a great many Indians are in the tourist business. That they show themselves off, perform parts of old ceremonies for gain, and peddle their wares, does not mean that they are frauds or have lost their integrity. It means only that they like eating regularly as much as we do.

For the same reasons, a number of Indians made their way to Hollywood and others pick up some badly needed cash at times when motion picture companies come out their way on location, even though often they know that how they are dressed and what they are told to do is ridiculous. A source of constant anger to Indians is the way they are represented in the majority of movies. Above all they are sick of the eternally repeated lie that makes them out as savage aggressors against innocent whites.

The tourists come with many preconceived notions. An Indian in a business suit disappoints them. Some years ago a visiting newspaperman went to see the Corn Dance, a major ceremony, at the Pueblo of Cochití, New Mexico. He concluded that the thing was a fraud because the supervisor of the dance was a young man with a crew haircut who worked at a white-collar job in the atomic center of Los Alamos. The newspaperman published a foolish article to this effect. He was too blind to see the truth, which was that the ceremony was so genuine and the belief so deep that this very modern young man would take several days' leave of absence to perform his part in it. Many Indians, learning what tourists expect, make efforts to give it to them. They don war bonnets and imitations of Plains leggings and do other things that are little more than theatricals. In quiet, they laugh their heads off and make fun of the tourists and of themselves.

A good many tribes, as a result of all the jostling and shoving around and hardship to which they have been subjected, have lost the externals of their old cultures, forgotten their rituals, forgotten their way of dressing. At present a synthetic, Pan-Indian culture is spreading among such tribes, largely based on Plains costume and Plains modes of dancing. They take it up because they crave a means of asserting that they are still Indian.

I wrote above of Indians laughing and making fun of others and themselves. There are exceptions, of course, but almost everyone who knows some tribe well will tell you of its people's extraordinary sense of humor and their love of laughter. Usually, each man who goes among Indians has his favorites, so that when Indian Service employees, anthropologists, and other such come together, you will hear arguments as to whether the Apaches, the Papagos, or the Sioux (or whatever tribe each man has known best) have the keenest humor and are the most fun to be with.

Again with some exceptions, Indian family ties are deep and strong, and Indians are passionately fond of children and delightful with them. Indian children are well brought up, but in most tribes they are never struck. The family

Taos Hoop Dance, a dance of no religious significance, intended to show off the agility of the performers. The dancers maintain a fast step while putting their feet through one or more hoops, passing the hoops over their bodies, and performing similar gymnastics. The dancers wear elaborations of Plains-type roaches, while the plump character in the background is decked out in war bonnet and beaded leggings, quite unknown to his ancestors.
U. S. Dept. of Interior.

Navaho schoolgirl learning weaving. *U. S. Dept. of Interior.*

Modern Northwest Coast wood carving, exhibited at the Golden Gate Exposition, 1939-40, tribe not identified.

U. S. Dept. of Interior.

Modern Iroquois wood carving, showing an Iroquois-style tug of war. *Rochester Museum of Arts and Sciences.*

"War Dance," by Keahbone, a Kiowa artist. The Kiowas began painting under the influence of members of the University of Oklahoma, as a sort of secondary effect of what was happening among the Pueblos. Keahbone's work keeps something of the mingled stiffness and real liveliness of primitive Plains painting. *U. S. Dept. of Interior.*

Dancing of the "war dance" type, by the Kiowa artist Mopope. As he intended this painting for a mural at Wichita, Kansas, he has put a grass lodge in the background. *U. S. Dept. of Interior.*

Zuñi potter, New Mexico. *U. S. Dept. of Interior.*

Maria Martínez of San Ildefonso, most famous of all modern Indian potters, and her husband, Julian Martínez. They were photographed polishing two pots preparatory to painting the designs on them. On Mrs. Martínez' left is a pot that has not yet been polished. Among other honors, this remarkable lady received the medal of the American Institute of Architects and the French Palmes Académiques. The pottery revival sparked by the Martínezes worked an economic revolution at San Ildefonso, where lack of water and farming land had resulted in great poverty. *U. S. Dept. of Interior.*

"Women's Buffalo Dance," by Lorenzo Beard, Cheyenne-Arapaho, a reminiscence of a ceremony similar to the Mandan dance shown in Chapter V. The picture has an interestingly primitive and strongly symbolic quality.

U. S. Dept. of Interior.

"Koshare of Taos," by Pablita Velarde of Santa Clara Pueblo. The Taos sacred clowns make a mixture of comedy and ritual out of climbing the pole to get at the food hung at the top as part of the annual Taos fiesta on St. Jerome's day—a good example of the Pueblo pattern of Christian and non-Christian side by side. If the clowns fail to get to the top of the pole, it is an extremely bad omen. The men standing with blankets wrapped around them are typical of present-day Taos Indians in their best dress; the watchers with hats on. are from other Pueblos, or Jicarilla Apaches. The pole to be climbed is in reality at least twice as high as Miss Velarde has painted it. *Philbrook Art Center.*

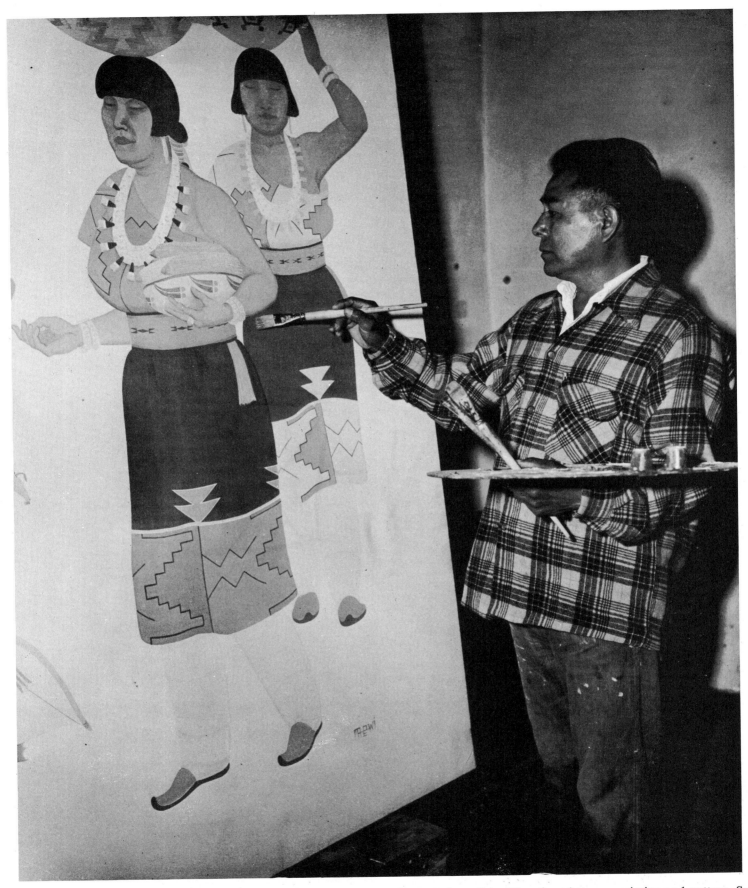

Velino Herrerra or Ma-Pe-Wi of Zia Pueblo, working on a large mural. Modern Indian painting, except for some work done in Oklahoma, began at San Ildefonso Pueblo about 1917, when scientists asked the Indians to make records in water color of what were thought to be dying ceremonies. From this sprang a school of painting which spread rapidly, first through the Pueblos, then to other tribes. Meantime, between painting and pottery, San Ildefonso grew prosperous, its population stopped decreasing and began to increase, Today, in addition to farming and arts, the tribe receives a considerable income from wages earned at the neighboring atomic research center of Los Alamos—and the "dying" ceremonies still go on. *U. S. Dept. of Interior.*

Hunting deer on horseback, by Tsinnahjinnie, one of the most gifted of modern Navaho artists. With a bit of fantasy, he has depicted something he never saw. *U. S. Dept. of Interior.*

Model of modern Iroquois false-face dancers. Their costumes are modern; their masks remain unchanged.
Courtesy of American Museum of Natural History.

Navaho weaver, also by Tsinnahjinnie. This artist, who came from one of the most primitive parts of the Navaho Reservation, arrived at the Indian boarding school in Santa Fe when he was sixteen. He began by copying the work of Pueblo painters there, then established a strong style of his own that was copied by other Navaho and Apache painters. *Philbrook Art Center.*

feeling reaches wide, to grandparents, brothers and sisters, cousins, uncles, aunts, children, nieces and nephews. It is unthinkable to abandon them or refuse them help. From this arises one of the serious problems of the Indian who goes to the city to earn his living. In his family are old people, children, perhaps a sick or crippled relative, going hungry at home. He supports them. If they follow him, he takes them in. Even if he has worked himself up into semi-skilled or skilled employment, the load is so heavy that you could say he shares their poverty, rather than that they share his comparative wealth.

An Indian seeking employment has a tough time. Thin-skinned, proud, shy, and thoroughly uneasy in his new situation, he is readily discouraged, and usually appears stupid and unable to talk. Until employers have had experience with Indians, they are likely to be prejudiced against them. The foreman's way of giving orders may be normal to us, but shockingly insulting by Indian standards. The idea of absolute regularity, of turning up *every* day, at the *same* hour, has to be learned. Once Indians have got past all these hurdles and learned how the system works, they do very well, and are particularly desired in jobs requiring fine manual skill.

So there they are, nearly a million of them. They have a tough struggle, and it is no wonder that many get discouraged, yet they refuse to give up. One of the amazing things about them is their loyalty to the United States. Their record in World War I, World War II, and the Korean and Viet Nam wars is magnificent, not only in the armed forces, but in the way that, out of their poverty,

they scrimped and scraped to give to the Red Cross, buy war bonds, help in every way they could. The grandmother of one Indian I know joined a Red Cross knitting group during World War II. Somehow she just could not learn to knit properly, partly because of her rheumatism, so her grandson learned and did her stint for her, thus saving her face until he was drafted and went on to distinguish himself in Europe. Many Indians, registering for the draft, turned up with their rifles, ready to go.

The Iroquois made a fuss about being drafted. In the First World War Indians were exempt, so the League of the Iroquois had passed its own draft act and sent its young men into the National Guard. They took it as an insult to be called up under compulsion.

All the Indians are struggling. They want and need help to help themselves, and they are worried and angry because government policy so often seems to deny them the opportunity to do so.

The picture is generally a dreary one, but still these remarkable people can drum and sing, joke and laugh—even if some of the jokes are bitter. They have not given up. They do not want handouts or charity; they want the guidance and help that is necessary to enable them to help themselves. With a little understanding from their fellow Americans, they still may attain their goal, which is to be as healthy, as competent in all our ways, as active contributors, as solidly self-supporting as the rest of us, and still hold to traditions, generosities, and ancient knowledge that will add greatly to the richness of the American scene.

School's out at Santa Ana Pueblo, New Mexico. There must be hope and a future for youngsters like these. *U. S. Dept. of Interior.*

Index

Figures in *italics* refer to illustrations.

definition, 15
early history, 15
geography, 15, 106
religions, 109
Spanish, 27, 35, 36, 149, 192
abandoned in Southwest, 144
attitude toward Indians, 143
contributions to Pueblo culture, *118, 143*
rebellion against, 143
repression of Indians, 143
settlement of Southwest, 142
spears, 12, 32, *94,* 196
spinning wheel, *241*
spirit, 52
squash blossom hairdress, 122, *126*
Stalking Turkey, *36*
Standing Bear, 248, 250 ff.
star cult, 100
state sovereignty, opposed by Indians, 242 ff.
status of Indians today, 250
Stedham, John, 37
Stinkers, 25, 34
stockades, 45
Stone Age people, 13
stone boiling, 182, 196
stone chisel, *199*
stone hammer, *74*
storage bin, *25*
storage box, food, Tlingit, *212*
storage box, Haida, *213*
storage pit, Hidatsa, *91*
succotash, 79
"Sun, The," 25
Sun Dance, *166,* 168, 176–77, *177, 178,* 240, 265
enclosure, *178*

T

Talking God, *128*
Tanoans, 110, 123, 150, 162
Taos Hoop Dance, *269*
Taos Pueblo, *107*
tattooing, 27, 114, *188*
Tavibo, 225
Tecumseh, 37, 59, 98, 103, 225
Temple Mound Builders
art, 21
bowl, *23*
carved figurine, *24*
carved shell, *22*
culture, 21
farming, 21, 25
villages, 22
Temple Mound Building
Culture, 21, 27, 89. *See also* Mississippian culture
decline of, 24
variants of, 24
tents, 96
Teotihuacans, 14, 20
tepee, *96, 187, 229, 230*
Blackfoot, *153*
cars, *153*
Cheyenne, *153*
comfort of, 96
cover, *160*
hunting, *97*
Kiowa, *153*
large, made possible, 151
painted, *152*
size of, 98
termination, 256–57
Teyas, 148
Thayandanega, *59*
theocracy, 20
Thorpe, Jim, 237
Thunderbird, *211*
Timucuas, *27, 29, 33,* 35
Tlaolacha, *208*

Tlingit, 195, *199, 203,* 204
baskets, *200*
dagger, *199*
design, *203*
food dishes, *215*
food storage box, *212*
horn ladle, *214*
mask, *208*
potlatch, *216*
wood carving, *216*
wooden headdress, *209*
wooden helmet, *206*
tobacco, 100, 151
raised by men, 98
tobacco pipe, 54
toboggans, 98
Mandan, *99*
Toltecs, 14, 15, 20, 181
tomahawk, *46, 49, 54,* 88
trade, *84*
tombs, early Southeast, *25*
Tomochichi (Creek chief), *30,* 35
Tonkawas, 228
tortilla, 111
torture, 34, 57
absence of in Southwest, 109
among Western farmers, 100
by Iroquois, effect of, 57
symbolized, 100
totem poles, *70,* 201, 206, 213, *218, 219, 221*
insignia of rank, *219*
with door, 216, *219*
tourist business, 268
towns, independent, 28
towns, ruled by own chief, 28
trade, early, between Southwest and Mexico, 15
Trail of Broken Treaties, 261, *261*
Trail of Tears, 41
trailer and Quonset hut school, *147*
trailer school, *245*
traveler's bread, *131*
"Traveling," *151*
travois, 98, *150, 151, 186*
treaties with Indians, 233
Treaty of 1868, 234
Treaty of Guadalupe Hidalgo, *123*
Tribal Court, *253*
tribal enterprises, Navaho, 138, 235
tribal history, types of, 233
tribal saw mill, Navaho, *244*
tribal self-government, modern, 254–55
tribal store, 265
tribes, organization of, 26
tribes, Southwest, democratic, 29
trousers, 50, *119*
trust land, 242
Tsimshian, 195, 220
mask, *210*
potlatch, *208*
Tsinnahjinnie, *274, 276*
tuberculosis, 252, 254
tumpline, *74*
Tumucuas. *See* Timucuas
Tunicas, 27, 34
Turner Group of mounds (Ohio), carved figure from, *24*
Turtle Dance, *125*
Tuscaroras, 57, 81

U

Umatilla, *184*
un collín, 220
"Uncle Tomahawks," 261
United Sioux Tribes, 264
U.S. Bureau of Indian Affairs. *See* Bureau of Indian Affairs
U.S. Public Health Service, 244

Ute, 110, 160, 177, 181, 183, *184,* 256
Uto-Aztecan languages, 110, 181, 183

V

Velarde, Pablita, *125, 273*
village, Mandan, *90, 94*
village, Omaha, *97*
village, Wichita, *96*
villages, fortified, 93
villages, Papagos, 111
Virginia, 1612 map of, *80*
Virginia chiefs, dress of, *64*
Virginia Indian ceremony, *64*
Virginia Indians, sixteenth century, *73*
Virginia shamanistic ceremony, 74
visions, 98, 112, 116, 164, 182, 184, 228
drugs for, 191
vote, Indian use of, 250

W

Wakonda, 100
Walapais, 183
"Walking Purchase" treaty. *See* Penn Treaty
Walpi, Arizona, *117,* 248
Wampanoags, 233
wampum, *48, 49, 50, 54, 55,* 58, 81
belts, *77*
counterfeit, 77
headdress, *81*
making of, Algonkian, 62, 77
used as currency, 77
uses of, 48
Wappo tribe, *190*
war
among Iroquois, 56
Apache attitude toward, 32
attitude toward in Southeast, 32
attitude toward in Southwest, 109, 144
based on religious revivals, 224
bonnets, 102, *102,* 161, *268, 269*
chiefs, 98
dance, 101, *271*
Ghost Dance Cult doctrine, 225
honors, 161
Iroquois attitude toward, 56
Navaho attitude toward, 141
northern Algonkians wiped out, 81
organizations, 123
rituals, 110
Southwest, described, 32
War Eagle, *161*
war game, 156
War of 1812, 59, 103
warfare, true, 160, 205
warfare as outlet, 31, 34
warpaint, *39*
warrior, steps in becoming, 27
warriors, training of, 141–42
wars
against Algonkians, 77
against Plains Indians, 180
Washakie, *187, 193*
Washington, George, 58, 59
water rights, 259
Watkins, Senator Arthur, 256
Wau-ho-ra-be, *104*
Wauneka, Mrs. Anne, *251*
weaving, *119,* 134, *270*
Northwest Coast Indians, 203